Boomers on the Loose® South Sound

Boomers on the Loose®
South Sound

Retirees Staying Active in South Puget Sound

Boomers on the Loose®

Lacey, Washington

Photographs by the author unless otherwise noted.

Editing by Bill Cowles and Barbara Crawford

Cover Illustration by Joshua Cleland (JoshCleland.com)

Cover Design by Lyn Birmingham

The intent of this book is to provide ideas as to leisure activities available to retirees in the United States. A large portion of the information included is based on information publicly published on the Internet and was believed to be accurate approximately 60 days prior to publishing.

ISBN: 978-0-9989871-3-2

Table of Contents

Do More Of It

Seems a lot of people, spend a lot of time
Trying to get happy, and finding peace of mind
To me it's very simple, to live your life and love it
Just find what you like to do, and do more of it

To some it's driving fast in a car
To some it's flying high with the stars
To some it's traveling near and far
To some it's staying right where they are

Some like dancing all night long
Some like singing and playing a song
Some folks live as if it's a race
While others like a slower pace
Doesn't really matter, what puts a smile on your face

All I'm really trying to say
You want to have a better day?
Just find what you like to do, and do more of it
Yes, it's really very simple, to live your life and love it
Just find what you like to do, and do more of it

Tim Flumerfelt, Musician, Songwriter
1954 – 2022

INTRODUCTION

It's a great time to be a Baby Boomer in Washington State's South Puget Sound. If you're embarking on your retirement journey in or near the surrounding communities of Pierce, Kitsap, Thurston, or Mason counties, this book is for you!

Every day, South Sound Boomer retirees discover that "retirement" is simply a journey toward "re-inventment!" Life isn't winding down for Boomers – it's amping up! And that's why this book is full of exciting retirement ideas and choices – to make it easy to discover exactly how you want to stay meaningfully active in this exciting new life chapter.

Research shows that Boomers want to live with purpose and fulfillment. They want to be active and productive. They want to dig in the dirt, plant, and harvest community gardens, and restore wetlands and wildlife habitat. They like to guide groups around nature centers, art galleries, and museums. Shelve library books. Serve on public committees. Teach kids to read, play music, dance, garden or create art. Learn music, lead hikes, paddle dragon boats, count birds, and clean up parks. Retirees learn new skills and start new careers and businesses. They study the world, meet new people, volunteer, improve their communities, travel, have fun, and lots more.

As I first heard Tim strum and sing "Do More of It" – it struck me – his lyrics were a simple, clear expression of my book's purpose and example of someone who, through his music, lived it.

"To live your life and love it, just find what you like to do and do more of it."

Boomers on the Loose® South Sound will help you with the "find" part, the "do" part is up to you.

We hope you're getting the idea that South Sound Boomer status can be pretty darn exciting!

We also realize that retirement can be intimidating – *"What do I do now?"* That's exactly why *Boomers on the Loose® South Sound* was created – to guide you on your quest for "what's next?" In this book, you'll learn more about why, how, and where to pursue your existing or hidden interests or develop new ones.

In this book, we share our excitement for retiring – *Washington style*. We emphasize the importance of filling your time our unique part of the county pursing activities that are meaningful and true to us. And… helping you discover the *why's*, *how's* and *where's* of doing just that.

Staying Healthy, Active, and Engaged

More and more research (and often our own experience!) is uncovering the activities and lifestyle choices that enhance retirement. As you explore the abundant options available to you, consider weaving these life-enriching practices into this next life chapter.

- **Maintaining physical health.** When healthy, we live longer, happier lives. Living our best retirement lives means making good lifestyle choices about exercise, sleep, and food.

- **Boosting brain health.** Physical and mental health are related. Activities that deliver more oxygen to the brain improve brain health. Among a long list of brain-nourishing activities are being outside, exercising, learning, volunteering, and social activities.

- **Learning new things.** We enlarge our life by immersing ourselves in a hobby, attend, or teach a class, learn more about ourselves, our world, and communities, or delve into our creative side with art and crafts, writing, performance, photography, music, or similar pursuits.

- **Giving back.** Your time and energy make the world a better place through volunteering and community service. Volunteering enriches our lives with purpose and the satisfaction of helping others.

- **Engaging socially.** We are hard-wired social creatures. Our interactions with family and friends create positive feelings of wellbeing. Closely related and equally important, we innately need to belong and feel valued in our communities.

- **Appreciating your world**. Enjoy the accomplishments of mankind, including your own. We find meaning in the advances of knowledge and expression of humanity in all forms. We explore that by traveling, reading, engaging in, and supporting cultural activities.

- **Getting outside.** Being outdoors is good for us. In the South Sound, we are blessed with amazing opportunities to experience and appreciate nature's beauty. Make fresh air and green earth a priority.

- **Taking time to be still**. Express gratitude every day. Put aside mind-clutter and to-dos and focus on just being silent. Be grateful for the abundant blessings and opportunities we enjoy in life.

How *Boomers on the Loose® South Sound* is Organized

To provide you with the best experience, *Boomers on the Loose® South Sound* is organized into three parts:

1. **Self-Understanding Section.** *CHAPTER 1: WHO AM I?* offers a series of questions to help you visualize retirement. It helps you look at your make up values, passions, personality, skills, experience, and other factors that influence what is meaningful to you. This takes you to the next step of focusing on specific types of interests that might attract you.

2. **Interest Area Section.** Chapters 2-25. *"Interest Areas" in this book are 23 broader categories of activities, for example, volunteering, arts, music, animals, outdoors, learning, etc., that are popular among retirees.*

   CHAPTER 2: INTEREST AREAS AT A GLANCE gives you a quick summary of each of the 23 categories that are described in greater detail in…

   CHAPTERS 3-25. In these chapters – making up the essence of this book – you'll learn more about activities and options that may naturally appeal to you. Each chapter offers a handy jump-off point for researching opportunities in your areas of interest in the **Resources Section** on pages 141-280.

3. **Resources Section.** The *APPENDIX: RESOURCES IN YOUR COMMUNITY* beginning on page 141 is packed with 160 pages of South Sound local and regional listings and information, also by interest area(s) on specific organizations, resources, opportunities, and activities, listed by county, city, and other geographic categories.

Note about the interest area of Volunteering: *Because volunteering and giving back is such an important focus for many retirees, volunteering activities are not only the focus of CHAPTER 3: VOLUNTEERING, and RESOURCES: VOLUNTEERING, but are also woven throughout many other interest area chapters throughout the book.*

How to Use This Book

You'll find this guide an invaluable multi-purpose resource an important reference wherever you are on your retirement journey.

- As a stand-alone planning and resource tool, it step you through a process to explore appealing, interesting retirement pastimes.

- As a pure reference guide to discover places to pursue your interests or develop new ones. Browse *APPENDIX: RESOURCES IN YOUR COMMUNITY* beginning on page 141.

Step-by-Step Guide

Using this book, follow the steps below to embark on your personal journey into your new life chapter, enjoying every step of the way.

1 Complete self-reflection questions.

CHAPTER 1: WHO AM I? Questions to prompt thoughts about your retirement vision, values, talents, life experience, personality, passions, and interests.

2 Identify your main area(s) of interest.

CHAPTER 2: INTEREST AREAS AT A GLANCE. Summaries that introduce the 23 categories of popular retiree interests and activities expanded in Chapters 3-25.

3 Dive into specific chapter(s) related to your interest(s).

INTEREST AREA CHAPTERS 3-25. Within these 23 chapters, you'll learn more about a wide variety of interesting pursuits and options to imagine and consider.

4 Check out the wide variety of resources in and around your local community.

APPENDIX: RESOURCES IN YOUR COMMUNITY. Browse extensive listings and descriptions of specific places in South Puget Sound to immerse in your interests.

5 Create your plan of action to get involved or do other research to see you've found a "good fit."

ACTION PLAN WORKSHEET. Use the Action Plan Worksheet below as a tool to create your game plan beginning with your interests and action steps to do learn more or participate in the activity.

Create an Action Plan

You can make the process as detailed or as simple as you want and create your own plan using the "Action Plan" headings below.

In the plan:

- Define your specific area of interest. For example, hiking and walking, community service, volunteering, etc.

- Specify the organization and/or type of activity of interest. For example, libraries, helping kids learn to read; swing dancing, boating, learning music, studying history, starting a business.

- Make notes; write your questions about what more you need to know about activities or organizations by continuing your research.

- Identify the next steps to take to decide if it might be a good opportunity for you. For example, search online for information about related activities and organizations, attend a meeting, contact an organization directly.

- Put specific action steps on your calendar. For example, join a meetup group, visit websites, research elsewhere, talk with a specific organization or talk with people involved in the activity, contact a group or club leader.

- In your Action Plan Worksheet, write in reference information such as contact name, phone number, email address, and questions, and notes regarding next steps.

- If you believe this might be a good fit, GO FOR IT!

Action Plan Worksheet

Use these headings as a starting point to create your own worksheet.

Area of Interest	Specific Activity or Organization	What More Do I Need to Know?	Action / Next Steps

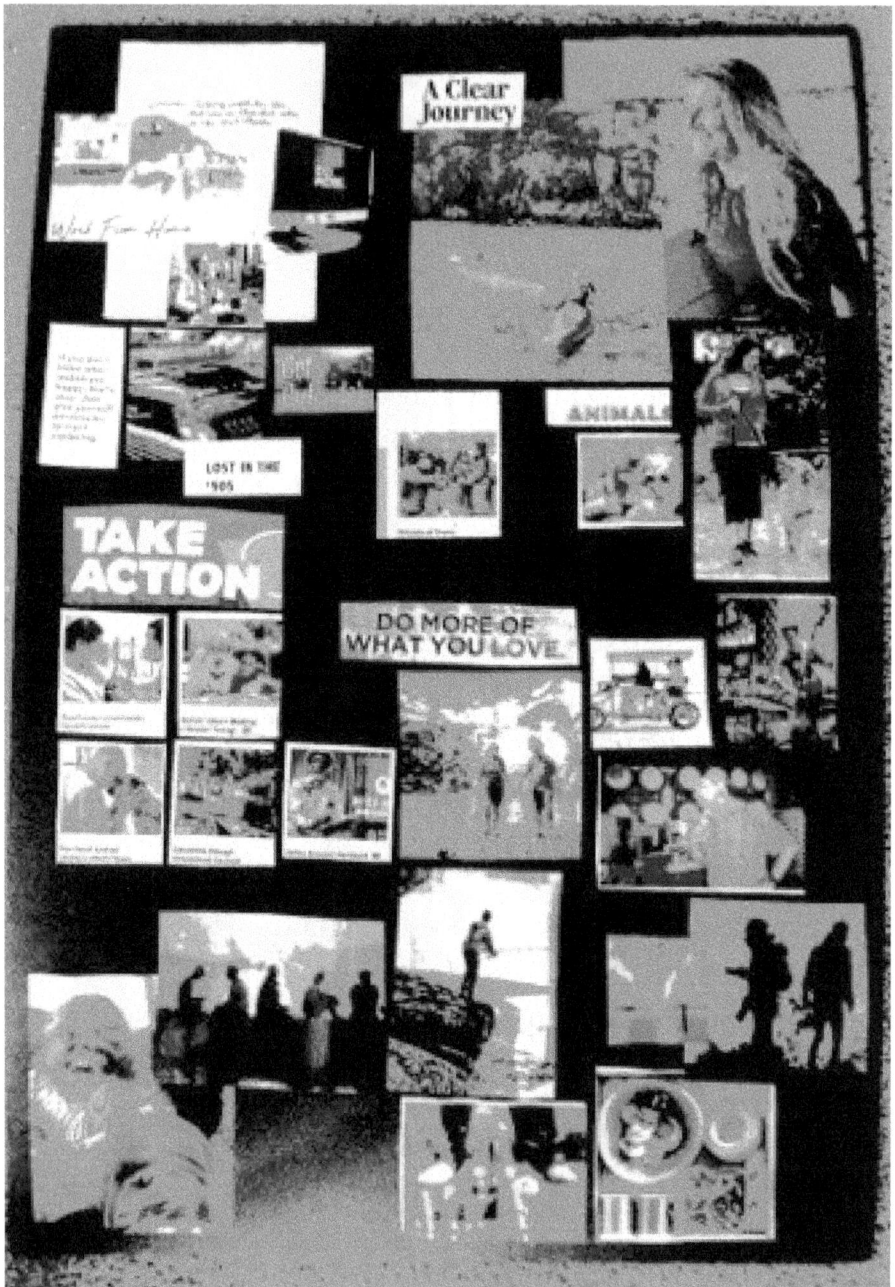

A Clear Journey

Work From Home

LOST IN THE
1905

TAKE
ACTION

ANIMALS

DO MORE OF
WHAT YOU LOVE.

CHAPTER 1: WHO AM I?

Transitions in our lives are a good time to go back to basics and think about what makes you, you. A clearer understanding of yourself and your retirement aspirations will help you zero in on the activities that appeal to you and where to go from here.

The following questions will help you be aware of your bigger vision and what you bring to this life chapter—the values that you live, your favorite natural and acquired abilities and skills, your passions, your general areas of interest. Think carefully about your responses, completing the sentence prompts with how they relate to you.

If you would like to explore these question prompts in greater detail, download the *About Me* questions, exercises, examples, and other self-understanding tools at boomersontheloose.com.

What Is My Vision?

Your vision is your mental picture of you in this next phase of your life. What does the future feel and look like to you? What do you want to see, experience, create, learn, and accomplish? Who do you want to experience life with? Probably even more important, what should retirement feel like? *What is meaningful to you?*

In retirement, I see myself… (what types of activities do you imagine yourself doing in retirement?)

For me, retirement should feel like… (include words that show how you want to feel in retirement, for example, happy, fulfilled, energetic, thoughtful, relaxed, etc.).

What Am I Passionate About?

Passions are experiences we get so immersed in that we lose track and sense of time and place. Passions are a major influence on our life choices. We may be passionate about the relationships in our lives, a cause, an activity, or a place. Our passion may be interacting in some way with animals, being outdoors, cooking, traveling, or a combination. Knowing our passions adds another piece of the "me" puzzle. Living our passions makes us smile.

The experiences in life that make me smile are… (describe the people, activities, and other experiences that truly bring joy and meaning to your life).

Activities that I enjoy so much that I totally lose track of time are…

What Values Do I Live By?

Our personal values are concepts, traits, or beliefs that guide the ways we live and work. What we value influences nearly everything we do – our lifestyle, decisions, behaviors, choices, and emotions. Examples of values are good health, commitment, fairness, integrity, sense of family, and honesty.

The values that guide my everyday life decisions and activities are… (describe the values that are reflected in how you live your life).

To help you examine the values that guide your life, download the *My Values* worksheet at boomersontheloose.com.

What is My Personality Like?

Each of us is made up of unique set of personality traits that come into play when we consider "what's next?" We are drawn to activities that line up with our personalities, as well as other preferences. Some people, for example, are highly social; others prefer solitude. Some want physical activity; others enjoy mental challenges.

The words I would use to describe my personality are … (describe a few of your dominant personality traits).

To help you define your personality traits, download the *My Personality* worksheet at boomersontheloose.com.

What Do I Do Well?

One goal of many retirees is to make the best use of what they do or know well – the skills, abilities, knowledge, and unique experiences acquired through work, volunteering, hobbies, and just doing life. For many, using our skills and knowledge in purposeful, meaningful ways enhances our retirement experience.

I am the proudest of my abilities to… (describe what you believe are your best skills and abilities, for example organizing, communicating, building something, cooking, sewing, managing, acting, playing an instrument, etc.).

The skills and abilities I'd most like to use in retirement are …

To help you examine the values that guide your life, download the *My Skills* worksheet at boomersontheloose.com.

What Life Lessons Do I Want to Apply?

At this time in our lives, we can usually point to specific life experiences that have impacted our lives and provided insight into ourselves, our priorities, and what we value. Examples are often found in personal, academic, career, or sports accomplishments, or experiencing a serious illness, the births and deaths of loved ones, and experiences involving college, travel, classes, books, and many others.

The life experiences that taught me the most were… (describe the most life changing experiences or events during your life).

The most important lessons I learned from these experiences were…

To help you explore and define important life experiences, download the *Life Lessons Learned* worksheet at boomersontheloose.com.

What are My Gifts to the World?

Each of us brings an individual package of values, skills, experience, expertise, passions, and interests with a unique-to-us view to the world. That package changes as we grow, mature, and experience transitions in our lives. Wrapping those within your vision, you'll discover a picture of what you uniquely offer in this world. Large or small, our gifts are uniquely ours. Many of us find meaning and purpose expressing that which only we can offer.

What makes me different and unique is… (describe what you uniquely bring into your world of retirement).

To help you discover and define your unique gifts you, download the *My Unique Gifts* worksheet at boomersontheloose.com.

What Else Should I Consider?

Other questions you might think about in this process include:

- *What have I always wanted to try? Is it time to go in a totally new direction?* Now might be that time to pay attention to a desire to learn renew a new or back-burner activity. For example, you've been a corporate accountant but always wanted to teach. *Is it time to switch careers to teaching or do something totally different?*

- *What are my family commitments? What family commitments do I need to work with or around? Should I spend more time with family and friends?*

- *What financial considerations do I have? What can I afford? Many pursuits are free or low cost. Is the availability or cost of transportation or other factors a consideration?*

- *What other limitations should I consider, such as health or physical conditions, location, or other obligations such as caregiving?*

CHAPTER 2: INTEREST AREAS AT A GLANCE

Our interests, along with activities that attract us, are influenced by our vision, values, skills, and personality, and often, our upbringing and many other things. Now that you've considered the package that is you, it's time to narrow your search and see what interests attract you.

Below you can browse summaries of popular interest areas (categories of activities) that make up the core chapters of this book. Looking at the summaries, you can begin to apply the self-understanding you acquired by working through *CHAPTER 1: WHO AM I?*

For the interest areas that speak to you, find its corresponding interest area chapter. Within each chapter, you'll find a more in-depth description of activities and opportunities within that category. Then visit *APPENDIX: RESOURCES IN YOUR COMMUNITY* beginning on page 141 for listings of places, organizations, and opportunities near you to pursue your interest(s) in the South Sound.

Or do your own research on specific options in interest areas outside the scope of this book that may appeal to you.

Popular Interest Areas

The following summarizes popular interest categories under which retiree activities are grouped and detailed in Chapters 3-25.

- **Animals.** Find your niche in organizations that rescue and care for dogs, cats and other small animals, horses, birds, and wild animals. Or get your pet certified as a therapy animal for friendly visits at places such as nursing homes and care facilities. See *CHAPTER 4: ANIMAL LOVERS* on page 43.

- **Art, Photography, Film.** Engage in your favorite art form, expressing yourself through art, photography, or video or filmmaking...or other art form. Take classes, visit your favorite gallery, or volunteer as a docent, curator, teacher, or in a behind-the-scenes office or another role. See *CHAPTER 5: ART, PHOTOGRAPHY, FILM* on page 47.

- **Business Building.** Turn a passion, interest, or hobby into a business. Examples are consulting, jewelry-making, writing, and blogging, on-line retail, professional services such as accounting and bookkeeping, and more. See *CHAPTER 6: BUSINESS BUILDING* on page 53.

- **Care for the Environment.** Look for opportunities in environmental organizations, friends-of-parks, parks and recreation activities, and public gardens. Volunteers restore parks, natural and wildlife areas, plant trees, shrubs, and flowers, teach and guide groups, and advocate for environmental causes. *See CHAPTER 7: CARE FOR THE ENVIRONMENT* on page 57.

- **Career Encores.** Explore options to stay in the workforce or ease into retirement such as continuing in another full or part-time role, changing careers or employers, seeking new training, or working for a nonprofit. See *CHAPTER 8: CAREER ENCORES* on page 61.

- **Community Service.** Volunteers give back to help people who are disabled, hungry, homeless, or face health and mental health challenges with many nonprofit and faith-based organizations. Work in direct service, outreach activities, technology and administrative areas. See *CHAPTER 9: COMMUNITY SERVICE* on page 63.

- **Exploring the South Sound.** Take advantage of all types of experiences in the South Sound. For information on local and regional places to visit, see *CHAPTER 10: EXPLORING THE SOUTH SOUND* on page 65, and *RESOURCES: EXPLORING THE SOUTH SOUND* on page 180.

- **Fitness, Healthy Living.** Options for staying fit and healthy in retirement are plentiful, from walking and hiking to skiing and water sports, golf, pickleball, swimming, or visiting the gym. To make the most of retirement, commit to healthy living. Pick out activities you enjoy and go for it! See *CHAPTER 11: FITNESS, HEALTHY LIVING* on page 75.

- **Gardening.** Release your inner, or outer gardener by hands-on dirt digging in your own garden, or volunteer to help care for a public or demonstration garden. Enroll in classes, teach one, or join a garden club. Help maintain gardens in community facilities. See *CHAPTER 12: GARDENING* on page 85.

- **Government Service.** Look into a wide variety of volunteer opportunities county, city, and state government agencies. Serve on a variety of advisory boards, commissions or committees; help out in parks and recreation programs, farmers markets, city events, and festivals; assist with various social and public safety services, or in justice and legal, or law enforcement offices. See *CHAPTER 13: GOVERNMENT SERVICE* on page 89.

- **Healthcare Volunteering.** Bring your healthcare experience or interest to a volunteer role in a hospital, community health, mental health, or hospice setting. Or work for health-related causes you are passionate about or naturally connect with. Help with office and administrative tasks, community outreach programs and events. See *CHAPTER 14: HEALTHCARE VOLUNTEERING* on page 93.

- **Hiking, Walking.** As the retiree exercises of choice, walking and hiking are easy and good for you. Take in the fresh air and natural scenery in nearby communities, parks, urban routes, trails, forests, mountains, rivers, and wetlands. Join up with friends or a walking and hiking club or walk in an event. See *CHAPTER 15: HIKING AND WALKING* on page 97.

- **Hobbies.** Move a long-time (or new) interest, or back burner hobby to the top of the list. What do you want to do more of, collect, make, collect, or play? To start, seek out online classes or workshops, take or teach a class, visit hobby stores, or join a club. See *CHAPTER 16: HOBBIES* on page 101.

- **Learn Something New.** Transform your curiosity into knowledge, understanding, and appreciation. Take advantage of abundant learning venues including libraries, community college classes, museums, parks and recreation programs, community centers, community organizations, retiree living communities, online classes and forums, and many other learning places. *CHAPTER 17: LEARN SOMETHING NEW* on page 105.

- **Literary Arts, Reading, Writing.** Retirees fulfill their reading desire at local libraries, using the technology of online readers, and downloads. And volunteer to help others. Many retiree authors find their own voice through self-publishing books. *See CHAPTER 18: LITERARY ARTS, READING, WRITING* on page 107.

- **Museums, History.** Dig into your favorite aspects of history at museums and learning places nearly everywhere. They preserve histories of natural features, communities, industry, art, architecture, transportation, and other topics. Volunteers help maintain museums and artifacts and in other administrative, marketing, and teaching roles. See *CHAPTER 19: MUSEUMS, HISTORY* on page 111.

- **Music.** Many retirees renew, revisit, or redirect their love of music as they attend concerts, perform in various venues, learn an instrument, improve abilities, or teach. As music volunteers, they teach for nonprofits, help with music events, and play music to help causes they care about in settings such as hospitals, hospices, and nursing homes. See *CHAPTER 20: MUSIC* on page 115.

- **Social Connections.** Innate to our humanity, we seek a sense of belonging and connection with others. We connect anywhere we gather around a common interest such as neighborhoods, faith organizations, hobby and interest groups, community centers, in volunteer activities, and many more places. See *CHAPTER 21: SOCIAL CONNECTIONS* on page 119.

- **Teaching, Speaking.** Share what you know with others through classes, workshops, and speaking in classrooms, libraries, and community centers or through service clubs, learning forums, and many other types of organizations. See *CHAPTER 22: TEACHING, SPEAKING* on page 121.

- **The Great Outdoors.** Follow your passion for the outdoors, check out opportunities, including volunteer activities, throughout several chapters of this book. Start your research with *CHAPTER 23: THE GREAT OUTDOORS* on page 129.

- **Theater, Performance**. Enjoy nearly unlimited ways to engage in all flavors of theater experiences. Those who enjoy performing roles on or behind the stage find community and regional theater companies a great place to join a volunteer cast or take tasks to bring performances to life. See CHAPTER 24: THEATER, PERFORMANCE on page 133.

- **Travel.** If travel tops your bucket list, options for fun, once-in-lifetime trips are plentiful. Or stay closer to home and explore your own state, region, or community. See *CHAPTER 25: TRAVEL CHAPTER 25: TRAVEL* on page 137, and *CHAPTER 10: EXPLORING THE SOUTH SOUND* on page 65.

- **Volunteering.** For many Boomers, retirement is a time to use our time, experience, and skills to give back. It's no secret that giving back enriches our retirement experience. See *CHAPTER 3: VOLUNTEERING* on page 25. Volunteering opportunities and options are also described within many other interest area chapters.

CHAPTER 3: VOLUNTEERING

Because so many retirees find meaning and purpose in giving back, the topic of volunteering appears here as a stand-alone chapter. Volunteering activities are also described in several other interest area chapters.

The spirit of volunteerism among Boomer retirees reflects our love of life, our world, and each other. And for those of us in the active Boomer community, it's our time to give back to make our communities better places to live both now and in the future.

Retiring Boomers have more time on their hands and feel the need to give back. Instead of looking for being paid, Boomers now look to pay back in their communities.

Some people are drawn to a particular organization; others to a cause or issue that speaks to them. Many enjoy working with a specific age group such as kids or seniors. Handy retirees want to use their skills in new ways or learn a new skill. Some volunteers join with others to improve their neighborhoods and communities. Others find their callings within groups to which they already belong, such as faith communities or professional organizations, and quietly fill needs they see around them. Opportunities to give back are endless.

Why We Volunteer

For many of us, retirement is a time to use our time, experience, and skills in a meaningful way. It's no secret that giving back enriches our retirement experience. Ask just a few of the millions of retiree volunteers across the county.

Volunteering, plain and simple, creates positive feelings and makes us feel better physically and mentally. Our brains are nourished when we feel purposeful, challenge ourselves, work in community, socialize, and, most importantly, help others.

The feeling of making a difference gives us a stronger sense of purpose and fulfillment. The activity associated with volunteering enhances our health. We find greater meaning by using our time, energy, and unique gifts to improve the lives of others. For many, retirement is a time to share what we uniquely offer to serve others.

What is your unique gift? What could you share that gives you meaning and joy?

At a time when we leave work and our social network all but disappears, volunteering opens us to new people and experiences. We naturally build new relationships, and learn new things, We broaden our social networks through connections with the people and communities we serve. Volunteering helps us enjoy a greater sense of camaraderie and community in sharing common causes and purposes.

It All Starts with You!

Confused about where to find a meaningful volunteer gig? Start with yourself, of course.

Finding the right opportunity means searching for organizations and situations that need what you can and want to do. You first need a good idea of your own reasons to volunteer, which include your preferred types of activity/service. Then you can look for the right organization or situation. Here's where to start:

1. Review your responses to questions in *CHAPTER 1: WHO AM I?* that helped you clarify your values, passions, and areas of interest.

2. Browse through the section below – *Popular Volunteer Paths* to see which may appeal to you or spark ideas for others. Many of the volunteer path descriptions refer to the related interest area chapters of this book for more information.

3. Next, find organizations with opportunities that match your skills, interests, and passions. These are as varied and diverse as the fabric of your community. Consider organizations that further causes you care about, the people they serve and how you can support them. Believe it, they want you!

4. If you're curious and adventurous, look into organizations you've never heard of, and just see what appeals to you. Sometimes friends can point you to an organization that you may want to look into.

5. Search for organization websites by your interest. Begin with the name of your community and type of organization. Visit their Volunteer pages or contact them directly for specifics.

6. Research the types of activities or organizations that match your interest through interest searches, then visit individual websites. Read their blogs and publications, and research news articles.

7. Check out the organization's vision, purpose, and mission. How does the organization carry out its purpose and serve its clients? Does it align with your values and personality?

8. Learn about the duties, responsibilities, and expectations of members or volunteers as well as the requirements and application process. Background checks of volunteers may be required.

9. See how their website represents the organization; for example, does the website feel welcoming to new members, volunteers, and others? Is information, such as ways to contact, easy to find?

10. Set up an appointment with the volunteer coordinator and visit the organization to observe volunteers at work. Talk with other volunteers or members for their perspectives on the activity or volunteer opportunity.

11. Try out an activity, if possible, with other members or volunteers. How welcoming are they to new people?

Popular Volunteer Paths

Below are summaries of interest areas that commonly attract Boomer volunteers. Look for a category that speaks to you and learn about the types of volunteers typically needed. Many of these volunteer paths are also described in more detail in the interest area Chapters 2-24. Those chapters are referenced in the descriptions below.

Animal Lovers

Retirees enjoy many options to make a positive difference in our world through our connections with animals. Get involved in any number of roles in small or large animal rescue, people-pet team therapy involving pets, horses, and other animals, and wildlife preservation. See *CHAPTER 4: ANIMAL LOVERS* on page 43 and *RESOURCES: ANIMAL ADOPTION AND RESCUE* on page 142.

Art, Photography, and Film

Behind-the-scenes volunteers in diverse art communities serve as docents and curators; they work in gift shops, sell concessions, or put teaching, writing, photography, website, and office skills to work in many types of organizations. They help design and build exhibits and perform other roles to enhance the experience for others. See *CHAPTER 5: ART, PHOTOGRAPHY, FILM* on page 47 and *RESOURCES: ART, PHOTOGRAPHY, FILM* on page 149.

Business, Career, and Professional Organizations

Your own professional organizations or unions represent opportunities to volunteer while staying current in your field. These organizations need volunteers from within the ranks to carry out projects and education programs for members and often the community at large.

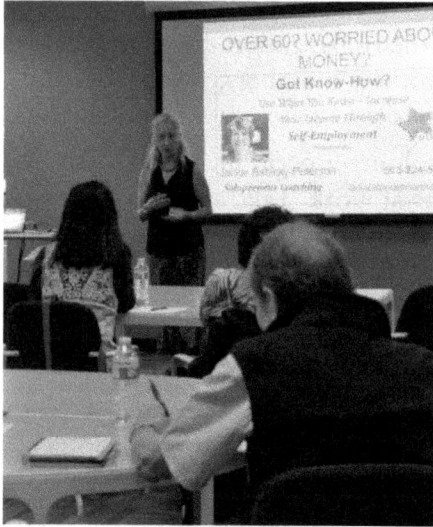

Business owners may associate with any number of organizations that need volunteers either in leadership or worker bee roles. Career and professional organizations help members with information and services that develop and advance their skills.

Community Service

Volunteers give back in direct or behind-the-scenes service to help the disabled, hungry, homeless, and people facing health and mental health challenges at faith-based organizations and nonprofits. See CHAPTER *9: COMMUNITY SERVICE* on page 63 and *RESOURCES: COMMUNITY SERVICE ORGANIZATIONS* on page 172.

Community Service Clubs

These groups serve the community through programs and projects that benefit various groups. In addition to leadership roles, their projects typically are operated entirely by member volunteers. They address the needs of various ethnic, cultural, religious groups, and age groups, through a wide variety of community projects, meetings, and events. Examples are Kiwanis, Urban League, Junior League, Lions Clubs, community health centers, and many other types of organizations. To find these organizations in your community, visit the websites of local Chambers of Commerce, community foundation organizations, or search for local non-profits at greatnonprofits.com. For listings of chamber organizations, see *RESOURCES: BUSINESS BUILDING, Economic Development, Chamber Organizations* on page 162.

Current Connections

Organizations to which you belong may offer the easiest way to "dip your toe" in the water of volunteering. Consider taking on a volunteer role with organizations in which you are active or have some other connection. Consider business and career organizations (see above), neighborhood groups, faith-based organizations, recreational and hobby clubs, and various clubs in retirement communities. You can serve as an officer or part of a project planning group or committee or help with a special event or fundraising event or taking on an occasional as-needed worker bee assignment.

See the sections in this chapter including *Business, Career, and Professional Organizations, Faith-based Organizations, Homes Associations, Neighborhood Service, Recreational, Hobby, and Special Interest Clubs*, and *Retiree Living Communities* for more examples.

Faith-based Organizations

By nature, faith-based organizations offer compassionate help to one another and others in some way. Retiree volunteers benefit from a sense of connection to something beyond themselves, and benefit from social connections and the satisfaction of helping others.

Many provide support services for needy citizens, including the homeless, children, and others. There are numerous opportunities to give back and carry out your faith teachings.

How could you get involved with your faith community service projects and programs? For example, could you collect and sort clothes, prepare and serve food for homeless people, baby sit, or mentor youth?

Farmers Markets

What could be healthier right? All that fresh food. Families walking. Homemade good-for-you products. People enjoying the summer outdoors in their community. Listening to bluegrass and just sometimes…classic rock.

Farmers markets need and welcome help in setting up and taking down the market, staffing an information booth, setting up signs, helping vendors, and many other behind the scenes and office chores.

Festivals, Events

The events and festivals we love so much need many behind-the-scenes volunteers to make them enjoyable. Volunteers help out at every stage of planning, holding the event, cleanup, and follow-up. A fun way to give back. If you've not done it before, look into a behind-the-scenes job at your favorite festival or event. Apply at least several months in advance to ensure that you get a spot.

Centered around a special interest, festivals bring together a sponsoring organization, a team of planners, vendors, and lots of volunteers. With all the work involved in coordinating many moving pieces and parts, volunteers are essential and very welcome. For the event and festival volunteer groupies, opportunities are nearly endless.

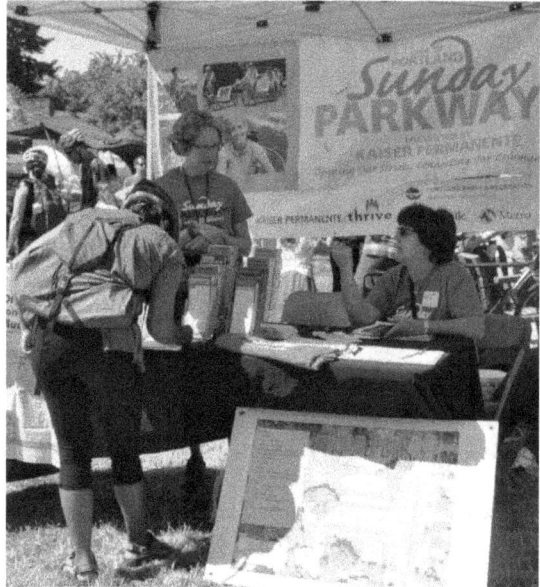

Depending on the type, behind-the-scenes volunteers get involved earlier in planning time and place logistics, working with sponsors, fundraising, and promoting the event.

Outdoor day-of-event roles vary widely from selling tickets and concessions, staffing information tables and booths, setting up stages, assisting with and coordinating activities, answering questions, assisting performers, and of course, cleanup!

You may also get to work with a favorite artist, performer, musician, athlete, or winemaker. Or you may get to hear music from the era of the old cars you're reminiscing about.

For lists of upcoming festivals and events, check calendars of your city or community, Chamber of Commerce, parks and recreation programs, community organizations, sporting goods stores, or special interest groups that promote events.

In this book, see *CHAPTER 10: EXPLORING THE SOUTH SOUND, Events, Festivals* on page 71. For listings of area art festivals, see *CHAPTER 5: ART, PHOTOGRAPHY, FILM, Where Art Lives, Volunteers Follow* on page 48; *RESOURCES: ART, PHOTOGRAPHY, FILM, Art Walks, Festivals* on page 155, and *Film Festivals* on page 159, and *CHAPTER 20: MUSIC, Behind* on page 117 and *Concerts, Festivals* on page 118.

Sporting and Active Outdoor Events

What sports do you love? Soccer, baseball, track & field, running, bicycling, and golf are only a few! Sporting events and local competitions, whether for a school, college, professional or community event, offer many ways to provide your support and enjoy the fun of competition.

One way to enjoy sports is to combine your interest in the sport with a volunteer job. And…possibly land a free admission ticket! If you enjoy youth sports, look into a mentoring or coaching role in school and community sponsored programs. Or take on support tasks such as maintaining equipment, setting up competitive events, or selling items.

Consider also volunteering at other types of community sporting events such as run-walk, cycling and golf events. Volunteers enjoy many interesting options from the logistics of months-in-advance planning, designing t-shirts and awards, working with sponsors, assembling goodie packets, setting up a course, handing out food or water on a course, staffing a finish line, and coordinating kids' events. In the South Sound, look into volunteering to help senior athletes at the Washington Senior Games held every July and August at various locations in the South Sound. For more information (or to compete!), visit washingtonstateseniorgames.com.

Find an event on your community calendar and check out its website. You'll have fun, meet other people, and enjoy the sense of community.

Government Service

Surprising to many retirees are opportunities at city, county, and metro area government agencies. Volunteers are always needed to serve on advisory boards, commissions, and committees; help at parks and recreation outdoor activities, farmers markets, city events and festivals; and assist with various social services, city, or county-sponsored activities, and in justice and legal, and law enforcement offices. See *CHAPTER 13: GOVERNMENT SERVICE* on page 89 and *RESOURCES: GOVERNMENT SERVICE* on page 216.

Healthcare

Healthcare volunteers assist with patients in hospital, community health, mental health, and hospice settings. They work for health-related causes about which they are passionate or are naturally connected. They help with office and administrative tasks, and community outreach programs and events. See *CHAPTER 14: HEALTHCARE VOLUNTEERING* on page 93 and *RESOURCES: HEALTHCARE VOLUNTEERING* on page 219.

Home and Remote Volunteering

For whatever reason, Boomers may want to volunteer, but physically can't leave home. So, what are some of the choices? With the widespread use of technology for communications and research, there are many options to explore.

For example: AARP, RSVP (createthegood.aarp.org) program. Using the AARP website, you can search for opportunities for remote volunteer tasks which can be performed from home. At the volunteer-search page, enter the keywords "Volunteer from Home," and your zip code, and other criteria.

Other options for volunteering from home include:

- *Can you use the phone and computer?* If so, you may find organizations that need volunteers to make calls, send emails or do administrative work remotely.

- *Are you interested in writing notes, thank you notes, or invitations by hand?* Find organizations that need people to hand-write invitations or thank-you notes or address envelopes.

- *Could you write for an organization's newsletter or blog?* Could you write and submit a blog or article on something you know?

- *If you have a skill such as knitting or sewing,* could you help make blankets, quilts, scarves, or hats for the needy?

- *Will organizations bring work to you?* Perhaps for assembling baskets, stuffing envelopes. Or putting together flower arrangements.

- *Consider starting your own organization* to collect, package, and mail items, or create cards for men and women serving overseas. Put together backpacks of items for foster children.

Homes Associations

The boards and committees of Homeowners Associations carry out the bylaws of neighborhood communities and make decisions regarding maintenance of properties. Serving on a board gives you a direct say in issues affecting quality of life, home values, safety, and security. If you're new to a neighborhood, HOAs are good place to meet your neighbors and become more involved in your community. Boards welcome people of all backgrounds who bring plain skills, experience, and just plain good common sense to various roles.

What opportunities are available in your HOA? Could you put a special skill to work on your board, such as finance, or taking minutes, or working on the landscape committee. Or how about welcoming new residents? Or would you be better suited to one-time worker bee projects?

Libraries

City and county libraries need volunteers throughout library operations. They assist in computer labs, help with events, shelve books, check in materials, assist patrons, perform office and administrative tasks, teach classes, work with books, and help with kid's programs, and arts and crafts classes. "Friends" groups support their libraries. *See CHAPTER 2: LEARN SOMETHING NEW, Your Library* on page 105 and *CHAPTER 18: LITERARY ARTS, READING, WRITING, Public Libraries: Retiree Reader Heaven* on page 107 and *RESOURCES: LEARNING PLACES, Libraries* on page 235.

Neighborhood Service

Boomers find and create fulfilling opportunities where they live. They get involved in both formal and informal groups of neighbors to support a project or a cause that benefits their community. They find a need and fill it, either individually or by joining together with others.

A good example is serving on, or starting, an emergency preparedness team. These teams help communities and individuals prepare for adversities ranging from power outages to chemical spills, to natural occurrences such as earthquakes, hurricanes, tornadoes, and floods.

Other volunteer opportunities within neighborhoods include maintaining community gardens and parks and creating informal groups to pursue common hobbies such as reading, sewing, woodworking, tennis, pickleball, or walking.

Without realizing it, many Boomers volunteer for caring activities in their neighborhoods by filling needs that arise in the community. For example, Boomers often watch out for and help their elderly neighbors with outdoor and pet tasks, grocery shopping, transportation, and little household chores, and provide a friendly visit to combat loneliness.

Are there needs in your own neighborhood that would improve security, or create a more inclusive, friendly community? Could you help with chores or run errands for someone having health or mobility problems? Or provide a regular friendly visit or call to people who are homebound and isolated?

Museums and Historical Sites

A wide variety of museums preserve histories of communities and states, industry, art, architecture, transportation, home life, military, and more. Volunteers help preserve history and help others appreciate the past. You can work with a particular facet of history or focus on the history of your community. Opportunities are endless. See *CHAPTER*

19: MUSEUMS, HISTORY on page 111, and on *RESOURCES: MUSEUMS, HISTORICAL SITES, SOCIETIES* on page 244.

Music

Many Boomers express their love of music as volunteer teachers and performers in nonprofits that help people learn and enjoy music. They perform for causes they care about and in settings such as hospitals, hospice care, and nursing homes. Music festival volunteering is another option. See *CHAPTER 20: MUSIC, Concerts, Festivals* on page 118 and *RESOURCES: MUSIC ORGANIZATIONS* on page 257.

Nonprofits

The broad and large category of "Nonprofits" refers to organizations that exist for a social benefit (not to make a profit) and are defined as nonprofit for tax purposes. Types of nonprofits include community service organizations, arts and cultural organizations, schools, churches, charities, homes associations, business associations, and social clubs; many of the types of organizations described elsewhere in this book.

Nonprofit organizations are an abundant source of opportunities to use your commitment, skills, and experience to give back. Nonprofits come in all shapes and sizes, with wide-ranging volunteering needs.

At the heart of all nonprofit organizations are committed volunteers who bring a wide variety of skills, interests, and talents to serve their communities and keep their organizations running. Whatever your skills and interests, you'll find a nonprofit eager to sign you up!

Especially welcome are volunteers with experience in business operations, or knowledge in the organization's area of focus or particular type of business. For example: healthcare, retail, marketing, or managing a nonprofit.

Volunteer tasks typically needed by nonprofits involve day-to-day operations, office and administration, marketing, technology support, and outreach. In many cases, nonprofits need lots of "arms and legs" volunteers ready to do whatever is needed to support their purpose. Volunteers get involved in working directly with an organization's clients or servicing them in some way. Assignments may be one-time projects, or ongoing daily, weekly, monthly, or seasonal. Volunteers also serve on governing boards and committees. Nonprofits of many types are represented throughout this book.

To research places to volunteer, visit the websites of organizations that connect with in some way. These include city and county government agencies, nonprofit associations, Chambers of Commerce, community foundations, United Way, and other community organizations. For a list of chambers of commerce, see *RESOURCES: BUSINESS* on page 162. For a list of organizations that connect volunteers to community opportunities, see *RESOURCES: VOLUNTEERING* on page 277.

Outdoor Volunteers

Opportunities for outdoorsy volunteers in the South Sound are plentiful in environmental organizations, friends-of-parks, parks and recreation programs, and public gardens. Volunteers help restore parks, tend natural and wildlife areas, plant trees, shrubs, and flowers, as well as teach and guide groups, and serve as advocates for environmental causes. See *RESOURCES: THE GREAT OUTDOORS* on page 129 and *RESOURCES: THE GREAT OUTDOORS* on page 271.

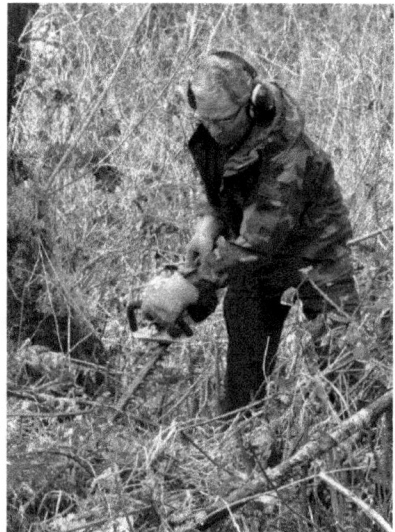

Recreational, Hobby, and Special Interest Clubs

No matter what your interest or hobby, there is a club for it. Whether it be sports, DIY, arts, crafts, music, parenting, writing, or nearly anything, clubs are a great way to learn more and enjoy the ideas of like-minded people. And volunteers, of course, are always needed for any number of tasks. Think about groups to which you belong are aware of, or want to join, and what you could offer. See *CHAPTER 16: HOBBIES* on page 101.

Retiree Living Communities

As retiree communities become more popular, residents volunteer within their communities to teach, organize, carry out special events, or informally volunteer to help others. You can find any number of one-time, seasonal, or ongoing ways to give back to the communities at large or serve on your community's board or committees.

Most communities always have open positions in areas such as communications, trips, education, entertainment, community service, and social activities. You may also have an idea for a hobby or special interest group that would also include volunteering. If so, start one.

How can you get more involved in your community's social activities and projects? For example, could you help with food, clothing, holiday gift drives? Could you adopt a nursing home or contribute time to a youth homeless shelter?

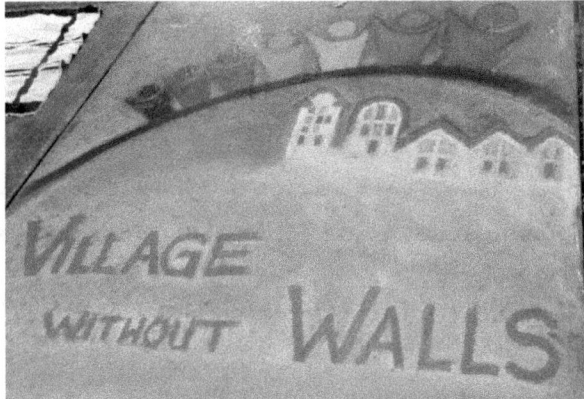

Senior Assistance

Senior assistance organizations are another way Boomers give back. "I volunteer for organizations that help seniors because I'll need that help someday," say retiree senior-support volunteers. "We provide a little help to help older adults age in place."

Volunteers pay it forward through nonprofits and other organizations that help seniors in daily living activities such as transportation, in-home assistance, grocery delivery and meals.

Many nonprofits, government agencies, faith-based and community service organizations sponsor programs to help seniors in daily living activities such as transportation, meals, learning, social activities, in-home assistance, grocery delivery, and many others. Organizations also help seniors with day-to-day needs. Senior centers provide a wide range of health, recreation, fitness, education, and social activities for seniors. Retiree volunteers bring their own special connection and understanding of the needs of these services and make great volunteers. See *RESOURCES: SENIOR SERVICES* on page 264.

Senior and Community Centers

Located in communities throughout the state, senior centers provide a wide range of social services to help seniors live, learn, thrive, and socialize. Senior Centers also offer a variety of services including legal aid counseling, health and fitness education programs and activities, e.g., dancing, tai chi, yoga.

Among the many volunteer roles in senior centers are teaching classes in fitness, arts and crafts, writing, history, and many more topics, maintaining libraries, cooking and serving meals, assisting with technology and computers, and leading trips.

For more information, contact the senior or community center in your community. For a listing of area centers, see *RESOURCES: SENIOR SERVICES, Senior and Community Centers*, on page 267.

Sharing Wisdom

Boomers who want to pass along the benefits of THE wisdom, knowledge, and expertise accumulated over a lifetime have some unique options for giving back.

Examples are organizations that work with mentoring children, young adults, and intergenerational groups.

If you are a retiree who looks to apply the insight gained from life experiences, consider nonprofits and other organizations that specifically tap into the life skills and experience of seniors to carry out their missions. These programs recognize the valuable contributions of older adults who make a difference in their communities.

They volunteer for any of several types of organizations that are specifically built upon the life skills and experience offered by retirees. Skills are sought in areas such as teaching, training, management, accounting, working with youth, and many other areas. See *RESOURCES: VOLUNTEERING, Sharing Wisdom* on page 279.

Teaching and Speaking

What knowledge or expertise could pass along to others? Teach what you know through classes, workshops, and speaking in classrooms, libraries, and community centers or through service clubs, learning forums, and many other types of organizations. See *CHAPTER 22: TEACHING, SPEAKING,* on page 121.

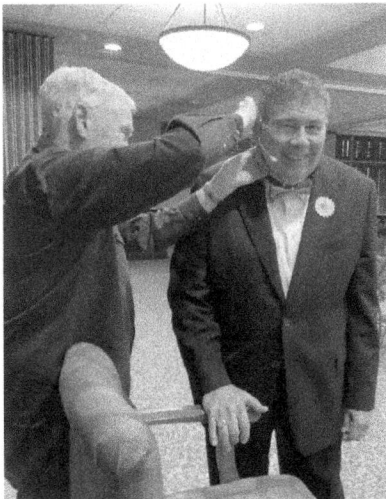

Theater and Performance

Theater lovers enjoy many opportunities to enhance the theater experience for themselves and others. Look for community and regional theater companies to join a volunteer cast or take on any number of behind-the-scenes tasks to bring performances to life. *CHAPTER 24: THEATER, PERFORMANCE* on page 133 and *RESOURCES: THEATER, PERFORMANCE, South Sound Performing Arts Companies and Venues on page 273.*

Unique, Informal Giving Back

Many people become naturally involved in informal volunteering using their unique interests and skills. Doing repairs, organizing youth baseball games, taking a disabled neighbor to lunch, playing music in a hospital waiting room, and checking with neighbors during an emergency are examples.

Think again about the skills you've acquired in a past or current job or career. Are you good at building or fixing things, or figuring out technology? Calligraphy? Assembling something? Plumbing, carpentry, or electrical work? Car repair? Look for places that could use that skill, including many of those described elsewhere in this book. Some people turn their special interest into a Meetup group (meetup.com) to help others learn and participate in their interest.

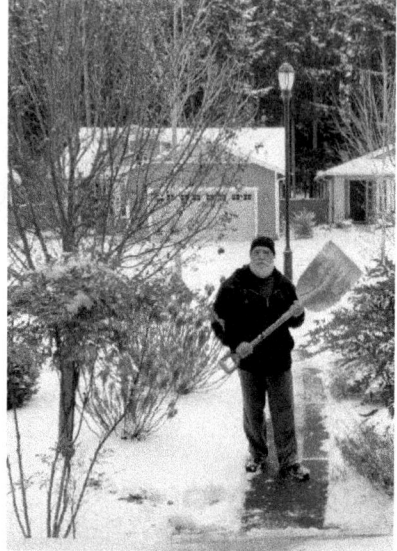

So how do you find informal opportunities?

- Look around for needs that you could fill in your neighborhood or daily activities. Include your friends. *Who needs your help? Those who are elderly or disabled? New arrivals? Parents with young children? Someone who experienced a serious health setback or lost a loved one?*

- Think about how to share your interests. *Pet lovers, could you walk dogs, or take your friendly pet to bring a smile to those in nursing homes?* (You'll need to get some training!) Or could you offer to help care for pets who reside with owners in assisted living facilities.

- Think about something you enjoy such as woodworking, jewelry making, or art, or some type of craft. *Could you donate your items to a nonprofit auction or gift store?*

- *If you knit, crochet, or sew, could you make blankets, hats, or scarves for needy adults and children?* Do some research. You'll come up with as many ideas as there are people with needs.

Volunteer Websites and Organizations

Another way to narrow your search for a volunteer opportunity is to visit websites of organizations post volunteer opportunities for many organizations. These include community-minded organizations such as chambers of commerce, city and county websites, United Ways, and community foundations. Some post job openings for their member businesses and organizations, and their nonprofit partners.

One popular site is VolunteerMatch.com which nonprofits throughout the country post volunteer opportunities. You can search for a gig that matches your location, interests, skills, availability, and any other criteria you choose. For example, you can narrow it to one-time or ongoing projects, outside or inside, long-term, or short-term. Work with kids, adults, or seniors. In groups, or singly. See *RESOURCES: VOLUNTEERING* on page 277 for other organizations by that connect volunteers to community opportunities.

More on Volunteering

This process described in this section is intended as a starting point and path/process to lead you to meaningful volunteer work. Keep in mind:

- An important part of taking on a volunteer role is to understand your "why." In other words, how will you also benefit. Many who volunteer want to use their knowledge and skills in a meaningful way, learn new things, feel useful and appreciated, and make a difference. The social aspect of a common cause may also be extremely satisfying.

- Finding the right opportunity is an ongoing process. Much like a career, your ideas and interests change as you discover and pursue more options. While the basic you is still you, you may unexpectedly discover interesting new ways to give back. As the world changes, so do the options available to you. There are new life lessons to learn. Expect to try a number of new things and enjoy it as part of life-long learning process Stay open to possibilities.

- You may find what appears to be the "perfect" volunteer opportunity but then find that it just doesn't feel right. If intuition or common sense tells you otherwise, address it in a positive way, look at what you've learned, respectfully back away and move on.

CHAPTER 4: ANIMAL LOVERS

As humans, we share this planet – earth, water, air, and space – with other animals of every imaginable size, shape, and type. Many feel the calling to make the world a better place through love for, and connections with, other living creatures.

Animals we're closest to – our pets – give us a sense of purpose and meaning, motivate us to exercise, reduce isolation, give us a feel-good non-judgmental companion, and help us care for something outside ourselves.

If animals occupy your special heart place, get involved in animal-related volunteer work. You'll discover interesting, fulfilling and some out-of-the ordinary opportunities:

- Adopting and caring for our own pets.

- Volunteering at pet rescue and shelter organizations.

- Teaming up with a pet for joyful visits with adults and children confined to hospitals, nursing homes, and other care facilities.

- Working or volunteering with therapy animals such as cats, dogs, and horses to help people heal from physical and mental illness.

- Speaking out to advocate for animals in a variety of organizations.

- Caring for wild animals at zoos.

- Volunteering with wildlife and habitat preservation organizations.

Animal Adoption and Rescue

Every day, Boomers pour their love for animals into many channels of volunteer work to improve the lives of rescue cats, dogs, horses, birds, and other animals.

If your heart goes out to homeless, sick, abandoned, or abused animals, volunteering in animal rescue and adoption may be a rewarding activity for you. Many types of animal shelters are found in most communities and rely on volunteers to fulfill a wide variety of shelter caregiving jobs.

Small animal shelters always need volunteer help with animal feeding, socializing, fostering and adoption, transportation, and veterinarian care. Many also volunteer their time doing office and administrative work, or in outreach, marketing, and special events. Others offer their skills in photography, writing, graphic design, and technology.

To find places to adopt a pet or volunteer in a pet shelter, search for animal shelters in your community. For listings of area animal adoption and rescue organizations see *RESOURCES: ANIMAL ADOPTION AND RESCUE, Cats, Dogs and Other Small Animals* on page 142.

You can also visit any of these websites which allow you to search for available pets by city:

- Adopt a Pet. Nonprofit pet adoption search site. adoptapet.com

- Humane Society. National animal protection organization. humanesociety.org

- Pet finder. Searchable database of animals who need homes petfinder.com

- Animal Shelter. Animal adoption website. animalshelter.org

- Best Friends. National organization that saves lives of homeless pets (bestfriends.org).

Horse rescue operations care for at-risk horses that have been abandoned, abused, neglected, lost, or simply unwanted. They care for them until permanent homes can be found. Some combine horse rescue with equine-assisted therapy. See *Equine Assisted Therapy Programs* below. Horse rescue involves similar tasks – feeding, grooming, cleaning stalls, fundraising, helping with special events, clerical work, and other jobs. For a list of area horse rescue organizations, see

RESOURCES: ANIMAL ADOPTION AND RESCUE, Horse and Large Animal Rescue, Rehabilitation on page 146.

Find other places to work with shelter horses with searches for equine or horse rescue in your community or on these national websites where you can search by city.

- Rescue Shelter. Provides links to horse rescue operations throughout the U.S. (horse.rescueshelter.com).

- Horse World Data. Provides links to horse rescue and retirement operations throughout the U.S. (horseworlddata.com).

Advocacy is another important function of animal rescue and adoption organizations. Animal advocates are the voices to protect animals in legislation and ordinances addressing animal treatment, speaking out and getting involved in causes to protect animals and prevent cruelty.

Animal-assisted Therapy Programs

People-animal teams seek to improve the lives of others through friendly visits. They bring smiles to those they visit in hospitals, hospice care, nursing homes, mental institutions, treatment centers, and other places. Their visits calm the emotionally challenged, give confidence to the disabled, and connect to those with special needs.

Many libraries offer programs that help children improve reading skills by reading to special dogs, which by nature are non-judgmental listeners.

Special training is often required to certify people-pet teams for animal-assisted therapy visits. Start with programs that offer training for animal-human teams such as:

- Love on a Leash. Animal therapy certification (loveonaleash.org).
- Pet Partners. Animal therapy certification (petpartners.org).

Equine-assisted Therapy Programs

If you enjoy working with horses and want to make a difference in the lives of people, volunteer in an equine-assisted therapy program. Health professionals conduct animal-assisted programs as part of an individual's therapy. In equine-assisted therapy, for example, individuals receive hands-on training in horsemanship to address various disorders and disabilities. Look for websites of equine-assisted therapy programs in your area.

Wildlife Organizations

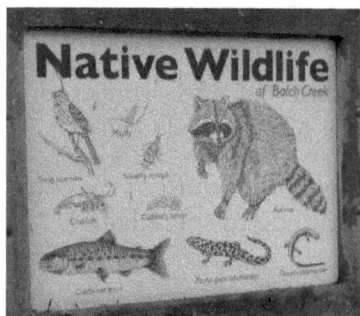

By participating in wildlife organizations, retirees contribute to the bigger picture of protecting our natural resources for the wellbeing of animals and humans alike.

Options to get involved include volunteering, advocacy, fundraising, and activities at state and local levels. Check out the websites of wildlife organizations in your own community or national and international organizations. See RESOURCES: ANIMAL ADOPTION AND RESCUE, Wildlife Organizations on page 147.

CHAPTER 5: ART, PHOTOGRAPHY, FILM

Does your interest gravitate to some aspect of visual art? If so, you'll discover a variety of places in your community to interact with your favorite art form by learning, teaching, volunteering, or participating in art-full communities of artists, photographers, and filmmakers.

You can attend exhibits ranging from the highly regarded collections at the Seattle and Tacoma Art Museums, to local and regional shows at community art centers, to collections throughout public and private venues. You're surrounded by art in all media embedded throughout community landscapes and within regional and local exhibits at art museums and galleries, cultural centers, universities, and festivals.

Art is everywhere. You'll find collections and shows of every imaginable size and type of space and venue – public art galleries, museums, public and private buildings, spacious and tiny outdoor spaces, parks, colleges, businesses, airports, senior communities, corporations – you name it. To explore abundant visual art experiences in South Puget Sound, see *RESOURCES: ART, PHOTOGRAPHY, FILM, Visual Arts Spaces and Cultural Centers* on page 149.

Art festivals offer retirees a place to display their creations and experience art in an interesting venue. For a list of art festivals, see *RESOURCES: ART, PHOTOGRAPHY, FILM, Art Walks, Festivals* on page 155.

Similarly, the emerging film scene offers film-lovers places to experience all genres of film as a viewer, a filmmaker or aspiring filmmaker. Several annual film festivals bring the excitement of new, innovative, and diverse releases to area audiences. For a listing of area film festivals, see RESOURCES: ART, PHOTOGRAPHY, FILM, Film Festivals on page 159.

Photographers also find inspiration in the area's diverse lush, sometimes wild landscapes, rugged coastline and wilderness areas and all flavors of cityscapes and people. Photographic expressions are found in galleries and centers and changing exhibitions around the area.

Learn, Teach, Speak Art

If it's time to release your inner artist, no matter what your media, look for classes in museums, arts, and cultural centers, community colleges, parks and recreation classes, community and senior centers and retirement communities. Other places to learn and practice art are visual arts, and film and photography clubs and organizations.

To enjoy your art through teaching or speaking, look for opportunities at the same places. For more ideas on where to learn or teach, see CHAPTER 17: LEARN SOMETHING NEW on page 105 and CHAPTER 22: TEACHING, SPEAKING on page 121 and RESOURCES: ART, PHOTOGRAPHY, FILM, Photo, Community Colleges on page 161.

Where Art Lives, Volunteers Follow

A variety of art-related volunteer opportunities are available to retirees. Boomers express their art-loving sides in volunteer roles that range from working in a cultural center to helping youth learn about art, film, and photography. Most cultural nonprofits – regardless of size – rely heavily on volunteers to make exhibits, events, and programs available.

At larger galleries, many volunteer as docents – people who guide groups and help bring exhibits to life. Volunteers, including those with certain specialties perform a variety of other tasks such as working with artists, staff, and visitors, and setting up exhibits or writing blogs. Tasks may involve greeting visitors, assisting in a store or with office work, and helping at previews, receptions, fundraisers, and other events.

To research places to volunteer in the arts, see *RESOURCES: ART, PHOTOGRAPHY, FILM, Visual Arts Spaces and Cultural Centers* on page 149.

Festivals and events are another interesting option for artsy volunteers as they often need lots of volunteers for day and weekend shows. Festivals offer a more relaxed atmosphere, and volunteers may enjoy the benefits of free passes and refreshments, with some fun thrown in. Tasks include setup and take-down, ushering and hosting, and on-the-ground festival coordination and outreach. For a listing of art festivals, see

RESOURCES: ART, PHOTOGRAPHY, FILM, Art Walks, Festivals on page 155, and *Film Festivals* on page 159.

Youth Program Volunteers

Volunteering in youth art programs is another way to give back while expressing your artsy side. Volunteers help young people learn through classes, workshops, and special events. Find out more by researching places to teach youth art in your community such as family and youth nonprofits, schools, youth organizations, parks and recreation classes, arts and cultural centers, and after-school programs.

Art Commissions and Alliances

Art lovers like you help bring art to others by serving various community, city, and county arts boards, committees, and commissions. These commissions invite and welcome participation in planning and overseeing community art projects.

By joining an art commission, you'll help promote the growth of arts and culture through public art projects, grants, advocacy, and special events, making art accessible to everyone. For more information, research the commissions and committees of your city, county, or regional planning entities.

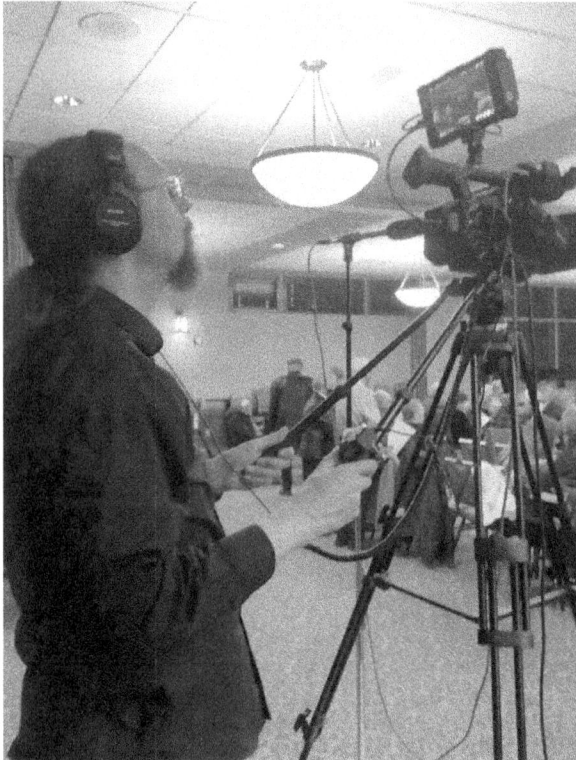

Volunteer Your Art and Graphic Skills

You also can volunteer your artistic talents in graphic design, illustration, or desktop publishing for behind-the-scenes work with any number of organizations. Many need design and graphic arts skills in writing and photography, and creating websites, printed programs, brochures, posters, mailings, invitations, and more. To find graphic arts volunteer opportunities, research organizations in your interest area.

Photography, Video, Film

Opportunities to practice, learn, teach, and volunteer in photography and filmmaking are similar to those enjoyed by other types of art enthusiasts. Photographers find learning and teaching opportunities in art and cultural centers, community colleges, community and senior centers, parks and recreation classes, clubs, and Meetup groups. The popularity of film and video media also has led to a growing number of college and university offerings in screenwriting and production.

Photography and Film Volunteers

Photographers with an interest in volunteering should look into stand-alone photo galleries, or galleries within art or historical venues. Opportunities may include serving as docents, maintaining collections, and helping at events and festivals, or in back-office roles. For a listing of area film festivals, see *RESOURCES: ART, PHOTOGRAPHY, FILM, Film Festivals* on page 159.

Other options, whatever your skill, are community service and nonprofit organizations. For example, many animal shelters and rescue groups need photos for outreach and marketing activities. It's a great, fun way for amateurs to gain experience and add to a portfolio.

Other options for graphic arts volunteers include teaching in youth nonprofits, or other places such as community and senior centers, retirement communities, parks and recreation programs, and libraries. Start your research for arts volunteers at individual nonprofit organizations in your interest area, libraries, or volunteering websites such as voluntermatch.com.

CHAPTER 6: BUSINESS BUILDING

Have you ever felt called to start and run your own business?

Some people find that turning their passions into businesses is the best way to express themselves and make their personal connections with the world. Their businesses are natural extensions of themselves and another way to live their passion or purpose.

Boomers who release their inner entrepreneur and go into business are in good company. We're aptly labeled Encore Entrepreneurs, and those who go it alone are called "Solopreneurs."

We're driven to run our own shows, challenged by turning our expertise and knowledge into a business. We create new uses for our experience – consulting or writing for example. We turn hobbies and passions into successful "lifestyle businesses." We offer products or services that we find meaningful and make a difference to others. Encores also embrace technology and the Internet to start and operate businesses. Add a touch of creative spirit, and Boomers find this an ideal time to go for their dreams.

Popular Business Options

While business opportunities are unlimited, examples of typical types of businesses Boomers engage in are:

- Consulting. Return to employers or an industry as consultants.

- Lifestyle. Turn an interest such as jewelry-making, crafts, woodworking, or collecting into a business.

- Writing and blogging. Share life experiences and expertise in a book or blog, or as a freelance writer.

- Online. Establish an Internet or a website business to sell products, services, information, or some combination.

- Retail. Sell specialty products such as gifts, clothing and accessories, or food at a physical location.

- Public speaking, teaching, tutoring, or coaching. Inspire others and teach what you know in pursuits such as music, art, writing, sports, crafts, technology, and many others.

- Hang your shingle. Provide professional services such as writing, bookkeeping, accounting, marketing, or personal services.

- Turn a hobby into a business. Examples are fishing guides, teachers of art or music, crafters of all sorts, and gardeners.

Ask Yourself...

Questions you might ask:

- What is my personal goal for having a business? Earn money, express myself in the world, follow a dream, etc.

- What type of business do I want to start?

- What ability, skill, or interest could I turn into a business?

- How do I make my business unique and stand out from others?

- Who are my customers and how would my business benefit them?

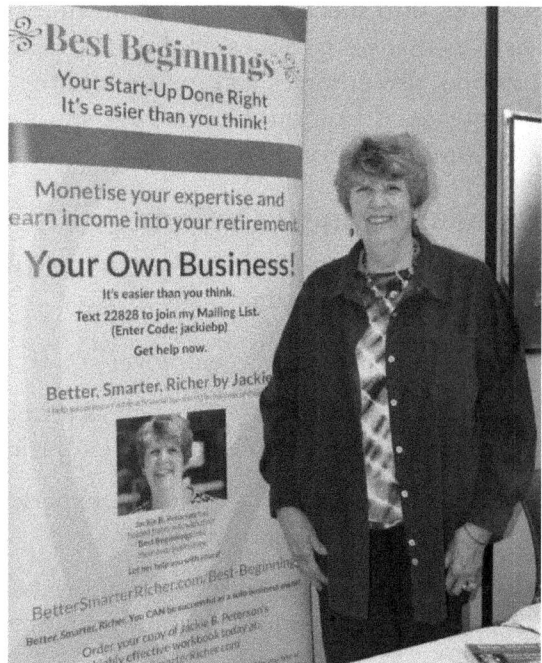

Getting Started

Want-to-be entrepreneurs often don't know where to begin. Owning even a simple business has many pieces and parts to address, starting with decisions such as business name, form of business, state registration, and other legalities.

You need to determine specifics about your product or service, your customers and how to reach them, and how and where you will operate. Need employees? Physical equipment and supplies? What about office technology, website, credit cards, bank accounts?

Not the least among your decisions are how to finance and grow your business. All this leads to the necessity of a business plan. Fortunately, abundant help and resources are available to Encores no matter where you are with your business.

Small Business Development Centers

Small Business Development Centers (sba.gov) throughout the country provide aspiring and current small business owners with a variety of free business consulting, low-cost training services and informational tools. Many area colleges and universities host regular SBDC activities.

SBA-sponsored local chapters of SCORE provide free mentoring and low-cost workshops. Working and retired executives and business owners donate time and expertise as business counselors. (score.org)

State Business Offices

Washington State provides easy-to-navigate information for businesses within the state. Information includes steps on how to start a business, practical and legal information about business names and structure, business plans, registrations, taxes, licenses, permits, and ongoing business requirements. Contact business.wa.gov.

Other Resources for Entrepreneurs

Other types of organizations with resources to help with launching and running a business include:

- Economic development organizations. As supporters of job creation, state and local economic development and chamber of commerce organizations provide access to resources and sponsor workshops for new business startups.

- County and City Business Services. Educational resources and business toolkits are provided by several cities and counties.

- Libraries and Community Colleges. Both online resources and in-person classes can be found at libraries and community colleges.

See *RESOURCES: BUSINESS* on page 162 for listings of economic development and chamber organizations, SBA, and other resources for South Sound businesses. For a listing of community colleges see *RESOURCES: LEARNING PLACES, Colleges, Universities*, on page 233. For a listing of Libraries, see *RESOURCES: LEARNING PLACES, Libraries* on page 235.

CHAPTER 7: CARE FOR THE ENVIRONMENT

You love the outdoors and are willing to spend time caring for and helping preserve our natural assets. Our area has a lot of environment to care about. In fact, your area may be known for it. Look at your favorite natural area, park, forest, river, lake, watershed, or wildlife habitat and you'll find all types of groups who help preserve and protect it.

Options to give back to nature are plentiful. You'll find groups that adopt or friend their favorite community park, wildlife refuge, natural area, forest, river, wetlands, or garden. Connect with advocates who speak up and teach about nature. Volunteer with city, county, and parks departments who are eager to sign you up for park duty. Sign on with organizations in your own neighborhood that partner with cities and parks departments to keep parks healthy and safe. For information on the area's

Dig In, Clean Up, Party On!

Sign up for a work party. You can be part of a weekend or weekday (you're retired, remember) work group at a park, natural area, garden, or wildlife reserve. Unearth your boots, gloves and shovels to plant flowers, trees, and shrubs; pull weeds or build flower beds. Count birds and wildlife. Be an active learner and educate others on causes you are passionate about.

Organizations generally are flexible and will match your schedule to their activity. Choose a one-time project or clean-up or be on a regular volunteer schedule. Get dirty working outside or skip the dirt and mud and work in an office or an outreach program. Take photos, write for blogs and websites. It all makes a difference.

You'll take away the satisfaction of connecting with Mother Earth, doing your part to keep the world healthy, growing, and green. Along

the way you'll meet new people and learn something new about your area's unique ecology. And don't forget how outdoor exercise benefits brain health! It is so very win-win.

Friend or Adopt a Natural Area

Dedicated "friends of" and park stewardship groups everywhere work to preserve local and community parks and natural areas. Often, they

team up with city or county parks organizations. Park warriors participate in park planning, clean up, work parties, identifying problems, and getting involved in park education and advocacy issues. Most Friend groups are free or low-cost to join. Friend groups are perfect places to get your hands dirty, socialize, and learn more about park ecology. And get outdoors!

Look for activities you can enjoy with kids and grandkids. Guaranteed you'll be digging around with young old people like us. For information on area groups dedicated to preserving local parks and natural areas see RESOURCES: CARE FOR THE ENVIRONMENT, Protecting Ecological Areas, on page 166.

Ecological Preservation Groups

These volunteer groups tackle environmental preservation in expansive and dramatic spaces of rivers, watersheds, wetlands, and wildlife habitats. Examples include projects in forests that focus on the park's ecological health; many maintain trail systems. Volunteer jobs at wildlife refuges range from conducting tours to habitat restoration. Friends groups of large natural wonders work to preserve sprawling, complicated outdoor

spaces and protect the scenic beauty though work parties, discovery hikes, and community education.

Volunteers at wetlands preserves help at education centers and on crews that remove invasive plants, maintain trails, and work with marshes. State affiliates of organizations such as the Nature Conservancy sponsor restoration projects that benefit natural areas in many states. (nature.org)

For information on area groups dedicated to preserving ecological areas, *see RESOURCES: CARE FOR THE ENVIRONMENT, Protecting Ecological Areas*, on page 168.

Advocacy and Education

If your passion is sharing knowledge, many environmental organizations welcome outreach and education volunteers. Ecological preservation groups advocate for their areas in public and political forums. Organizations such as the Sierra Club (sierraclub.org) get involved in the nitty gritty of Environmental Impact Statements and in influencing public policy decisions – legislative, legal, administrative, and electoral.

State-specific groups communicate with the public regarding political issues involving the public wildlands, wildlife, and waters. Outreach programs may also include workshops, classes, and models of environmental preservation in action at their sites. Other local environmental nonprofits bring environmental education to the community through on-site education programs in schools and at community events.

For more about area groups involved in environmental advocacy, see *RESOURCES: CARE FOR THE ENVIRONMENT* on page 165 and visit the websites of groups of interest.

CHAPTER 8: CAREER ENCORES

While many Boomers eagerly trade jobs and career for a leisure retirement, others opt to stay in the workforce. An increasing number want or need to work for the money. Others do because they just enjoy their jobs, the daily routine, and their daily contact with co-workers. Not to mention they find their work satisfying and feel valued. Sometimes, it's just hard to let go.

Turning Points, New Chances

Retirement age for many retirees is a turning point. It's finally time to look elsewhere for a more meaningful career or job, or better situation. Some prefer a gradual transition to retirement by working part-time or consulting. Others are ready to do what they love or fulfill a life purpose. For them, it's time to realize a dream and turn skills, experience, and interests into a business or independent work.

Change Careers, Profession, or Situation

Popular stay-in-the-workforce options among Boomers are:

- Transitioning to another role within an organization, applying expertise to areas such as training or mentoring.

- Shifting to a flexible or part-time schedule or working from a home office (or coffee shop).

- Taking a similar position at a new situation in the same industry.

- Taking business skills and experience to a favorite nonprofit.

- Seeking out a new batch of education or training to pivot to an entirely different career, profession, or industry.

Where to Start the Process

Either within or outside your current situation, a good job search involves research and networking. The process starts by evaluating skills, experience, and expertise, and defining an "ideal" job. Among the many parts of ideal are hours, work environment, location, work culture, interaction, projects, compensation, and camaraderie.

Research the types of industries and organizations that would be a good fit. Learn more through internet searches, talking with friends, acquaintances, and many others. Take advantage of the tools, resources, and people available to you, many at no or low cost. Today's online world delivers job search guides, checklists, and other tools to your desktop or other devices. From building a resume to interviewing, to networking, to researching, it is all out there.

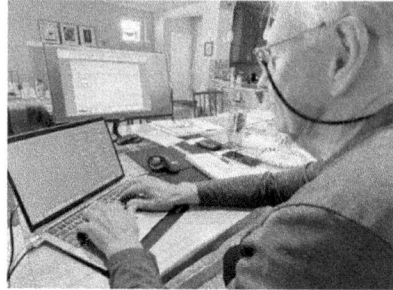

Resources for Career Change

Hands-on job seekers can enroll in live and online classes and seminars at community colleges. Companies and industry groups, and even AARP (aarp.org), sponsor job fairs and career classes. Networking is key to finding a new gig. Spread the word among friends, former employers, workout buddies and others. Social media such as LinkedIn, Facebook, and other social media platforms are good ways to connect; use them as appropriate for you and your situation. Below are examples of organizations retirees can tap into to land a new job.

- AARP. Jobs, Work & Resources by city. Job hunting articles and links to job hunting sites, niche sites, and social media. (aarp.org)

- AARP Tek Academy. An online connection to job search tools and online career fairs. (learn.aarp.org)

- Community Colleges. Check out local community colleges for career and technical programs See RESOURCES: LEARNING PLACES, Colleges, Universities on page 233 for a list of area colleges.

- Job search websites such as Career Builder, Career One Stop, Indeed, and Monster. Search for openings by location and job type.

- Libraries. Visit the websites of libraries within the Pierce County and Timberland Library systems resources and classes for job seekers. See RESOURCES: LEARNING PLACES, Libraries on page 235 for a list of area libraries.

CHAPTER 9: COMMUNITY SERVICE

In this chapter, community service refers to organizations that serve individuals, families, and youth facing challenges with addictions and mental health, food insecurity, homelessness, and other human issues.

Retirement is a great time to explore community service opportunities and give back to make our communities better places to live. Our communities care deeply about the needs of health-challenged, less fortunate, and underserved populations. We want to help people out of the mainstream who are homeless, hungry or need other types of help.

Many community service organizations are nonprofit and depend heavily upon volunteers. Many are grass-roots groups and others are sponsored by churches and civic groups. Many people – like you – start and run them. Volunteer roles are as varied as the organizations and need all types of skills, or just the desire to do whatever is needed to meet their clients' needs.

Types of Service Organizations

Many types of organizations provide services to those in need and welcome volunteers to serve in a variety of roles.

- Addictions and Mental Health. A wide variety of organizations serve the community through mental health treatment, education and support for adults, families, and children. Volunteers perform in many support roles such as mentoring, answering calls, development, communication, teaching, and helping at events.

- Disability Services. These organizations support adults and children with disabilities to help people realize their potential and provide opportunities in areas such as housing, recreation, fitness, daily living, transportation, and socializing. Volunteers assist with programs, camp activities, work parties, social events, learning and education, transportation, fundraising, and administrative support.

- Emergency Services. Emergency food, shelter and other services are provided to individuals and families by a variety of nonprofit, faith-based, and other agencies. Volunteers assist in shelters, food pantries, clothing rooms, and thrift stores; they serve meals, help with care and office tasks, drive, and teach.

- Food Banks and Gardens. Food pantries provide food for low-income individuals and families, and people who are homeless. Volunteers help unpack, repackage, sort and box food, and serve clients. Garden and farm volunteers help plant, weed, harvest, and deliver fruits and vegetables to food banks.

- Hunger and Homeless Services. Resources for homeless people include shelters, meals, clothing, healthcare, training, transitional programs, and other services provided by nonprofits, faith-based, and government organizations. Volunteers help in shelters, prepare meals, interact with clients, help with child and animal care, staff clothing and food rooms, teach, and outreach and maintenance.

To find examples of these types of community services organizations in Kitsap, Mason, Pierce, and Thurston Counties, see RESOURCES: COMMUNITY SERVICE ORGANIZATIONS on page 172.

CHAPTER 10: EXPLORING THE SOUTH SOUND

Welcome to South Puget Sound

Looking for FUN Things to do in South Puget Sound? Whatever your interest or home base, Washington's unique South Sound area offers unique, interesting exploration destinations. In this chapter you'll find short summaries by area counties and natural geographic areas – each with its own characteristic vibe. And other starting points for exploring and references to good sources of information.

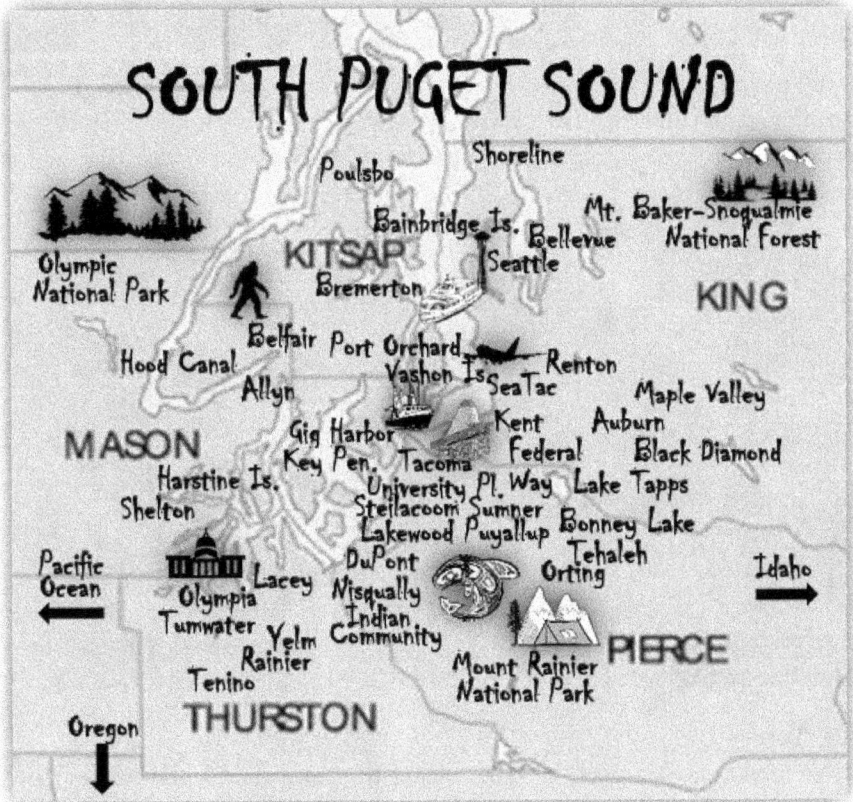

Kitsap County

Kitsap County includes inlets in west Puget Sound to the North, and includes the Kitsap Peninsula, Bremerton and its shipyards, and smaller

coastal communities of Poulsbo (a great bakery), Port Orchard, Port Gamble, and Kingston, which connects via car or walk-on ferry east across the south to King County and Seattle.

Mason County

Mason County, also on the west side of the Sound and inland, is a more sparsely populated area. It's characterized by small coastal towns, thick old forests, natural areas and waterways, mountains, and sits east of the Olympic Peninsula. Shelton is the largest city in the county.

Olympic Peninsula

In Washington's west corner, the expansive Olympic Peninsula awaits those who wish to experience the iconic rainforests, mountains, and

ever-changing rocky coastline. Turnout points give visitors spectacular viewpoints of shifting driftwood piles and hiking cliff vistas.

Further in are the mid-and small size Puget Sound coastal towns, many built up from and around remnants of once larger logging, fishing, and oyster operations. Other places to see are areas along the Hood Canal, numerous state parks and mountain lakes, estuaries, and hiking trails.

Pierce County

Going to the east Sound, is the more populated Pierce County, the Port city of Tacoma. Its suburbs of Dupont, Steilacoom, Lakewood, University Place, and Gig Harbor border the Sound. Inland area suburbs including Puyallup, and several smaller communities. All communities within

Further north up Puget Sound sits the large Port City of Seattle – Washington's largest city – and its suburbs that roughly make up King county. Itself a major visitor destination for many of the activities listed in this book.

Thurston County

Thurston County, on the southern tip edge of the Sound, is home of the State Capitol, Olympia, and its surrounding communities of Lacey, Tumwater, the Nisqually area, Yelm, and further south, Tenino.

So, Get Busy!

With landscape ranging from the iconic irregular coastline, to the lush rainforests of the Olympic Peninsula, to modern waterfront cities, and picturesque waterfront villages and towns backdropped with majestic

Mt. Rainer majestically visible from nearly anywhere – you can imagine there's a lot to explore and do in Washington's South Sound.

Day trip to big, medium, small, and micro-towns. Dig out the cultural attractions, historic sites and museums. Discover where communities blend new urban with refurbished old and real old, still original, and somewhere in between.

While many places can only be reached by car, others may be near to public light-rail-streetcar-bus systems, or ferry systems, or hiking trails. Venturing out, you'll find more than just big trees growing taller. You'll

find that just a little research – in your libraries, the local sections of bookstores, Chamber of Commerce offices, and visitor's centers – will bring you pleasant surprises as you explore your own backyard.

While we can't even begin to cover all resources available for exploring, we can point you to some easy starting places to start. Below are some ideas to whet your local journey appetite and the tip of the iceberg when it comes to exploring the many unique and diverse communities, including your own, in the South Sound.

- Pick cultural destinations from your area's collection of art galleries, museums, historical sites, live theater, and other cultural centers.

- Enjoy the unique character, history, and ambiance of other Puget Sound small towns and communities. Walk about, visit local shops, bakeries, eateries, coffee shops, and points of interest. Make several trips to experience the unique vibe and hidden surprises of each.

- Visit city, chamber of commerce or visitor center websites for maps, lists of attractions and walking tour maps of historical or natural interest. See lists of these websites in RESOURCES: *EXPLORING THE SOUTH SOUND*, beginning on page 180, and include attractions listed by county, city, and natural wonders.

- Get near water. Enjoy scenic river walks, excursions; try clamming.

- Tour campuses of colleges and universities, especially for wonderful surprises of art, architecture, sculpture, and landscaping.

Washington Tourism Website

As a starting point for your South Sound journeys, visit the State of Washington Tourism website. There you'll find information by region, city, area, type of activities and attractions, numerous free maps, guidebooks, and many other handy resources. Get free visitor guides and newsletter, and learn about hundreds of things to do, places to go, road trips, events, and trip planning. stateofwatourism.com

EXPERIENCE A STATE OF WANDERLUST

City, County, and Visitor Websites

Then localize your search by visiting visitor websites of counties, cities, areas and economic development, chamber of commerce and tourist organizations. They're a friendly, helpful source of abundant information on local and regional events, fun indoor and outdoor facilities, attractions, parks, natural areas, arts, music, and concerts, and their area's signature events, entertainment, festivals, museums, travel information, and on and on. For listings of all sorts of exploring websites, see *RESOURCES: EXPLORING THE SOUTH SOUND* on page 180.

Or do your own online search for popular travel and visitor sites.

Outings with Senior and Community Centers

If you'd enjoy like-minded company travelers, several area offer group single or multi-day trips, tours, and outings to various local and regional destinations. Senior centers that offer trips include:

- Bremerton Senior Citizens Center. 1140 Nipsic Ave, Bremerton. 360-473-5357. bremertonwa.gov

- Buckley Senior Activity Center. 811 Main St, Buckley. 360-761-7894. cityofbuckley.com/seniorcenter

- Greater Maple Valley Community Center. Senior activities, trips, and services. 22010 SE 248th St, 425-432-1272. maplevalleycc.org

- Mason County Senior Activities Center. 50 and Better Activities Center. 190 W Sentry Dr, Shelton. 360-426-7374. mcsac.net

- North Kitsap Senior Citizen's Lounge. 18972 Front St NE, Poulsbo. 360-779-5702. poulsboseniors.blogspot.com

- Olympia Senior Center. 222 Columbia St NW, Olympia. 360-586-6181. southsoundseniors.org

- Point Defiance-Ruston Senior Center. 4716 N Baltimore St, Tacoma. 253-756-0601. franketobeyjones.com

- Puyallup Activity Center. 210 W Pioneer Ave. 253-841-5555. cityofpuyallup.org

- South Park and Community Center. 4851 S Tacoma Way, Tacoma. metroparkstacoma.org

Events, Festivals

Add events and festivals to your South Sound experiences. Through festivals we celebrate our love for art, music, reading, theater, and ethnicity. We enjoy events and festivals around food and beverage, cars, nature, books, being outdoors, sports, and many other interests.

We turn out for events that celebrate our cities, towns and communities, our holidays, and our sports. We get involved in large and small events that support causes in our communities. And we delight in events that are just plain fun and sometimes just weird.

While warmer seasons naturally bring more events and festivals, you'll find celebrations and events year around. New ones pop up all the time. Festivals and events are a perfect way to have healthy fun with friends and family and celebrate our communities. For listings of area festivals, see *RESOURCES: ART, PHOTOGRAPHY, FILM, Art Walks, Festivals* on page 155, *Film Festivals* on page 159; and *CHAPTER 20: MUSIC, Concerts, Festivals* on page 117.

Navigating Water, Land Transit

The challenges of travel between locations between the jagged coastline of Puget Sound is made a little easier and faster with the area's ferry network. While a necessity for commuters between islands and mainland, ferries offer explorers an enjoyable alternative to driving or other transportation.

Area transportation is provided by city and county systems of accessible bus, rail, light rail, vans, ferry, and bicycle routes that work together. Fortunately, good information on route planning, maps, schedules, and other details is readily available and easy to navigate. However, public transportation between city and county jurisdictions may require patience in piecing together schedules published both in print and on-line.

As you discover the transportation mode(s) that fit your exploring style, try to include the ferry system as its own unique experience. You'll see Puget Sound from an offshore point of view, enjoying

backdrops of tall firs, mountains, diverse modern-mixed-with-vintage shore towns, neighborhoods, rocky shorelines, inlets, and estuaries.

For information on area public transportation systems, see *RESOURCES: EXPLORING THE SOUTH SOUND, Water, Land Transit* on page 189. For information about bicycling routes, *RESOURCES: FITNESS, HEALTHY LIVING, Cycling Clubs, Maps* on page 199.

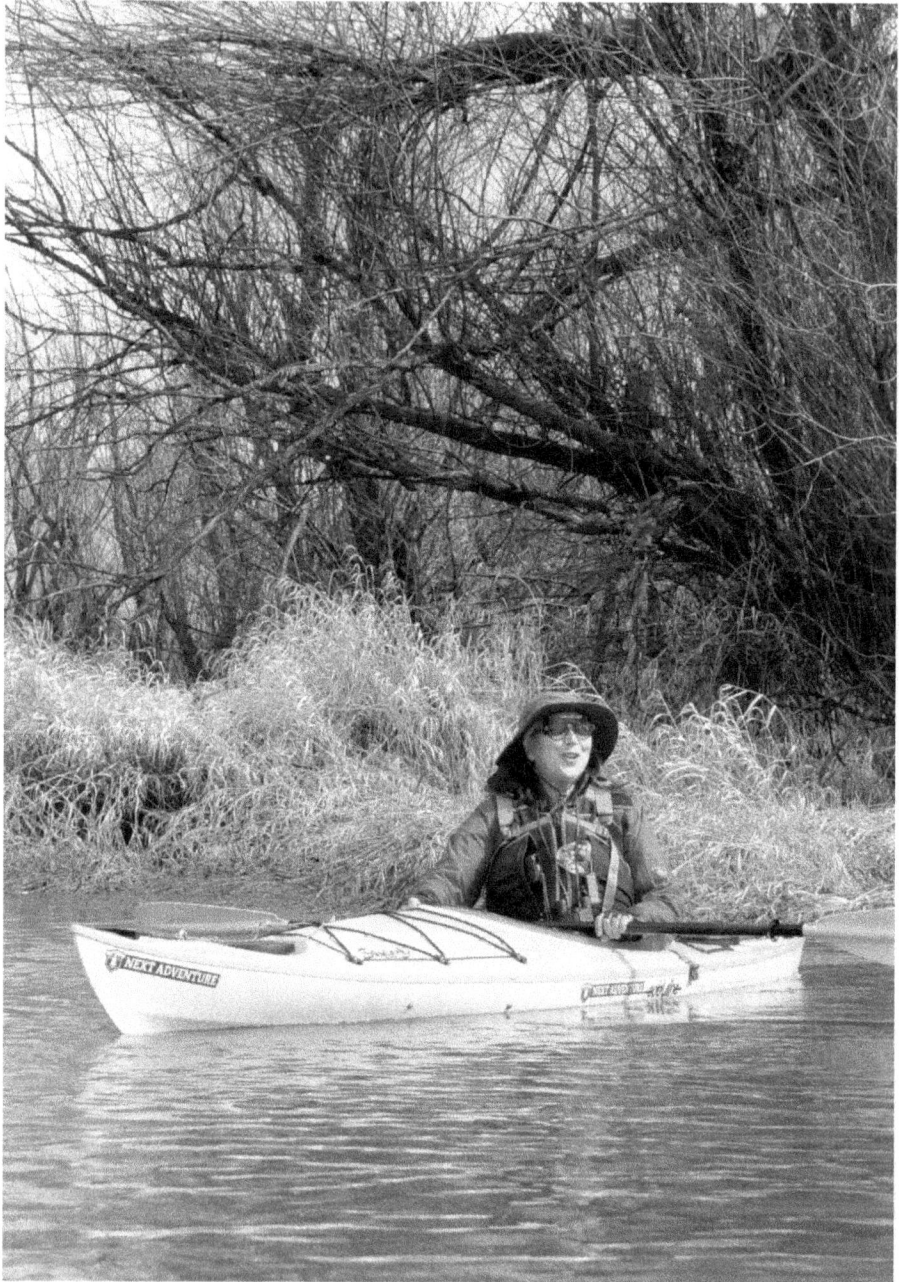

CHAPTER 11: FITNESS, HEALTHY LIVING

Boomers heading into their next chapters want to be healthy and fit enough to enjoy it. And the secret formula is really no secret – exercise and diet are the best "magic pills" we have for a healthy quality of life. And doing something fun for fitness with people we enjoy = a "super magic pill."

Exercise is essential because it strengthens our hearts and nourishes our brains. Being healthy and fit helps our mental fitness, balance, stamina, flexibility, strength, mobility, and ability to ward off disease. Boomers who exercise regularly feel better and can do more.

Already healthy and fit? Try a new activity to help keep you on track. Or, if you had a sedentary, butt-in-the seat job, look for a gradual program to start exercising. Try these three steps:

- Step One – Fit activity into your life by thinking about what activities you enjoy or always wanted to try. *Do you like the outdoors? Do you prefer being indoors for fitness classes or water exercise? Always wanted to dance? Play Golf? Garden, do yard work? Walk the dog? Paddle a kayak? Ski or snowshoe?*

- Step Two – Next think about your goals. *More energy, stamina to keep up with your spouse, friends, kids, or grandkids? Weight loss? Better body image? Improved quality of life? Better sleep? Make new friends?*

- Step Three – Scope out your options. Fitness opportunities – outdoor and indoor – surround Boomers in our own communities.

Choices of places, programs and classes for your fitness quest are endless. Add the huge benefit, yes benefit, of age – many fitness activities are either free or discounted for adults and older adults. Look for them. Two of them – Silver&Fit® and SilverSneakers® – no cost fitness programs included in many senior health plans and group retirement plans.

Important advice from fitness experts is to continually challenge yourself in some small way and set goals. Goals can be a cycling distance, walking in an event, or taking on a ski or snowshoe trail.

Mix up your schedule with activities to experience something new, make friends, and boost the health benefits.

Now, check out our rundown of Boomer-popular, fun, and readily available fitness and exercise options below.

Walk, Hike, Ski, Snowshoe to Fitness

One of the easiest ways to start a fitness program is by walking. So easy, and important, that a whole chapter – *CHAPTER 15: HIKING AND WALKING*, beginning on page 97 – is devoted to these popular forms of exercise.

Get a comfortable pair of walking or hiking shoes, comfortable socks, and workout clothes. Join a group of like-minded people. Join a walking group or Meetup. Find a walking buddy to keep you both on track. Head out in your own neighborhood, take in the scenery, the people, parks, and gardens. Step it up and venture to other walking destinations around town.

Ratchet it up further and hike! Hiking trails are plentiful around the South Sound, taking in plenty of forests, estuaries, mountain and water vistas, and unique little towns. Plan trips to the unique forests, lakes, and Olympic Peninsula coastline and take in the scenery of Mt. Rainier. To find scenic hikes, maps, and other information, see *RESOURCES: HIKING AND WALKING, Find Hikes in* Natural, *Wildlife and Scenic* Areas on page 226, and

RESOURCES: EXPLORING THE SOUTH SOUND on page beginning on page 180.

Check a neighborhood's walk score (walkscore.com/score) which tells you how easy and safe it is to walk to shopping, recreation activities, and transportation.

In winter, extend your local-motion to snow sports – join other retirees in fitness activities such as downhill, and cross-country skiing or snowshoeing or snowboarding. Check out the outdoor clubs and Meetups, or classes to find eager companions and group trips. Visit the website, stateofwashingtontourism.com for snow and other winter destinations in Washington's mountains, hills, forests, or flatlands.

Cycling: Ride, Boomers, Ride!

Ready to cycle into your next phase of leisure living? It's a popular way to experience outdoor activity with family and friends, exercise, or just enjoy the calming peace of a solo ride. Given the availability of "electric assist" cycling, there's no reason not to.

Good news – look no further than your own community. Thanks to bicycle advocacy groups and transportation programs, city and county planning in many communities encourage bicycling both as recreation and

transportation. Check out your area's cycling options including bike lanes, multi-use trails, and off-road trail riding options. Cycle around town, in commuter lanes to work, and side roads. Learn to trail ride. Or sign-up for community biking events and group rides.

Places to Bike, Maps

Start by search on these sites:

- Rails to Trails Conservancy, an on-line source for 30,000 trail maps, searchable by location. (TrailLink.com)

- Mapmyride.com. Search for bike routes by community.

- The department of transportation websites of your city, county, and state, parks and recreation programs, and bike shops.

Cycling Clubs, Events, Meetups

No matter where you hang your helmet, or whether you are a recreational or competitive cyclist, there's a group for you. Meetups (meetup.com), groups formed around a single interest, are a popular option for Boomers seeking all things outdoors, including cycling. And cycling events of all sizes and types are plentiful throughout the area.

For more about cycling resources, see *RESOURCES: FITNESS, HEALTHY LIVING, Cycling Clubs, Maps,* on page 199.

Running, Jogging

Are you still jogging along, no doubt a bit slower than you did in the running craze of the 60s, 70s and 80s? Or is jogging or running for fitness on your bucket list? How about a 5K? 10K? Marathon? Aerobic activities such as jogging and running raise your heart rate and are important to good heart health and brain fitness. Start with a good pair of running shoes, comfortable socks, and workout clothes (no cotton!) and get moving. You can jog practically anywhere. Prefer some company? Show up for group runs sponsored by a club or local running store. Look into running meetups. Most clubs welcome all abilities, and you'll have plenty of company no matter what your pace.

Put a 5K or 10K event on the calendar. Running events attract hundreds and even thousands of joggers, runners, and walkers of all shapes, sizes, and abilities. Many Boomers jog with their kids and grandkids. Most races are family friendly with kids' races and walks. What's not to like about them? It's also wise to look into group training sessions that help prepare you for a race.

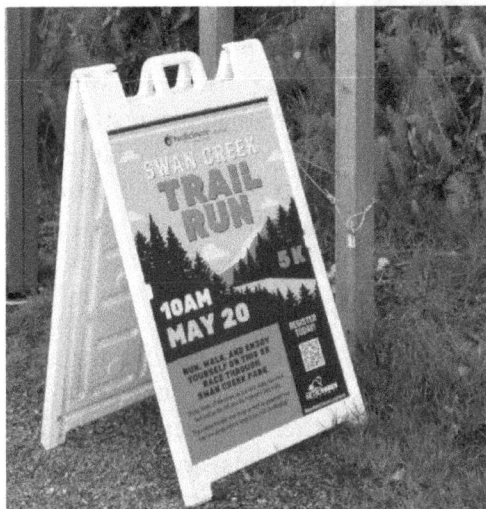

For more information, check the websites of local running and walking clubs, or visit these websites to find one in your area:

- runningintheusa.com. A website where you can search for local event schedules by city. Find one and sign up. Register on-line.

- Road Runners Club of America, search for a club by state. (rrca.org/find-a-running-club)

Just Keep Swimming

Boomer swimmers love the gentle all-body workout water exercise gives them, making swimming a popular year-around fitness activity. Lap swims, lessons, and water exercise are available at aquatic centers, parks and recreation facilities, community colleges, and public swimming pools. Not to mention lakes, rivers, and beaches. Exercise pools are also a common amenity for residents of retirement communities. *RESOURCES: FITNESS, HEALTHY LIVING, Parks and Rec, YMCAs* on page 204 to find fitness facilities in your community.

Tennis or Pickleball Anyone?

Tennis and pickleball are each fun, fit-friendly and social activities that go beyond just moving exercise. Racket sports connect your brain, and eyes to your racket hand and then (hopefully) to the ball. To keep relationships harmonious, you can partner with, instead of against, a spouse or friend.

Pickleball has become a wildly popular sport among Boomers. Much like tennis, players hit balls over a net on a smaller court, using a solid paddle and a ball similar to a whiffle ball.

Get lessons through many community programs and find classes, schedules, and other Boomer players at activities sponsored by parks and recreation programs, and pickleball and tennis organizations and facilities. For information on area pickleball clubs and court locations, see *RESOURCES: FITNESS Pickleball on page 200.*

Golf, Of Course

Tired of driving past beautiful, lush, expansive golf courses on your way to work? Does dreamland take you to an early round, where you breathe fresh air, get exercise, and enjoy buddy banter?

Wait no longer! You're retired, or soon to be, right? It's time to trade the laptop for a 5 wood and hit the fairways (at least as many of them as possible). So, do it now, especially if learning or playing more golf is a bucket list item.

Hundreds of communities around the country are golf wonderlands for everyone – from beginner to old pros alike. Courses range from tour class to forest and farmlands-bordered hills, to ocean-hugging links, to mountain backdrop cactus fields, in large and small towns, and everything in between.

Never swung a club? Many golf courses and clubs offer all levels of instruction and rental equipment. To find a course near you, search for courses in your community, or state golf associations. Golf classes are also offered through parks and recreation programs and community colleges. (And friends or your spouse, of course, will eagerly offer you much welcomed advice.)

Golf Volunteers

If you enjoy the fresh air and fun of attending tournaments, look for opportunities to volunteer at one. You'll get a free pass to walk with your favorite golfers, along with helping others enjoy the experience. Check tournament schedules at golf organizations in your community and contact the golf course hosting the event for information.

Volunteers also can help others learn and enjoy golf. Opportunities are available with many state associations to help with adult and junior golf tournaments, and administrative duties within the state. The First Tee organization, for example, relies on volunteers to carry out its mission in many states – to introduce the game to young people.

For more on finding golf courses playing, and volunteer opportunities in your area, see the Washington Golf amateur golf association, serving golfers in the Washington and Northern Idaho. 3401 South 19th St, Ste #200, Tacoma. 206-526-8605. wagolf.org

Shall We Dance?

Remember when Boomers twisted, watusied, hitchhiked, strolled, loco-motioned, hully-gullied, mashed potatoed, discoed, and hustled though the 60s and 70s? Today, Boomers find their way back to all forms of old as well as new dance floor moves from ballroom and country to contra and Latin, and everything in between.

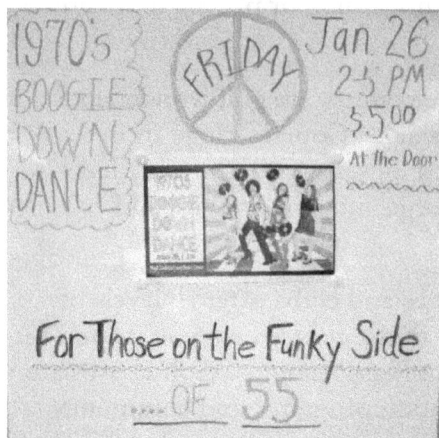

1970's
BOOGIE
DOWN
DANCE

FRIDAY Jan 26
2-5 PM
$5.00
At the Door

For Those on the Funky Side
.....OF 55

Can you guess why? To stay fit, learn something new, meet new people, and for the best reason, bring back those fun times.

For places to break out your unique dance style or learn distinct dances, look for websites of community retirees' or social clubs, private dance studios, or dance Meetups or clubs. Many ethnic organizations teach their signature folk dances, a fun way to socialize. Other places to learn and practice vintage and modern dances are community colleges, community and senior centers, and parks and recreation classes. Take classes in your own retirement community.

See *RESOURCES: LEARNING PLACES, Colleges, Universities* on page 233 and *RESOURCES: FITNESS, HEALTHY LIVING, Parks and Rec, YMCAs* on page 204.

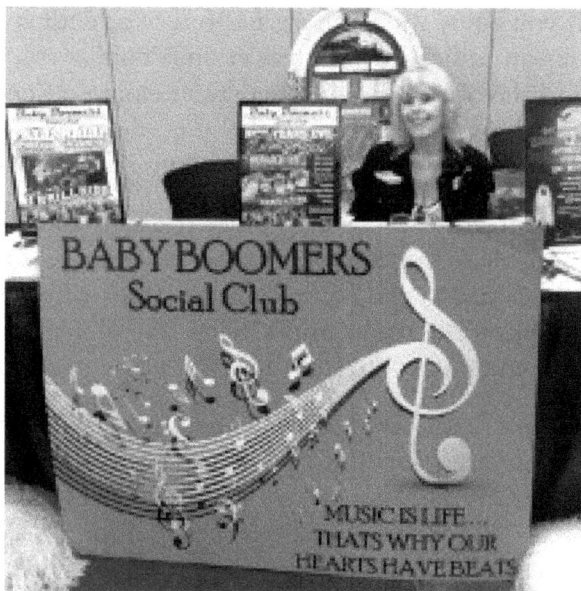

BABY BOOMERS
Social Club

MUSIC IS LIFE...
THATS WHY OUR
HEARTS HAVE BEATS

Join a Senior or Community Center, or YMCA

Health and fitness – both physical and mental – are a main focus of senior centers, community centers, and YMCAs that gear activities to different ages, abilities, and interests.

Senior centers offer services and activities to help seniors live, learn, thrive, and socialize. Depending on the community, retirees can take advantage of fitness classes in strength training, dance, aerobics, Tai

Chi, yoga, and other popular exercises. Many offer healthy lifestyle classes and activities and post schedules of classes on their website.

For listings of area senior centers, see *RESOURCES: SENIOR SERVICES, Senior and Community Centers* on page 267. For parks and recreation and YMCA organizations, see *RESOURCES: FITNESS, HEALTHY LIVING, Parks and Rec, YMCAs* on page 204.

More Choices: Community College, Parks Programs

In addition to community centers, retirees can sign up for a wide range of fitness classes offered by community colleges, and parks and recreation departments and YMCAs of their cities. Find descriptions and schedules on their websites and current activities catalog on their websites. Many locations offer both in-person and virtual programs.

For a listing of area community colleges, see *RESOURCES: LEARNING PLACES, Colleges, Universities* on page 233. For parks and recreation organizations, see *RESOURCES: FITNESS, HEALTHY LIVING, Parks and Rec, YMCAs,* on page 204.

Find Healthy Lifestyles at Healthcare Organizations

Area healthcare organizations also promote healthy living through classes and events in their communities. Many provide online classes and videos and schedule information on their websites.

For a listing of area healthcare organizations, see *RESOURCES: HEALTHCARE VOLUNTEERING, Healthcare Organizations* on page 219.

Fitness Activities Meetups

No matter what your fitness level or interest, there's a club or Meetup group for you. Meetups are formed by individuals around common or multiple interests, in this case fitness and exercise. Joining is either free or inexpensive and gives you online access to the Meetup's scheduled activities. Search for Meetups in your area at meetup.com.

CHAPTER 12: GARDENING

Got a little dirt under your nails? Have a need to pluck weeds and water flowers? If so, there's probably a gardener growing in you!

Look around. Seems like everyone either wants to start or spend more time in a garden, for good reason. Gardening grounds us. Clears our brains. Expresses our creativity. Gives us solitude. And makes us patient.

If you're a Boomer gardener or want-to-be, it's time to unearth gloves and shovels, and get to the garden of your choice. Most communities are garden friendly to beginners and experts alike – gardeners love to share their knowledge.

Enjoy Public and Demonstration Gardens

Start by venturing out to see all the luscious gardens that bless your area (and beyond). Some public, some private by invitation. Then bring your inspiration back in photographs to start applying those ideas to your own yard, containers, patio, or balcony.

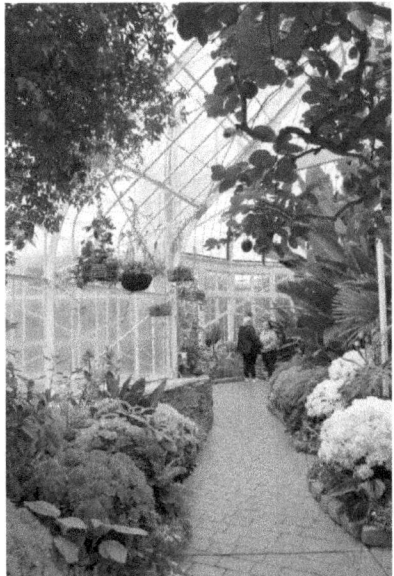

Whether you're a beginner, expert, or appreciator, you'll discover endless ways to enjoy gardens in parks, botanical gardens, wildlife areas, public buildings, university campuses, and many other places unique to your state, city, or county.

Gather inspiration by wandering through demonstration gardens in your areas that offer the latest on new plants, trees, and growing techniques.

Depending on where you live, you'll find places that focus on fruit growing, organic gardening, and gardens as wildlife habitat, as well as techniques to manage factors such as water usage, soil enhancement, and safety.

Volunteer at a Public Garden

All public gardens need and welcome volunteers of all skill levels and interests. Great for beginners! Tasks range from hands-on planting,

weeding, and mulching, to helping at special events, or working in gift shops or offices. You can show up at one-time work parties or join others in ongoing year-round maintenance. Some branch out into community and youth learning projects.

Take volunteering a step further and join a friends group that adopts and maintains their favorite public garden. For listings of public gardens *see RESOURCES:* GARDENING, *Public and Demonstration Gardens* on page 207.

Community Gardens

When you enjoy growing things, but lack space to plant your personality, you've probably discovered community gardens. You enjoy the satisfaction of beautiful flowers or healthy vegetables and meeting others with the same interests. Share tips, seeds, and even recipes. Carry that a step further, and help others enjoy gardening by teaching, speaking, or volunteering.

Most communities offer residents garden plots and various gardening equipment and services for gardeners. By volunteering to teach or provide gardening tips, you'll enrich your own experience by helping others learn what you love.

Garden volunteers with a community service interest should check out organizations that help people grow their own food. Volunteers help build organic, raised bed vegetable gardens in yards and balconies, or volunteer time in food growing orchards and gardens that donate fresh food to food banks. Some offer tool-sharing.

Garden Clubs

Garden clubs are a fun, social way to learn and share information on all things gardening and enhance the beauty of your community. Garden clubs offer opportunities to share your knowledge as a speaker or help put on workshops, plant shows, plant sales and exchanges, and tours.

Members also maintain flower beds in their cities, and encourage the appreciation of wildflowers, birds, insects, and the wise use of natural resources. Moreover, members share the fellowship of like-minded gardening enthusiasts.

For more information, search for garden clubs in your area. They may be affiliated with a state association and listed on its website. Garden clubs typically welcome all aspiring green thumbs and are eager to help and share their knowledge. For listings of area garden clubs see *RESOURCES: GARDENING, Garden Clubs* on page 211.

Gardening Classes, Workshops, Seminars

Gardening for most of us is evolutionary – there's always more to learn. Discover new design, seeds, soils, watering, plants, color, harvest – it goes on and on There's no shortage of places to learn more, get advice, attend classes and seminars, and hang out with other gardeners.

To really dig into gardening, attend Master Gardener classes typically offered through state universities. They often cater to the serious gardener, who in turn shares their knowledge through gardening-related demonstrations, lectures, seminars, and workshops in communities throughout their state.

Other options are community education gardening classes typically held in spring and fall. Search for gardening classes and workshops offered through community colleges and nurseries and garden centers. For a listing of area community colleges, see *RESOURCES: LEARNING PLACES, Colleges, Universities* on page 233.

Home and garden shows are still another source of classes and workshops to inspire and educate gardeners. Also, look for garden clubs and community gardens that invite the public to their classes.

Like to share your knowledge? Contact your favorite garden club, public or community gardens, community college, community or senior center, or nurseries to teach a class. For places to attend classes or ideas or places to share your knowledge, see *CHAPTER 22: TEACHING, SPEAKING,* on page 121.

Green Thumb Groups

Boomer gardeners should check out gardening groups or Meetup groups (meetup.com). Meetups are formed by individuals around a common, or multiple interests, in this case, gardening. Joining is either free or inexpensive and gives you on-line access to the Meetup's scheduled activities.

CHAPTER 13: GOVERNMENT SERVICE

Do you enjoy an active interest in your local government? Are you interested in being part of discussions and decisions affecting your community's parks, public safety, or art and cultural events and activities?

Many community-minded Boomers are and find that joining a county or city board, committee, or commission is a rewarding experience.

Boards and commissions advise city and county agencies and bureaus on community issues and policies. They value the experience and the variety of expertise that retirees and seniors bring to the local governing process.

Counties and cities stress the importance of citizen advisors who represent the full range of diversity in their communities.

Volunteers can opt to serve on standing committees or citizen advisory groups that deal with specific issues. Websites of each county and city describe the functions and the makeup of their boards, committees, and commissions, including how to apply. Many counties and cities also have committees for citizen involvement that focus on getting diverse groups of citizens active in government processes.

Regional Government

In large metropolitan areas, government entities with regional jurisdiction provide regionwide planning and coordination to manage growth, infrastructure, and development issues that cross jurisdictional boundaries. They may get involved in: regional research; management of parks, trails and natural areas; transportation; large-scale visitor venues such as zoos and convention centers; performing arts theaters; and utilities such as solid waste and recycling facilities.

Members of the community serve on various committees that shape public policies, transportation, funding, and more. Learn about current opportunities by visiting the advisory committees, citizen involvement, or the volunteer pages of the government website. You also may find information on other volunteer opportunities at facilities they manage, such as parks, theaters, and entertainment venues.

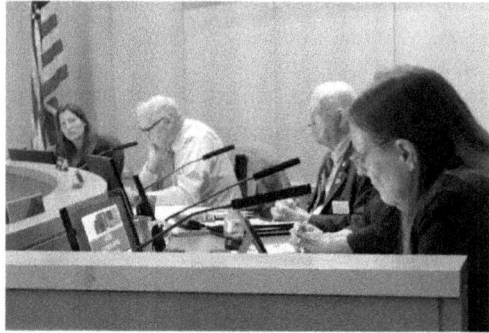

County Government

Citizen volunteers in county government take active roles in shaping policies, programs, and decisions supporting specific county activities and goals. Advisory boards and committees deal with areas such as aging, animal control, bicycle and pedestrian safety, libraries, budgets, clean water, historic preservation, parks, public health, arts, building codes, telecommunications, tourism, traffic safety, and more.

Individual counties typically offer opportunities based on the unique features of its community. For information, visit the citizen involvement or volunteer pages of your county website. For listings of area county government offices, *see RESOURCES: GOVERNMENT SERVICE, County Government* on page *217*.

City Government

Citizen volunteers serve on boards and commissions much like those of counties. Depending on the city, citizen committees support parks and recreation, city-owned facilities, budgets, architectural review, libraries, planning, arts and culture, tourism, citizen involvement, finance, water, zoning, public safety, transportation, and utilities.

Boards and commissions play a critical role in supporting city functions and advising the city leaders on a variety of issues and topics. Cities find that citizen involvement is essential to incorporating the community's voice in city decision-making. For information, visit the citizen involvement or volunteer pages of your city's website. For listings of area county government offices, see *RESOURCES: GOVERNMENT SERVICE, City Government* on page 216.

Law Enforcement Volunteers

Many communities need volunteers in special law enforcement programs involving various safety, parks, and outreach programs. For example, volunteers may participate in bike safety projects and community outreach crafts and games. In some communities, police volunteers help with car seat clinics, clerical duties, home security, and similar programs.

Another program some communities offer is a reserve officer program which trains volunteers for uniformed, armed duties or non-uniform, unarmed duties. For information, visit the law enforcement or police department pages of your city's website.

Other Local Government Opportunities

Other areas within your local government that may welcome office volunteers include city attorneys, events at government-owned facilities such as theaters, and special community projects and events such as a city-sponsored festival.

Other popular places to volunteer with city and county managed areas are parks and recreation departments and libraries. For more information, see *RESOURCES: FITNESS, HEALTHY LIVING Parks and Rec, YMCAs* on page 204.

Federal Government

Through the website Volunteer.gov, you can search for a variety of volunteer assignments with Federal government agencies and their state and local governmental partners. Its purpose is to provide an efficient way to connect volunteers with volunteer opportunities within natural and cultural resources agencies.

One popular activity among retirees who enjoy RVing, camping, and meeting new people, is working as a volunteer campground host at Federal facilities. Hosts stay at site in their camper or RV, and provide visitor information, recreation planning, and help with maintaining facilities. Opportunities are available throughout the country.

CHAPTER 14: HEALTHCARE VOLUNTEERING

Are you interested in applying your healthcare or caregiving experience to a volunteer role? Or just interested in volunteering in healthcare?

Boomers who have retired from healthcare careers, or those interested in healthcare, can find a wide assortment of places and ways to offer their help in an area with many volunteer opportunities. Your involvement is welcomed by all types of medical and healthcare organizations, including these described below.

Community Healthcare

Nonprofit community health clinics bring low-cost or free healthcare to underserved, disadvantaged, low-income populations, the elderly, families, children, and others.

Often working with limited budgets, these organizations depend heavily on volunteers with medical and non-medical skills for day-to-day operations. Professionals such as doctors, nurses, clinicians, dentists, technicians are always needed, as are volunteers who serve as medical advocates, screeners, interpreters, and translators. Also welcome is a background in office support, technology and computers, graphic design, communication, fundraising, as well as other skills.

Community Mental Health

Community Mental Health nonprofits serve the mentally ill, as well as adults and children with addictions. These organizations are supported by private and faith-based organizations, and city and county governments. Specialties include family and individual mental health and addictions.

Volunteer opportunities range from mental health professionals and those who assist them, to childcare, education, manning crisis phone lines and socializing in residential facilities. Volunteers also work in office settings, gardens, thrift stores and at special events.

Health-based Organizations

These familiar organizations focus on advancing cures and treatment of a specific condition or disease, and services and support for people and families affected by the disease. Examples of organizations that support the people and families afflicted by disease include the American Cancer Society, American Heart Association, MS Society, and Alzheimer's Association, all with local chapters. Examples of other conditions addressed by support organizations are diabetes, hearing, blindness, Asperger's syndrome, brain injuries, Down syndrome, and muscular dystrophy.

Retirees often choose organizations that speak to their hearts – the disease or condition may have touched them or their families or friends. Organizations seek volunteers in roles that support their mission and activities. In general, volunteers help provide services, educate the public, and raise money. Many sponsor large community fundraising events and need lots of volunteers to put on the events.

They also work in office roles, maintaining databases, files, and answer phones. On the communications side, volunteers may help with websites, social media, graphic design, photography, and writing assignments. Many work at large and small community fundraising events where they are involved in planning, outreach, setup, engaging with participants, operating information booths, and cleanup. For listings of area health-based organizations, see *RESOURCES: HEALTHCARE VOLUNTEERING, Health-Based Organizations* on page 223.

Hospice and End of Life Care

Volunteers provide important services to hospice organizations and the people they serve. Whether providing companionship to a person in the final months and weeks of life, offering support to family and caregivers, or helping with community outreach and fundraising, the contributions of volunteers are essential to the important work provided by hospice programs.

Every hospice relies on volunteer support to provide excellent end-of-life care to each patient and family. In fact, Medicare requires that a portion of patient care time be provided by volunteers.

For listings of area hospice facilities, see *RESOURCES: HEALTHCARE VOLUNTEERING, Hospice and End-of-Life-Care* on page 225.

Hospitals and Medical Centers

By this time in our lives, most Boomers are no strangers to medical centers. We often recall the kindness of volunteers who showed us to a room or brought us flowers or a newspaper. Volunteers bring joy to people at stressful times. Most hospitals offer volunteer positions throughout their operations.

Duties of hospital volunteers vary widely depending upon the facility. Volunteers may work in staff reception areas and gift shops, file and retrieve documents and mails, take out trash, clean up after nurses and doctors, provide administrative backup, assist with research, help visitors, visit with patients, or transport various small items such as flowers, gifts and cards from unit to unit.

Other "advanced volunteers" are those who work on health care teams and are given special training to work with patients. They are more common in large hospitals, particularly university-affiliated and teaching hospitals.

The best source of information on volunteering with healthcare organizations typically is the volunteer page of their website.

For a listing of area healthcare organizations, see *RESOURCES: HEALTHCARE VOLUNTEERING,* on page 219.

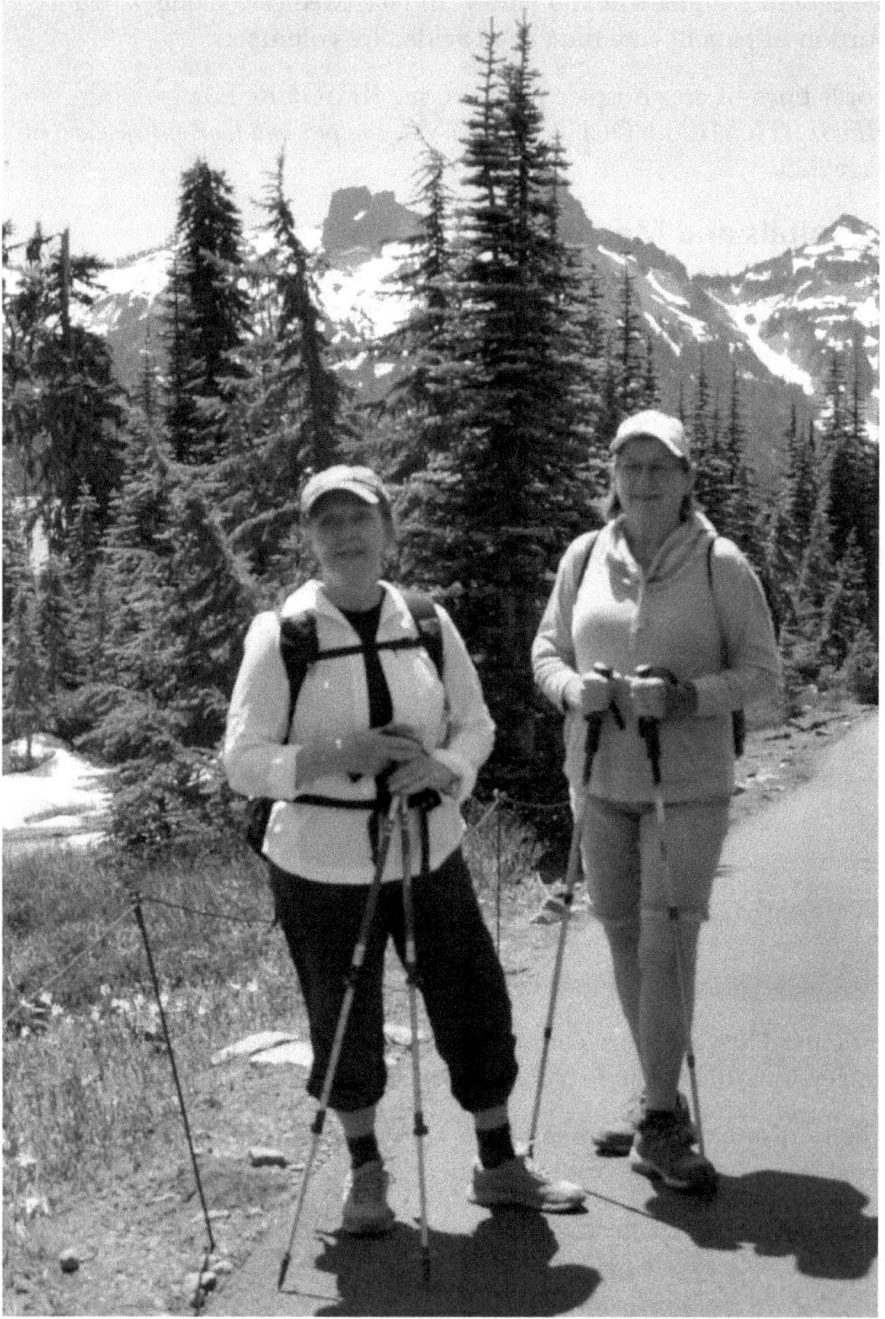

CHAPTER 15: HIKING AND WALKING

Why are hiking and walking retirees' exercises of choice? Easy – they are abundantly good for you and opportunities are plentiful. With no shortage of water, forests, mountains, scenic towns on vast rugged coastlines, unique opportunities await hikers of all interests and abilities. Nearly unlimited places to hike and walk in many communities make it easy and enjoyable to get your weekly 150 walking minutes.

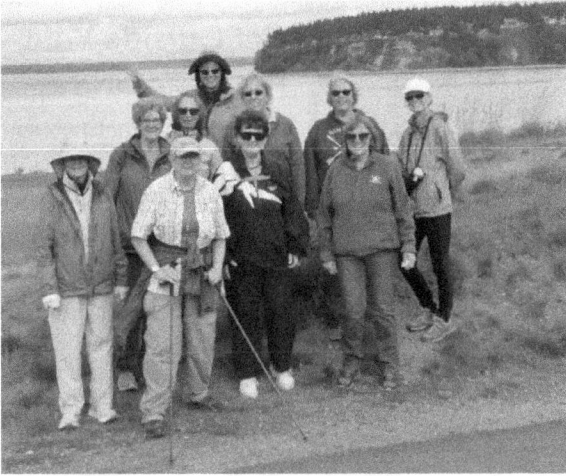

Multi-taskers can bundle walking with other leisure goals and hobbies. Pare down that paunch, give your partner space, feed your brain, or listen to nature. Explore communities beyond your own; discover out-of-the-way parks, trails, and fun little towns. Surround yourself with real forests and mountains, rivers, and wetlands. Make hikes and walks an excuse to see more of your family and friends or meet new people. Or just connect with nature in meditative hiking.

And – good news here – you needn't always traipse about a forest, park, or mountain trail to reap great health, aesthetic, and social benefits. Look for interesting urban or historic hiking routes and walkable neighborhoods, maybe your own!

Walk the Neighborhood

Not sure where to start? Get a good pair of walking shoes, comfortable socks, and workout clothes. Find a walking buddy to keep you both on track. Head out into your own neighborhood. Take in the scenery, the people, and the tucked away neighborhood parks and gardens. Gradually step it up and venture to other communities. In many areas, you can check a neighborhood's walk score which tells you its "walkability." (walkscore.com/score). As you gather confidence, gather your friends, pick a destination, download a map and head out.

Get Outside Your Home Zone

To find interesting explorable neighborhoods beyond your own, check out your city's (possibly a transportation page) or local parks and recreation website for maps and other information about walkable neighborhoods. Other sources of maps include the websites of outdoor, walking, or hiking clubs and meetups, outdoor stores, and local walking safety programs.

Other interesting walking options are mapped, informational walks through historic sites, neighborhoods, parks, cities, or sections of cities. They typically explore an area's history and culture. Look for these on the websites of history organizations, cities, or visitor organizations. Or check out the website of local Volkssport groups which offer events and route maps to enjoy at your own pace.

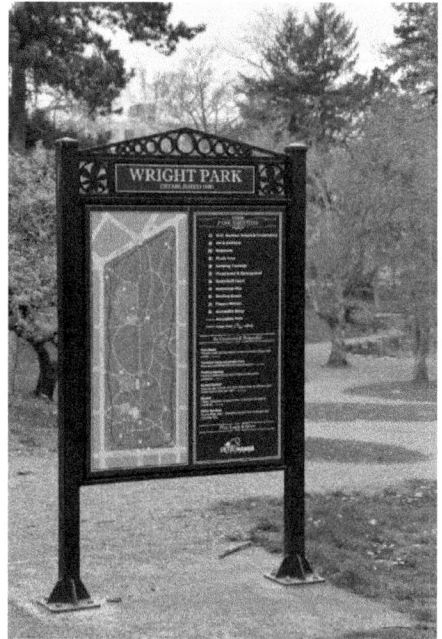

Birding

Bird lovers find birding an enjoyable way to walk and observe the diverse habitats and habits of their feathered friends. Look for outings sponsored by local Audubon groups, parks programs, nature centers, and community centers. For more information on walking through natural areas, see *RESOURCES: HIKING AND WALKING, Find Hikes in* Natural, *Wildlife and Scenic* Areas on page 226.

Step Out with Clubs or Meetups

Age-friendly outdoor clubs and Meetups everywhere welcome non-members. Most offer different levels of activity and are a good way to meet like-minded Boomers. Many schedule activities on weekdays at times preferred by retirees. Many clubs offer multi-activities such as hiking, walking, snowshoeing, cycling, kayaking, and backpacking. For a listing of area outdoor groups. See also *CHAPTER 11: FITNESS, HEALTHY LIVING, Walk, Hike, Ski, Snowshoe to Fitness* on page 76 and *RESOURCES: HIKING AND WALKING, Outdoor Hiking, Walking, Snow Sports Groups* on page 228.

Art and Cultural Meanderings

Add a little cultural variety to your walk. Log your miles when you show up for "first-something" art walks or stroll through regular or seasonal art walks held in many communities. Look on your city, county, Chamber of Commerce, or visitor websites for routes and public spaces where you can experience art up close and personal.

For examples of art walk options, see *RESOURCES: ART, PHOTOGRAPHY, FILM, Art Walks, Festivals* on page 155.

You'll also get your steps in on guided or self-guided tours of historical sites, homes, buildings, farms, and gardens. Similarly, take advantage of events at expansive walk-around attractions such as arboretums, botanical gardens, nature parks, and zoos, as well as community food, art, brew, and wine walks.

For examples of these, see *RESOURCES: GARDENING, Public and Demonstration* Gardens on page 207, and *CHAPTER 10: EXPLORING THE SOUTH SOUND, Events, Festivals* on page 71.

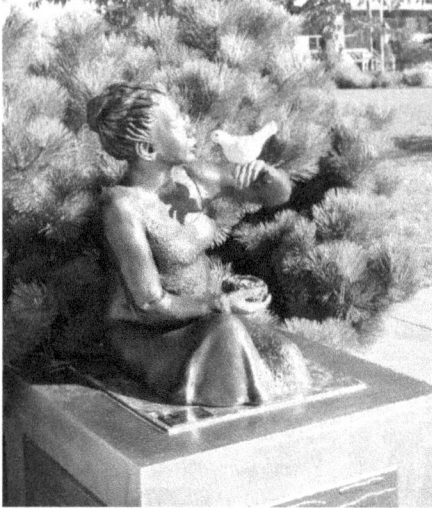

Community Walks

In many communities, you can choose from a few to dozens of walking and walker-friendly events. Some are multi-sport, multi-distance family events such as running races and fundraisers. Walk and multiply the benefits – your registration supports a good cause, and you get exercise, healthy treats, camaraderie, an event t-shirt, and other freebies.

Community College, City Parks Programs

Browse the catalogs of your area's community colleges and city parks and recreation organizations for seasonal outdoor senior programs and walk and hike activities. Popular among retirees are hikes, walks, walk tours, nature and historic tours, nature center visits, and similar activities.

For a list of area community colleges, see *RESOURCES: LEARNING PLACES, Parks and Recreation* on page 233. For a list of area parks programs and YMCAs, see *RESOURCES: FITNESS, HEALTHY LIVING, Parks and Rec, YMCAs* on page 204.

To find more on walking and hiking places in the South Sound, see *CHAPTER 10: EXPLORING THE SOUTH SOUND* on page 65 and *RESOURCES: EXPLORING THE SOUTH SOUND* on page 180.

CHAPTER 16: HOBBIES

Research tells us that engaging in a creative or fun hobby tops the list of best activities for your brain. Maybe, now that we have the opportunity, it's time to move that hobby up the list.

Are you ready to express yourself with oil or watercolor? Start or expand a 60s record collection, make jewelry, take photos, drag out old bins of scrapbook material? What about restoring – toys, a car, furniture? Or building a model train track?

You might like to visit quaint antique shops of antiques. Sell stuff on eBay. Write a blog, memoir, or your family history. Learn the guitar or mandolin. Or build or restore one. Create or expand a garden. Express your out-of-the-box side with rock balancing, pigeon racing, blacksmithing, or beekeeping. There are endless possibilities.

Hobbies sprout from any interest – something you make, build, create, engage in, collect, fix, read, or learn about. Maybe it's a sport, art, music, books, history, or an outdoor pursuit such as fishing. By yourself or in a group, or both.

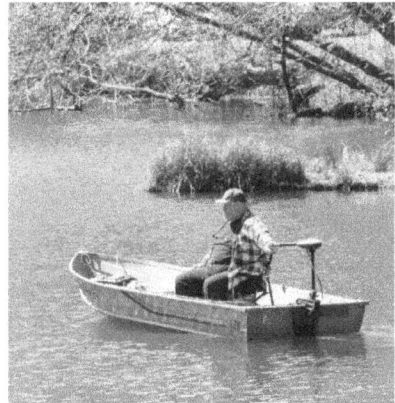

Where to Start

Searching in our digital world brings almost unlimited information and how-to videos right to your computer or phone screen. Search by hobby name and city and see what pops up. Other good places are hobby shops.

Most of your favorite learning places offer both in-person and online instruction and classes. Some examples are:

- Arts and Cultural Centers. Look into community's cultural center(s) for classes in all forms of art, crafts, music, theater, performance,

  dance, history, and more. See *CHAPTER 5: ART, PHOTOGRAPHY, FILM* on page 47 and *RESOURCES: ART, PHOTOGRAPHY, FILM, Visual Arts Spaces and Cultural Centers* on page 149.

- Community College Continuing Education.

  Many offer classes on a wide spectrum of life-long learning interests including art and crafts, music, cooking, dancing, photography, reading, language, sports, woodworking, and more. Look in seasonal print or online catalogs. *See CHAPTER 17: LEARN SOMETHING NEW* on page 105 and *RESOURCES: LEARNING PLACES, Colleges, Universities* on page 233.

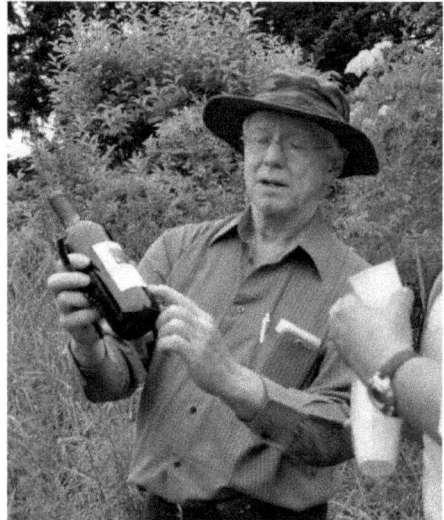

- Senior and Community Centers. These friendly places are built around hobbies such as reading, dancing, card playing, arts, crafts, exercise, fitness, computers and technology, sports, and day trips. Groups always welcome beginners and are eager to share knowledge. See *RESOURCES: SENIOR SERVICES, Senior and Community Centers* on page 267.

- Libraries. In addition to hobby books and media, libraries sponsor a variety of usually-free in-person and online programs on all sorts of hobby topics. Or you can suggest a class, or even teach one. See *CHAPTER 17: LEARN SOMETHING NEW, Your Library* on page 105 and *RESOURCES: LEARNING PLACES, Libraries* on page 235.

- Meetups, Clubs and Social Groups. People in these groups share a common interest. From arts, hobbies and crafts, to writing, culture, DIY, and many other activities, Meetups might be the place to look.

- Online Sources. Online classes on the hobby of your interest will bring you abundant information. Websites such as YouTube.com provide a wide selection of how-to videos on every imaginable hobby topic. See also the websites of retailers of hobby supplies, and hobby enthusiast organizations. Or create your own online class, webinar or workshop.

- Parks and Recreation Programs. Check the quarterly activities calendars of area parks programs for adult and senior group classes and activities such as creative arts, crafts, music, dance, bird watching, outdoor activities, games, sports, history, travel, and many more. See *RESOURCES: LEARNING PLACES, Parks and Recreation* on page 237.

Depending on your interest, Other ways to pursue hobbies are classes at cultural centers such as art galleries, museums, and literary organizations, and programs sponsored by outdoor organizations and hobby supply stores.

See *RESOURCES: ART, PHOTOGRAPHY, FILM* on page 149 and *RESOURCES: MUSEUMS, HISTORICAL SITES, SOCIETIES* on page 244, and *RESOURCES: LITERARY ARTS: WHERE TO READ, WRITE* on page 240.

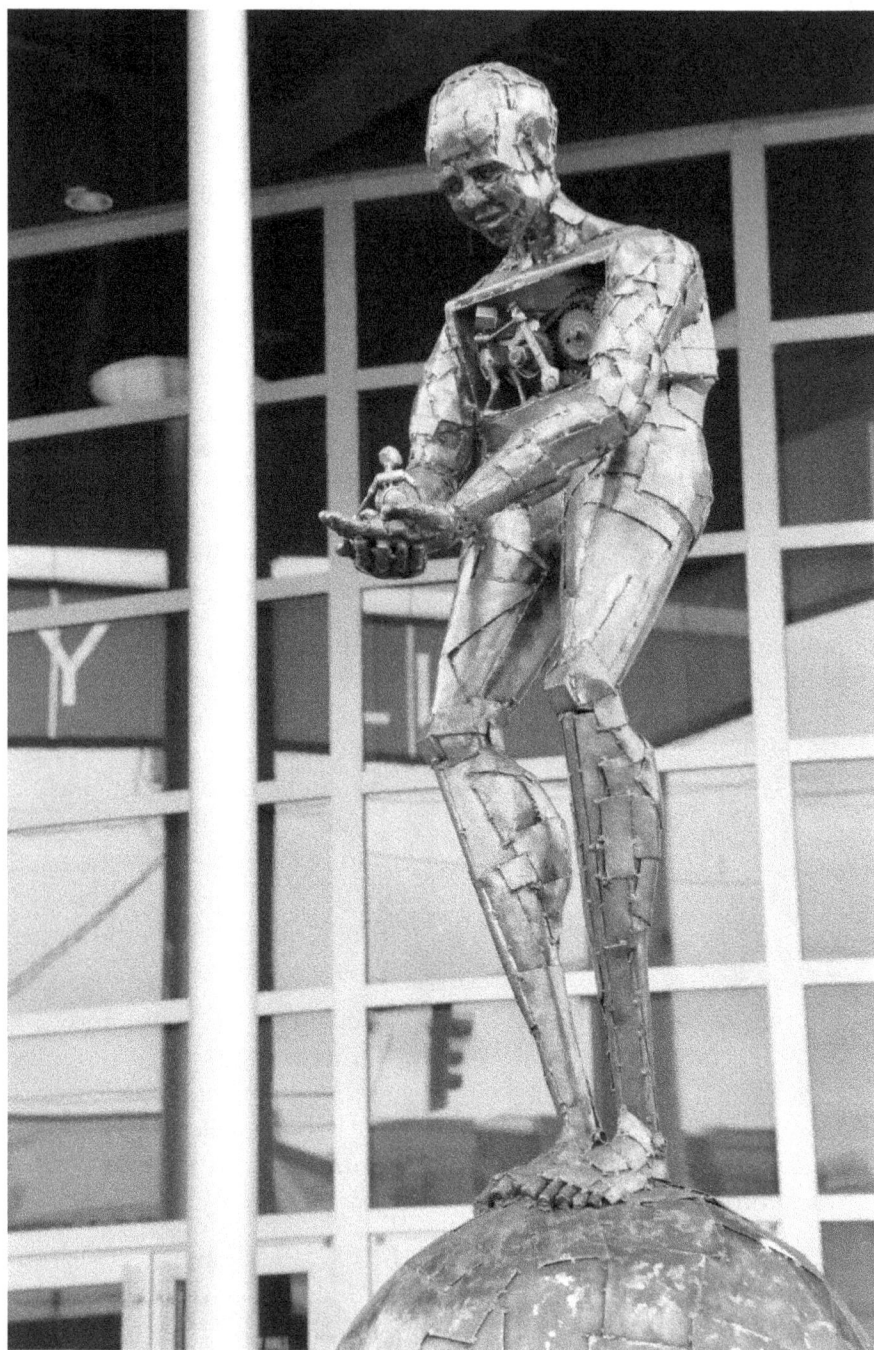

CHAPTER 17: LEARN SOMETHING NEW

There's no limit to what you can learn, and there's no limit to where you can find what you want. Most communities offer opportunities that transcend degree chasing and focus on more expansive interests that you might never find in a traditional classroom. Current events, some historical curiosity, some unexplored mystery of life? Now that you have more time, your interests may turn to learning more about topics that fascinate you in your country, state, or community.

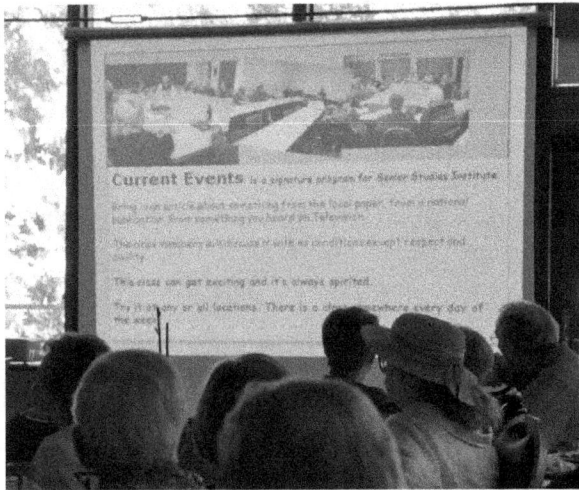

Online Learning

Computer learning has expanded rapidly, opening learners to more opportunities and a wide choice of topics available online. Feeding the popularity of online learning are the convenience of learning from a home computer. Many common learning forums have created learning programs via popular devices such as computers, phones, and tablets.

Your Library

Area library systems offer abundant learning opportunities. Today's libraries host classes and workshops, author readings, art shows, cultural festivals, lectures, and abundant hands-on learning opportunities for all ages. Multi-library city or county systems make it easy for patrons to borrow materials in all multiple viewing formats from any library in their system. For listings of area libraries see *RESOURCES: LEARNING PLACES, Libraries,* on page 235.

More Learning Forums

Other low- or no-cost learning forums in your community include:

- Adult and Senior Enrichment Programs. Typically sponsored by community colleges and universities and offer retirees a wide variety of in-person and online classes See *RESOURCES: LEARNING PLACES, Colleges, Universities*, on page 233.

- College and University Lectures. In many communities, public and private colleges and universities invite the public to attend both in-person and online lectures, classes, and events. See *RESOURCES: LEARNING PLACES, Colleges, Universities,* on page 233.

- Clubs and Social Groups. People in these groups share a learning interest. From arts, hobbies, and crafts, to writing, culture, DIY, and many other topics, Meetups offer many learning opportunities.

- Community Colleges. Offer credit and non-credit community education classes, in-person and on-line, covering a wide spectrum of learning interests and current events. See *RESOURCES: LEARNING PLACES, Colleges, Universities,* on page 233.

- Museums and Historical Societies. Museums are another place to pursue learning, especially for history buffs. Most museums offer a variety of programs, both in-person and on-line, about the history behind their collections. See *RESOURCES: MUSEUMS, HISTORICAL SITES, SOCIETIES* on page 244.

- Parks and Recreation. The seasonal lineups of city parks and recreation programs offer a wide variety of educational programs and classes that may be of interest. See *RESOURCES: LEARNING PLACES, Parks and Recreation* on page 237.

- Retiree Living Communities. One of the amenities offered at communities is a wide array of classes to learn more about current events, history, hobbies, the local area, and far more.

- Retiree Organizations. Other places to "never stop learning" are retiree organizations and groups. Many invite guest speakers on current topics. Check the website of your former employer or their retirees' organization.

- Senior and Community Centers. Many community and senior centers hold regular classes and special workshops on a variety of educational and historical topics. *RESOURCES: SENIOR SERVICES, Senior and Community Centers* on page 267.

For more information, visit the websites of these learning centers in your community.

CHAPTER 18: LITERARY ARTS, READING, WRITING

Two popular interests that Boomer retirees engage in more are reading and writing. That shouldn't surprise us because we enjoy more leisure time. We want to experience new lands, worlds, and even galaxies through books. We want to better understand our changing, complex world, current events, our communities, and the human journey.

And thanks to ever-growing technology, new books, and authors in every genre stream to us. We can instantly order, borrow, and download books on any subject, direct from bookstores and libraries to our computers, readers, or listening device.

On the flip side, many retirees are fulfilling their dreams to write. Whether crafting a memoir or coming of age story, a sci-fi, romance, fantasy or time travel, or non-fiction reference guide, Boomers are taking up their pens and keyboards to release their creativity, imagination, and desire to learn, grow, and help others.

Public Libraries: Retiree Reader Heaven

Many Boomers and retirees find their "reading heaven" at their local libraries. Far from becoming extinct due to technology, libraries have thrived, evolving into interconnected digital-age facilities. These virtual and community centers of learning have become inter-generational, multi-cultural gathering places, with 24-hour Internet access to places far and wide.

Starting with major library systems throughout areas large and small, Boomer readers discover abundant reading opportunities. Boomers still show up at libraries to learn, look up stuff and, yes, check out dear-to-our-souls printed books. And, just maybe for convenience, download digital books.

Beyond books, today's libraries feature art shows, gardens, and sculptures. They host cultural events, operate bookstores, provide computer and Wi-Fi services, home delivery, conference rooms, and a variety of community services. For listings of libraries in your area see RESOURCES: LEARNING PLACES, Libraries, on page 235.

Helping Others Learn

Libraries need curious people like you who are interested in helping people learn in one of your favorite places. Volunteers in today's libraries bring a wide variety of skills and interests to match the ever-expanding services libraries provide.

Beyond housing book and media collections, library programs help kids learn to read, seniors find services and adults navigate computers. Libraries need lots of volunteers – from teens to adults and seniors – who help throughout library operations. For example, they assist in computer labs, help put on public events and represent the library to the community. Inside, they shelve books, check in materials, assist patrons, perform office and administrative tasks, teach classes, work with books, help in after-school and summer programs, and arts and crafts classes. Many volunteers are multi-lingual, and if you have diverse language skills, you're in demand!

Library Friends

Library "Friends" groups support their libraries for charitable, literary, and educational purposes. They help to raise money to support literacy projects as well as for day-to-day operations. They help build library collections, purchase equipment, work in bookstores, and support activities such as summer reading programs. Another plus for Boomers, Friends groups are just that – a place to make new friends.

Other Libraries

Public libraries aren't the only places to express your interest in books, reading, or helping others learn. Many other types of organizations house their own library collections and rely on volunteers to make books easy to find, use and return.

The collections at art, history, and other types of cultural centers may be organized and managed by volunteers who blend organizational skills with their art or cultural interest. Library volunteers in retirement communities use their expertise to build and manage a collection for residents (usually based on donations), so that books are easy to find.

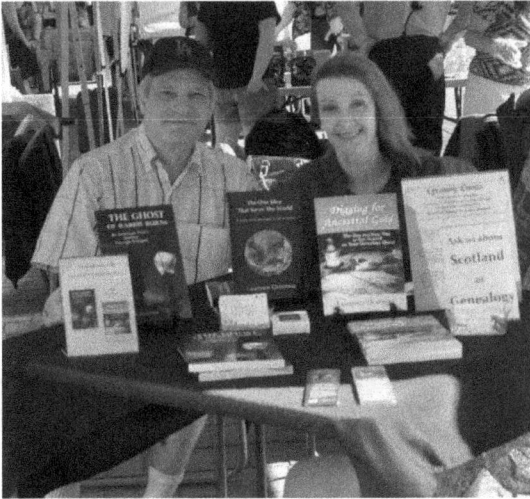

You can use your interest in books and libraries in other ways too. Self-styled "mini-libraries" housed in little structures commonly pop up in neighborhoods or on front porches where residents can exchange books easily. Volunteers at nonprofit thrift stores and faith communities may need help organizing their book donations so they're easy to browse through.

Other Book Connections

In addition to libraries, Boomers may have access to other fun connections with books such as book clubs, reader events at libraries and bookstores, author readings, and book festivals.

Book clubs are small reader groups who select, read, and discuss books. Book clubs are often formed around a genre or common interest. You'll find book clubs of every imaginable type in libraries, senior and community centers, faith-based organizations, bookstores, community organizations, retiree living communities and many other types of gathering places. In many communities, Boomers also can choose from a wide selection of book club Meetups (meetup.com).

Reading Festivals, Events

Bookstores, libraries, and literary organizations sponsor events such as regular readings, discussion groups, and book festivals to bring readers, books, and authors together. Check their websites for schedules and information about upcoming events and festivals.

The reading and book festivals sponsored in many communities need book-loving volunteers to work in planning, setup, marketing and outreach, and all phases of holding a book festival. In many instances, libraries either sponsor, or partner with festival sponsors such as literary organizations.

Retiree Writers, Authors

If writing is a bucket list item for you, there's no better time to realize your dream. Whether you are as aspiring author, poet, screenwriter, blogger, or playwright, you'll find resources to start your writing journey.

No matter what your writing interest, you'll find energetic organizations to help you learn, write, get feedback, publish, and socialize. A wide assortment of writing organizations throughout the area (and elsewhere!) offer more choices for authors, writers, bloggers, and poets of all interests and abilities. For a listing of writing groups, see *RESOURCES: LITERARY ARTS: WHERE TO* READ, WRITE, *Writing Groups, Conferences* on page 241.

Other places where all levels of writers and authors can practice and learn their craft include community colleges, parks and recreation programs, cultural centers, Meetup groups, and senior and community centers. You'll find writing classes in many genres including fiction, non-fiction, memoir, poetry, short story, screenwriting, business and technical writing, and many others. See *RESOURCES: LEARNING PLACES, Colleges, Universities* on page 233, *Libraries* on page 235, Parks and Recreation on page 237 and *RESOURCES: SENIOR SERVICES, Senior and Community Centers* on page 267.

CHAPTER 19: MUSEUMS, HISTORY

Is history your passion? Do you love digging into the facts and stories of your community's, state's, or county's past? Or could you take your passion deeper – dig into helping others learn and appreciate history.

Maybe there is a particular facet of history that has captured your fascination – art, architecture, military, politics, transportation, or home life, for example.

Depending on your location, museum exhibits may focus on art, film, architecture, photography, nature, maritime, industry, science, forests and habitat, transportation, cultural museums, private collections, and far more.

History museums in communities throughout South Puget Sound specialize in exhibits containing artifacts and stories of the state, city, and local communities and neighborhoods. Many museums offer regular events, programs, and tours to enhance the experience for their patrons. Many programs are presented on-line.

Other types of museums focus on more unusual, and often personal, collections such as puppets, hats, games, toys, rocks, and minerals. The list is endless!

For listings of museums in the area, see *RESOURCES: MUSEUMS, HISTORICAL SITES, SOCIETIES* on page 244.

Volunteering

Volunteers are the heart of most museums, large or small. Museums and historical sites offer a diverse assortment of roles to fit a volunteer's interests, time, skills, and experience. Whether you want to work with the public or behind-the-scenes, there is something for you.

A great way to share your passion for history is by being a docent or speaker. As a docent – defined as anyone associated with volunteer educational services to a museum – you connect visitors to what they see, conducting tours or talking with groups.

If you are handy with and enjoy working with tools or machinery, museums can use your skills to build and take down exhibits, set up or drive machinery and equipment, or maintain interactive displays. Modelers help build miniature versions of displays. Museums often need assistant archivists who work museum collections to categorize, clean, and store artifacts. Volunteers also may help research or transcribe oral histories.

Volunteers are always needed to greet the public, work in museum stores, help with events and tours, and perform office and fundraising tasks. Writers and editors, graphic artists, designers, and website designers support museum outreach, fundraising and marketing

activities. They also serve on advisory and planning committees.

Smaller museums are especially appreciative of volunteers who may take on multiple volunteering roles depending on the museum's needs.

Museum and historical site volunteers receive tremendous personal satisfaction through discovering, preserving, and sharing history. Many museums offer volunteer benefits such as memberships, discounts in museum stores, admission to special events, and recognition through group and individual events.

For listings of museums in the area, see *RESOURCES: MUSEUMS, HISTORICAL SITES, SOCIETIES* on page 244.

More Ways to Express Your History Passion

In addition to museums and historical sites, there are many other ways to express your love of history. And have a lot of fun doing it.

Many city celebrations are based on some aspect of its history or the history of a community's unique features, or something for which it is uniquely known. Examples of festival themes may be transportation, parks, unique crops, products, people, and cultures. These celebrations and festivals and celebrations help build a sense of community pride.

Look for opportunities to help these celebrations come alive. Sponsoring organizations such as cities, chambers of commerce, or historical societies need volunteer help in organizing, planning, and attending to hundreds of tasks needed for a successful event.

You can even combine interests with theatrics through reenactments of an historical period or event. With an eye on being authentic and true to a time-period or event, some of the most common are military encampments and battles, home, and rural life, and lots more.

If your interest lies in a special aspect of history, consider teaching or speaking about it. Look into giving talks in local museums, libraries, and community colleges. Ask around and you'll also find interest in your talk and knowledge at community and senior centers, retiree groups, and community service groups. See *CHAPTER 22: TEACHING, SPEAKING* on page 121 for more ideas!

If you enjoy writing about history, know that many large and small history museums could use your talent to document historical events or periods. You could also create interesting tidbits to publish in newsletters, blogs, and articles.

CHAPTER 20: MUSIC

Does your love of music play some role in your leisure time choices? Listen around, musical offerings are wonderfully diverse – bluegrass, folk, Indie rock, jazz, classical, pop, or some combination. The music scene offers a tremendous variety of ways to be involved, whether you sing, play an instrument, want to help young musicians learn, or just appreciate listening.

Many Boomers broaden their enjoyment of music by volunteering with organizations that perform, teach, and reach out to the music-loving community. Many organizations look for volunteer choral and instrumental musicians. Some ways Boomers express their love of music include:

Performing in Bands, Orchestras, or Choral Groups

It's not unusual to spot grey-haired and bearded Boomers performing both paid and volunteer gigs at farmers markets, fundraisers, community festivals, and other gathering places. Retiree musicians form small combos and garage bands to further their skills or for the plain fun of jamming with others.

Boomers also sing their way through retirement by joining choral groups in their communities and faith organizations, or entertaining at care facilities, retirement communities, and various music venues. Informal music sessions often gel and evolve into groups that write and perform their own music or perform old familiar music to appreciative Boomers and audiences of all ages.

You'll also find places to share your musical skills retirement communities, library programs, summer festivals, nonprofit fundraisers, and informal, impromptu get-togethers in a park or neighborhood. For a listing of music organizations in the area, see RESOURCES: MUSIC ORGANIZATIONS on page 257.

Performing at Care Facilities

Many take their music to people who are recovering or reside in facilities such as hospitals, nursing homes, assisted living centers, senior living communities, and hospice facilities. Musicians perform individually or as a group to brighten the days of people with health and other challenges.

Other places likely to welcome and appreciate your music include senior and community centers, libraries, and parks and recreation programs. Visit their websites or contact the coordinator of recreation programs.

Teaching Music

If you love teaching, consider helping others learn either as a paid or volunteer instructor. You'll find eager students of all ages – ready for sign up for private lessons or classes through music stores, community colleges, community centers, and parks and recreation programs.

Or consider doing behind the scenes work for nonprofits that help youth learn music. Youth music organizations rely on volunteers to help make music accessible to everyone. Volunteers help teach and mentor, maintain instruments, set up and host events, and help with fundraising and office activities. These nonprofits may require background checks.

Other places to teach music include senior activity centers, senior and retiree living communities, libraries, and parks and recreation programs. Visit their websites or contact the organization directly. For more about places to teach, see *CHAPTER 22: TEACHING, SPEAKING* on page 121.

Learning Music

Want to learn to play, practice, or improve your skills on a musical instrument? Check out learning places in your community such as community colleges, parks and recreation programs, and music stores. Ask local music stores or musicians for other unique starting places, for suggestions or private lessons. If you'd like to practice with others, consider finding jam sessions.

For a list of community colleges, see *RESOURCES: LEARNING PLACES, Colleges, Universities* on page 233. For a list of parks and recreation programs see *RESOURCES: LEARNING PLACES, Parks and Recreation* on page 237.

You'll also find lots of online music learning resources including books, live and video training, Facebook and other social media platforms, and online forums. Or search through the YouTube.com site's vast video library for musicians of all experience levels.

Behind Performances

Concerts in large venues rely on volunteers for a wide variety of roles such as greeting patrons, handing out programs, and ushering. In larger venues, you can join a "Friends-of..." group to fill the volunteer roles. In addition to working directly with performing artists and enjoying your favorite music, volunteer benefits may include concert passes, and patron and recognition events.

Music organizations also need volunteers in tasks such as office data entry and filing, answering the phone, fundraising, marketing, writing, graphic design, ushering, ticket taking, and serving refreshments.

Organizations that take music to their audiences may put you to work in outreach programs. Volunteering information typically is available on an organization's website.

Concerts, Festivals

An enjoyable summertime pastime is volunteering at outdoor concerts. Concerts are sponsored by parks and recreation programs or business groups all that welcome volunteer help in many roles.

Similarly, if you enjoy being part of the music festival scene, volunteer! Helpers work in all aspects of stage set-up and take-down, electronics, assisting performers, serving refreshments and activities unique to the concert. You'll probably land a free ticket, and opportunity to see up close your favorite performers.

Check out schedules of music festivals and concerts in your area posted on community calendars or by searching on the Internet for music events in your area. Visit websites well in advance to learn about volunteering roles and how to sign up. For more about places to volunteer at festivals and events, see *CHAPTER 20: MUSIC, Concerts, Festivals* on page 118 and *RESOURCES: MUSIC ORGANIZATIONS, Music Festivals, Events* on page 263.

Summer Outdoor Concerts

A great way to enjoy South Sound's picture-perfect summers is to grab your blanket or lawn chair and take in a free outdoor concert. Many are sponsored by parks programs and described on their websites. For a list of parks and recreation programs see *RESOURCES: LEARNING PLACES, Parks and Recreation* on page 237.

CHAPTER 21: SOCIAL CONNECTIONS

We are hard-wired to be socially active and engaged as a community. Research confirms what experience tells us – positive connections with

family and friends make us healthier and happier and improve everyone's lives. Without connections we become lonely, isolated, and just a touch crabby!

Retirees are no strangers to changes that upend lives. Life-changing events such as retirement and loss of daily people contact make us aware of our need for new social activities. Many view retirement as the time to make new friends as they try out new things! We find connections and community anywhere we gather around a common interest.

Places and Options for Social Groupies

Most communities in our country offer almost unlimited options for social engagement. In fact, as you browse this book, nearly type of interest and activity points to places where Boomers and retirees meet and connect with people around a common interest such as …

- Community, Adult, Senior Centers. Local community and senior centers are gathering places specifically designed for social activity. They encourage new and current members to take part in a wide variety of classes, workshops, excursions, and social clubs. See *CHAPTER 3: VOLUNTEERING, Senior and Community Centers*, on page 38.

- Community College Programs. Community colleges offer programs and activities on their academic schedules specifically for retired adults and seniors, or of interest to seniors, with emphasis on social learning activities. See *CHAPTER 17: LEARN SOMETHING NEW, More Learning Forums* on page 103 and *RESOURCES: LEARNING PLACES, Colleges, Universities* on page 233.

- Faith-based Organizations. Retirees benefit in many ways by involvement in faith-based organizations and the giving of their time and energy in causes their organization supports: a sense of connection to something beyond themselves, the connections and benefits of social aspect, and the satisfaction of helping others.

- Hobby Groups. The common interest we find in hobbies naturally connects us. Many hobbies bring us together to work on projects, study more about our pastimes and socialize. *See CHAPTER 16: HOBBIES,* on page 101.

- Meetups. These A-Z groups in your area groups formed around a common interest or activity, very social by nature. Meetups run the gamut of interests – from commonplace to unusual and everything in between. Visit meetup.com.

- Outdoor and Fitness Groups. Outdoor groups of all types are common everywhere. You'll find groups that walk, hike, run, play pickleball, swim, golf, garden…you get the idea. Outdoorsy types connect through a passion for their activity and being out in nature, as well as a liking for social gatherings. For information on outdoor and fitness groups, see *CHAPTER 7: CARE FOR THE ENVIRONMENT* on page 57; *CHAPTER 11: FITNESS, HEALTHY LIVING* on page 75; CHAPTER 12: GARDENING on page 85; *CHAPTER 15: HIKING AND WALKING* on page 97; and *CHAPTER 23: THE GREAT OUTDOORS* on page 129.

- Parks and Recreation Programs. Community recreation programs offer places to connect and socialize with like-minded seniors and adults. Programs include an ever-changing variety of classes and activities generally published in seasonal catalogs. *CHAPTER 17: LEARN SOMETHING NEW* on page 105.

- Retirement, Senior Living Communities. If you live in a retirement community, you already know that social engagement is a central attraction for many. These communities offer a variety of activities, centered on learning, healthy lifestyles, socializing, and fun!

- Volunteering. Part of our social nature is a desire to make our communities better places to live, work, and play. By volunteering we work side-by-side with others to help others. Learn more about volunteering in *CHAPTER 3: VOLUNTEERING* on page 25 and in *RESOURCES: VOLUNTEERING* on page 277.

CHAPTER 22: TEACHING, SPEAKING

How would you finish this sentence?

I would love to use my knowledge of _____
to help people such as _____ *learn about*
_____ -
_____ .

We each have acquired knowledge about and skills for something. We may have acquired it through school, work, a hobby, or people we hang with. Some came naturally; others we've had to learn. *So, is it now time to share that with others?*

For example, you may know how to create a quilt or knit a hat, build a cedar strip canoe, play the guitar, write a short story or poem, play pinochle, tie a fly, or kayak down a river.

Can you cook a specialty dish? Do you know how to set up a chart of accounts, put up a website, or use spreadsheet software? Maybe you're passionate about some interesting aspect of history, current event or issue, a biography, an artist, or a musician or author.

Think about it – if you're interested, others are too. Someone wants to know what you know. So why not help them learn? Find your own teach-talk-tutor-train niche and go for it! You have more to share than you think.

While we often use teaching, talking (speaking), tutoring, and training interchangeably, there are differences:

- TEACHING – Usually occurs in a formal group classroom setting, where you are the leader of a specific curriculum. A community college course on local history, for example.

- TALKING (SPEAKING) – Primarily from a platform before a group, where you are presenting as a keynote or workshop speaker. A civic, church, or social group speech on healthy aging, for example.

- TUTORING – Happens one-on-one, where you coach and guide another individual to learn from you. Helping students improve their math skills, for example.

- TRAINING – Can be for an individual or group, where you are guiding their learning and mastery of a specific set of skills. Guiding people on how to use a computer software program, for example.

Discover Your Niche

To figure out how best to position yourself, refer back to your self-understanding questions. Think about:

1. What is your passion and knowledge base?
2. Who wants to learn this knowledge?
3. Where can you reach those people and share what you know?

What to Teach?

What are you good at? What do you know a lot about? For what information do people come to you? What have you been invited to give presentations about?

Your past jobs and career are fertile discovery fields. *What did you enjoy most? For what do you have special knowledge and expertise in your field?*

Or do you have experience in a professional organization? For example, a special knowledge of technology, a product or service, current industry trends, or research?

What is your favorite hobby or pastime? Consider turning the hobby you love into your perfect volunteer opportunity. Help inspire others to learn from your expertise. *What about your hobbies or past hobbies? Do you build stuff? Make jewelry? Play cards, sew, knit, quilt, enjoy birding? Do you take photos or build models? Can you help others seek out local adventures? Do you write stories or novels?*

How about activities? What outdoorsy pursuits do you particularly enjoy and know about? Are you a special-interest gardener or a fisherman? Do you cycle, walk, hike, swim, play golf, tennis or pickleball? Would you love to help others learn?

Are there subjects you could tutor others on? For example, helping youth or adults with reading, math, science, writing, learning English, managing finances?

Who are Your Learners?

Next, think about the types of people who need the knowledge and experience you offer.

Are they children, adults, seniors, or some combination? What are their situations? How will you reach them? Are you interested in one-on-one, smaller, or larger groups? Narrow your choices down as much as possible.

Do you want to help people who are struggling with overcoming difficult life situations? Many social service organizations need people who can step in and serve in this important way.

Where to Share?

Where is your best place to teach-talk-tutor-train? Do you need the structure of an educational institution, library, or sponsor group? What learning situations would you prefer? Some may require formal education and credentials, others emphasize experience.

A multitude of teaching opportunities are found in and beyond traditional learning places – schools, universities, and community colleges. Many Boomers share their expertise in the less formal community education programs.

The following types of organizations may offer ways to share your knowledge and expertise. To find them, start by visiting the organization's website, viewing a course catalog, visiting the volunteer web page, or contacting the organization directly by phone or email. Ask for the appropriate contact person.

The following describes various organizations that you can contact for opportunities to share your knowledge and expertise.

The contact process will vary by type of organization so start by visiting the organization's website, viewing a catalog of courses, visiting the volunteer web page, or contacting the organization directly by phone or email to ask for the appropriate contact person.

Adult and Senior Enrichment Programs

Often sponsored by local colleges and universities, these programs offer seniors a wide variety of classes ranging from health and fitness, current events, local history, contemporary world problems, and many other topics of interest. Many feature talks by local speakers and authors. For a listing of area community colleges, see *RESOURCES: LEARNING PLACES, Colleges, Universities,* on 233.

Community and Senior Centers

Located in communities throughout the country, senior centers provide a range of social services, classes, and workshops to help seniors live, learn, thrive, and socialize. Many offer programs and speakers on a wide variety of topics such as various history and current events topics, health education programs and activities.

Suggest an activity or class you could offer on your specialty, favorite pastime, or interest. Senior and adult community centers offer programs on a wide variety of topics. Interested speakers should contact the center directly and ask for the person in charge of events and programs For a list of area community and senior centers, see *RESOURCES: SENIOR SERVICES, Senior and Community Centers* on page 267.

Community Business and Service Organizations. Depending on your area of expertise, all types of community and business organizations seek speakers on topics of interest to their members. Their programs vary from current events to interesting aspects of community businesses, organizations, history, unique features, and development. To find listings of community *RESOURCES: BUSINESS BUILDING, Economic Development, Chamber Organizations* on page 162.

Community Service Tutoring

Many schools and nonprofits seek tutors to help children and adults with reading, art, photography, music, sports, daily living skills, and social services. See postings on an organization's volunteer page. To find organizations, *CHAPTER 9: COMMUNITY SERVICE* on page 63 and *RESOURCES: COMMUNITY SERVICE ORGANIZATIONS* on page 172.

Libraries and Museums

Libraries invite speakers to share their knowledge, skills, and expertise on a wide variety of topics. Library programs include author talks, art shows, cultural festivals, lectures, and help with technology and language. Libraries also offer how-to programs and hands-on programs on all varieties of hobbies, arts, and crafts, writing and publishing, and much more.

Museums offer programs to enrich understanding of the history behind their collections. Many museums and historical societies offer teaching and speaking opportunities, especially for history buffs. And welcome local experts!

Because the contact process varies by organization, start by contacting the individual library or museum directly.

For a list of area libraries, see *RESOURCES: LEARNING PLACES, Libraries* on page 235. For a list of area museums, see *RESOURCES: MUSEUMS, HISTORICAL SITES, SOCIETIES* on page 244.

Medical Centers

Many healthcare organizations in and around Puget Sound offer health-related classes and events to their members and to the community at large. Some have online classes and videos.

Ongoing, popular classes are healthy eating, fitness and exercise, weight management, smoking cessation, healthy lifestyles, support groups, reducing stress, pain management, depression, yoga, and many other health topics of interest to seniors and retirees.

See the types of classes offered on their websites and contact the person in charge of community education. For a listing of area healthcare organizations, see *RESOURCES: HEALTHCARE VOLUNTEERING, Healthcare Organizations* on page 219.

Online Teaching

For a variety of reasons, more learning organizations offer a growing number and types of online classes. The flipside of online learning is online teaching. Consider turning your teaching or speaking expertise into an online class or talk. A digital recording of yourself teaching or speaking is also helpful when presenting your class as an option. Start with local colleges, community centers and other learning venues. Also, with the use of ever-changing online learning technology, consider that you can literally teach from anywhere to anywhere in the world.

Parks and Recreation Programs

Parks programs offer activities and classes for all ages. In addition to outdoor activities, many also offer indoor recreation programs such as music, dancing, healthy living, hobbies, and more. Those interested in teaching should view the organization's activity catalog and contact the person in charge of classes. Or contact the organization directly asking for the person in charge of classes and events, or the human resources or employment department. For a listing of South Sound Parks and

Recreation organizations, see *RESOURCES: LEARNING PLACES, Parks and Recreation* on page 237.

Schools, Universities and Colleges

In addition to credit and non-credit community education classes, many colleges offer other programs and activities that provide volunteer (and paid!) speaking opportunities. Look for contact information or applications in course catalogs. Interested speakers may also contact the college directly. Many schools and nonprofits also seek tutors to help children with reading, art, music, and sports, as well as social skills. For a listing of

community colleges, see *RESOURCES: LEARNING PLACES, Colleges, Universities* on page 233.

Senior Living Communities

Retiree communities offer a wide variety of programs for residents, eager (like you) to learn something new about a wide variety of topics. In your area, look for 55+ neighborhoods, independent living facilities, cooperatives, and similar living communities. Contact the community's program, activities, or education directors.

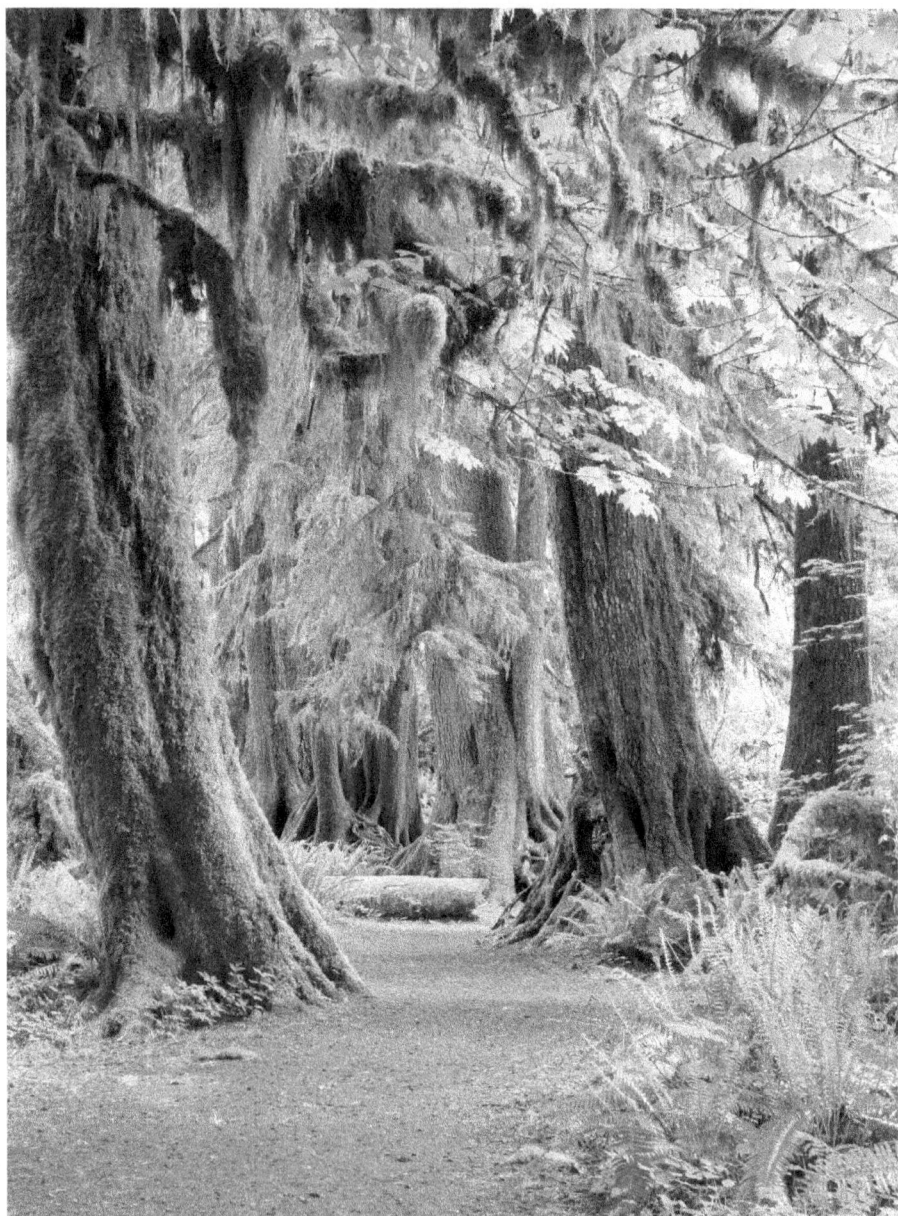

CHAPTER 23: THE GREAT OUTDOORS

Maybe you've spent years chained to a desk, your eyes radar-locked on a computer spreadsheet and now, on the cusp of your next phase, it's time for a change of scenery!

You can morph from corporate beige to green without a digital device. Experience tangible, touchable scenery. Photograph worthy landmarks. Go outside, away from all things electronic. Surround yourself with forests, nature parks, lakes, and rivers. Backdrop your tableau with blue, or grey sky – even the rain and snow have great beauty. Photograph blooming lavender, wander through forests of towering Douglas firs or collect oyster shells during low tide. Go to places where you can infuse fresh air into a foggy brain.

Ours is a county of rocky terraine, gentle coastlines, snow capped mountains, deserts, mountain trails, rivers, lakes, and out-of-the-way wetlands, watersheds, and natural dramatic features beckoning to be explored. Our large and small city towns display their own individual architectural interest, commercial uniqueness, and walkability.

Discover the abundant neighborhood parks right in your backyard. And don't forget your own community's unique features and hidden nature gems within walking, driving distance or a bus, train, or ferry ride.

On Land

In your next phase plan, then, turn electronics to "Not Now" mode, think about what appeals to you, and take yourself outside! Look for:

- Fitness Sports and Activities. Find places to enjoy the outdoors walking, running, cycling, skiing, jogging, swimming, pickleball, kayaking, and more. See more about outdoor health and fitness options in *CHAPTER 11: FITNESS, HEALTHY LIVING* on page 75 and *RESOURCES: FITNESS, HEALTHY LIVING* on page 195.

- Gardening. Get the dirt on local gardening and gardens; how to enjoy, learn, socialize, and grow stuff in a garden. See *CHAPTER 12: GARDENING* on page 85 and *RESOURCES: GARDENING* on page 207.

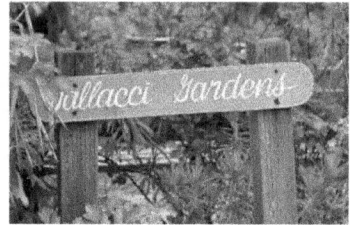

- Hiking and Walking. Choose from unlimited places to hike and walk in neighborhoods, in forests, parks, and cities, around outdoor art venues, on mountain trails, and unique local places. See *CHAPTER 15: HIKING AND WALKING* on page 97 and *RESOURCES: HIKING AND WALKING* on page 226.

- Local Adventures. Explore or day trip to new outdoor experiences. Seek out rivers, lakes, small towns, parks, estuaries, and nature centers. Check city, county, chamber, or tourism organizations. See *CHAPTER 10: EXPLORING THE SOUTH SOUND* on page 65, *RESOURCES: EXPLORING THE SOUTH SOUND* on page 180.

- Outdoor Concerts, Farmers Markets, Art Shows. Blend culture and outdoors in a seasonal festival. Look for those centered around art, music, food, ethnic traditions, history, city celebrations, and more. See *CHAPTER 10: EXPLORING THE SOUTH SOUND, Events, Festivals* on page 71 and *RESOURCES: ART, PHOTOGRAPHY, FILM, Art Walks, Festivals* on page 155, and *RESOURCES: MUSIC ORGANIZATIONS, Music Festivals, Events* on page 263.

- Outdoor Volunteering. Volunteer at parks, natural areas, wildlife refuges, trails, rivers, gardens, and many other places. See *CHAPTER 7: CARE FOR THE ENVIRONMENT* on page 57, *RESOURCES: CARE FOR THE ENVIRONMENT* on page 165, *CHAPTER 12: GARDENING, Volunteer at a Public Garden* on page 86 and *RESOURCES: GARDENING* on page 207.

On Water

Water sports are a great way to enjoy our connection to water and experience the amazing scenic waterways in our country. Water sports offer many opportunities for exercise and fun (or serious!) competition. Especially popular ways to do both are the row sports of canoeing, kayaking, dragon boating, and sculling.

Kayak and Canoe

Kayaking and canoeing offer gentle ways to experience nature's nooks and crannies in lakes, rivers, coastlines, and other waterways. These fresh air sports are easy to enjoy with family, friends, and grandkids.

Dragon Boating

Enthusiasts say that once you've tried it, there's no turning back. Dragon boating teams compete on their own circuit throughout the country. In some communities, over-55 paddlers can join their own team for fun and fitness. It's been said that old age and treachery overcome youth and ambition. (You'll have to see for yourself, of course.)

Paddle, Scull, Row

Paddle boarding has been the rage but sculling and sweeping are gaining fans. Sculling is another rowing sport popular in many waterways. In sculling, 1 to 8 people propel a scull by rowing with two oars, often in competition. Sweep rowing involves a pair of rowers, each using a single oar.

Sailing

You can make the sport of sailing as adventurous, peaceful, or playful as you want in the South Sound. Many sailing clubs and organizations offer inexpensive ways to get started, learn, and pursue sailing as a recreational pastime or competitive sport.

How to Start

Get involved in paddling and rowing sports on your own or in a group. Classes for all ages and abilities are conducted by community outfitters, city parks programs, community colleges, and other organizations. Clubs are another way to acquaint yourself with the paddle sports and find kindred spirits. Whether a beginner or white-water adventurer, there's a club for you.

Visit websites of area kayaking, canoeing and paddling clubs to find information about lessons and events. At the same time, find opportunities to share what you know about your favorite paddling sports by teaching or coaching, or volunteering at an event.

For lists of area paddling, rowing clubs, and other types of boating clubs, see *RESOURCES: THE GREAT OUTDOORS, Paddling, Rowing, Sailing Clubs* on page 271.

CHAPTER 24: THEATER, PERFORMANCE

Are you among the many Boomers who love live theater and performances and want to help enrich the theater experience in some way?

Do you secretly yearn to get on stage? Or volunteer behind the scenes? What resonates with you? Where can you get involved?

The Theater Scene

If you've secretly (or openly) wanted to be involved in theater, an ever-changing performance scene offers limitless opportunities to engage in all aspects of theater.

Many cities and communities beckon theater-lovers with rich, vibrant, opportunities for a broad range of interests. Large, established venues anchor the theatrical panorama, enriched with a delightful, diverse mixture of quality regional and local productions.

Depending on your area, your choices may range from innovative and experimental, to ethnic and social statement, ambitious blends with original music and visual arts media, and delightful homegrown productions. For a listing of theater and performance venues and companies, *see RESOURCES: THEATER, PERFORMANCE, South Sound Performing Arts Companies and Venues* on page 273.

Get on Stage: Acting and Storytelling

Want to lose the timid and get on stage? Haven't acted since junior high?

You're in the right place. Do a little homework first, though, because theaters have different needs and prerequisites for performers. Large and medium-sized professional theaters generally cast and hire equity and non-equity actors. Smaller and independent theaters may stage productions with a volunteer cast. Some train you in advance. Others give you on-the-set training.

Smaller community theaters are good starting places because of their all-volunteer cast and crew. In many community theaters, you can audition to act, understudy someone, or work hands-on behind the scenes. Tasks such as building and taking down sets, changing scenes, sewing costumes, running lights, and helping on show nights is a fun way to learn theater ins and outs.

Do you have a favorite story or two you'd like to share on stage? Storytelling is another great way to get in front of an audience. Tellers share vivid personal stories on stage, believing that to be human is to have a story to share. Classes and workshops sponsored by libraries, community colleges, and other groups help develop and present stories to live audiences. For lists of area libraries and community colleges, see *RESOURCES: LEARNING PLACES, Colleges, Universities* on page 233, *Libraries* on page 235, and *Parks and Recreation* on page 237.

Behind the Scenes Roles

Did you ever realize that performance by actors, directors, and other performers is simply the tip of the iceberg of the live stage?

Off-stage roles are filled with people like you who make the show go on. Volunteers enjoy being creatively involved in making plays happen and using a special skill or interest such as technology, construction, costuming, music, sound and lighting setup, organizing, or meeting the public. All desire to be part of the live theater experience up close.

Volunteers greet and usher. They design, build, and change sets, sew costumes, apply makeup. They manage lighting, sound, and music. Many work in the back office selling tickets, creating flyers, maintaining lists, and doing mailings. Others create brochures and programs and take photos. You might like to sell refreshments and gifts, meet the public at special events and outreach activities, or plan those activities.

Major Theaters

If you volunteer through a major theater, you'll join a well-established volunteer organization that may have hundreds of volunteers (lots of retirees), who donate hours as ushers, greeters, gift shop attendees, tour guides, reception desk attendants, office assistants, and receptionists.

Medium-Size and Regional Theater

Medium-size professional and non-professional companies perform in area downtowns and suburbs. Volunteers usher, sell concessions and merchandise, help patrons, do hands-on behind-the-scenes tasks, sew costumes, build sets, and work in outreach.

Local and Independent Theater

Smaller independent and home-grown performing groups are often scattered throughout a community. Theater groups entertain in theaters, converted buildings, churches, and warehouses. Many are all-volunteer – from actors and directors to many behind-the-scenes stage production, office, and administrative roles.

Dance

Dance-loving volunteers can also participate in performing arts. Performances in many cities range from ballet concerts to contemporary work by local companies and collaborations with other art forms. Many take their innovations to local communities. Volunteers perform various behind the scenes roles as they do in other performance genres.

For a listing of area Dance organizations, see RESOURCES: THEATER, PERFORMANCE, Dance on page 273.

CHAPTER 25: TRAVEL

While travel to "…someplace I've always wanted to visit…" is on many Boomer bucket lists, there are many more ways to create meaningful experiences through local, regional, national, or international travel.

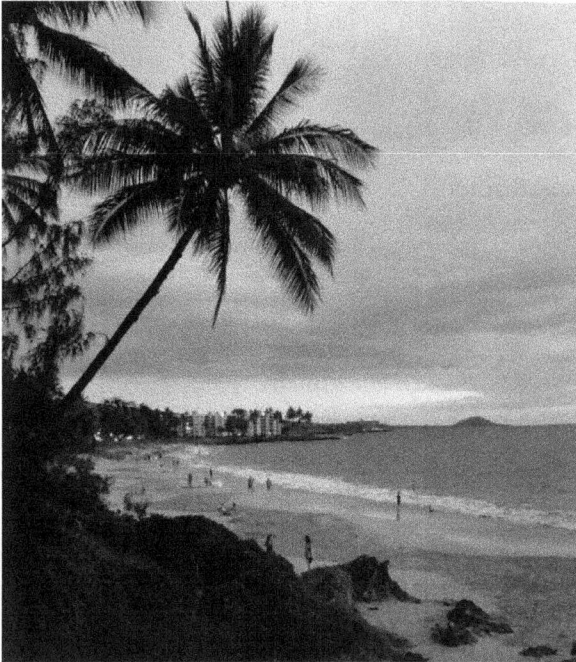

Start by thinking about your passions and interests, and the types of experiences you enjoy. Then look at the ways travel could enhance or enrich those. For example, if you enjoy cooking, you could enroll in classes in the country of your favorite food, take classes on a cruise, or enjoy either of these with your cooking group.

Another popular option are intergenerational trips, sharing a travel passion with kids, grandkids, grandparents, or others. For example:

- Heritage trips. Find places to research the history of your ancestors or study the history of an area of interest.

- Milestone trips. Celebrate a special occasion such as a birthday, anniversary, or retirement (Ta-Da!), to create a lasting memory.

- Hobby or interest. You have as many unlimited options as there are hobbies. Take classes, or just enjoy your hobby in other states or countries. Learn woodworking, art, music, sailing, hiking, culinary arts, or more about your favorite varietals.

- Sports and outdoors. Grab your clubs and rackets and skates, hiking boots, boards, skis, and whatever else you need to get up, get out, and take on your sport or activity at a new destination!

Good starting points to research travel are travel classes and group excursions offered by many community colleges and other travel and groups and organizations in local communities.

RV Travel

Another very popular bucket list option for millions of retirees is hitting the road by RV (recreational vehicle). Millions of RVers across the country express their wanderlust by either driving or pulling their shelter to thousands of get-away destinations near and far.

Weekend, months, or seasonal trips. They're off to leave behind yardwork and chores, experiences new places, and enjoy new and old friends, and companions. With groups or solo to remote areas.

If you're thinking that RVing may be for you, do your research. Consider ways to try out the lifestyle and responsibilities and costs before taking the plunge. Ease into RVing by visiting any number of online forums, discussion groups, and talking with people you know.

Local Adventures: Day Tripping

City websites. Visit these websites for listings of visitor information including local events, indoor and outdoor facilities, parks, arts, music and concerts, and other cultural events and festivals, museums, and many other attractions.

How often do we say, "I only visit local sights when guests come to town!" Well, it may be time to venture out as a tourist in your own town. You'll likely find no better day-tripping paradise than driving to destinations in your own local and regional communities. You may be delightfully surprised with new discoveries for everyone. Day trip solo, with friends, or find a group.

In many areas, you needn't travel far to enjoy a forest, wetlands, shipyard, river city, valley, beautiful garden, outdoor art collection, seasonal farmers market, art fair, history museum, local oddity, and on and on.

Good places to look for information on day tripping are:

- Washington Tourism Website. You'll find all types of visitor information on travel destinations by region, city, types of attractions, as well as access to guidebooks, maps and more.

- City websites. Visit these websites for listings of visitor information including local events, indoor and outdoor facilities, parks, arts, music and concerts, and other cultural events and festivals, museums, and many other attractions.

- Chamber of Commerce Websites. Chamber websites are a good source of visitor information on community events, local attractions and places of interest, and visitor amenities.

- Visitor Information Websites. These organizations focus on providing information to visitors on things to do and see, including events, lodging, local attractions, and entertainment.

For information and resources on these organizations, and exploring the many destinations in the region, see *CHAPTER 10: EXPLORING THE SOUTH SOUND*, page 65 *and RESOURCES: EXPLORING THE SOUTH SOUND*, beginning on page 180.

Group Day Trips

If group day outings appeal to you, look into organizations that offer group outings and trips such as community colleges, parks programs, retirement communities, and community centers. You'll likely find inexpensive, convenient ways to visit local and regional attractions, natural landscapes, and diverse off-the-beaten-path destinations.

For lists of area libraries and community colleges, see *RESOURCES: LEARNING PLACES, Colleges, Universities* on page 233, Libraries on page 235, and *Parks and Recreation* on page 237. For a list of senior centers that offer local trips, see *CHAPTER 10: EXPLORING THE SOUTH SOUND, Outings with Senior and Community Centers* on page 71.

Travel Abroad

Many retirees find the lure of international travel irresistible and set out to learn about and experience different cultures up close. Today's interconnected world brings abundant resources and information right to our electronic devices. Connect to vast libraries of travel information, on-line blogs and chats, podcasts, newsletters, classes and more.

Experts emphasize the importance of doing extensive research on foreign county designations. Visit the U.S. State Department website for visa information and travel advisories. Sources of information include travel agencies, community colleges, and community centers. Many colleges sponsor international travel as a part of their curriculum, and senior centers partner with travel organizations to provide group planning and pricing. For a listing of area community colleges, see *RESOURCES: LEARNING PLACES, Colleges, Universities* on page 233.

APPENDIX: RESOURCES IN YOUR COMMUNITY

RESOURCES: ANIMAL ADOPTION AND RESCUE

The following are animal rescue and care organizations in and near Mason, Thurston, and Pierce Counties. They provide temporary care, shelter and adoption services for unwanted small and large pets and other animals. Most, if not all shelters need and welcome animal lover volunteers. Visit animal shelter websites for more information.

Cats, Dogs and Other Small Animals
Kitsap and Mason Counties

- Adopt-A-Pet. 940 East Jensen Rd, Shelton. 360-432-3091. adoptapet-wa.org

- Animal Rescue Families. Animal rescue, fostering, adoption. animalrescuefamilies.org

- Assistance Dogs Northwest. Provides children and adults with special needs special needs with professionally trained dogs to assist them. Bainbridge. 206-321-0592. assistancedogsnorthwest.org

- City of Shelton Animal Shelter. 525 W Cota St, Shelton. 360-427-7503. sheltonanimalshelter.org

- Companion Animal Care Project. P.O. Box 903, Shelton. animalshelter.net/shelter/7382/companion-animal-care-project

- Humane Society of Mason County. 24070 State Route 3, Ste 3, Belfair. 360-275-9310. hsmcwa.org

- Kitsap Animal Rescue and Education. Silverdale. 360-602-6717. nwkare.org

- Kitsap Audubon Society. Poulsbo. kitsapaudubon.org

- Kitsap Humane Society. 9167 Dickey Road NW, Silverdale. 360-692-6977. kitsap-humane.org

- Kitten Rescue of Mason County. 420 SE State Rte 3, Shelton. 360-427-3167. kittenresq.net

- Paws Adoption Center. 4688 Lynwood Center Rd NE Ste 11, Bainbridge Island. 206-842-2451. pawsbink.org

- PAWS of Bremerton. 3306 Perry Ave, Bremerton. 360-373-7043 pawsofbremerton.org

- Rescue Every Dog, Mason County Chapter. PO Box 1937, Belfair. countyoffice.org/rescue-every-dog-mason-county-chapter-belfair-wa-41f

- Shelton Mason County Parrot Rescue, 81 East Daniels Rd, Shelton. sheltonmasonparrotrescue.rescueme.org

- West Sound Wildlife Shelter. Wildlife rehabilitation and education. 7501 NE Dolphin Dr, Bainbridge Island. Call ahead. 206-855-9057.

- Wild Felid Advocacy Center of Washington. 3111 East Harstine Island Road, North Shelton. wildfelids.org

Pierce County

- American Cocker Spaniel Rescue. 624 191st St, Court East, Spanaway. countyoffice.org/american-cocker-spaniel-rescue-spanaway-wa-eea

- Angels In Flight-Avian Rescue. 18708 229th Ave, East Orting. 253-941-5896. countyoffice.org/angels-in-flight-avian-rescue-orting-wa-eeb

- Animal Rescue. PO Box 814, Puyallup. 206-535-0937. petfinder.com/member/us/wa/puyallup

- Auburn Valley Humane Society. 4910 A St, SE, Auburn (King County). 253-249-7849. auburnvalleyhs.org

- Binky Bunny Tales Rescue. Rabbit rescue. South Hill. 253-651-4462. binkybunnytalesrescue.com

- Bob's Amigos, A Pet Rescue, 10605 122nd Ave, Kp N, Gig Harbor. animalshelter.org/shelters

- Cascade Animal Protection Society. PO Box 2085, Sumner. 253-863-8004. myrescuesite.org/caps

- Cascade Bulldog Rescue Rehome, Inc. PO Box 436 Buckley. animalshelter.net/shelter/7374/cascade-bulldog-rescuerehome-inc
- CHEW Dog Rescue. 5803 125th Ct NW, Gig Harbor. 253-265-6235. chewdogrescue.org
- English Setter Rescue. 96 Park Ave NW, Gig Harbor. 360-830-4427. countyoffice.org/english-setter-rescue-gig-harbor-wa-eee
- Feline Rescue. 4410 70th Ave Court West, University Place. 253-565-1769. countyoffice.org/feline-rescue-university-place-wa-eef
- Harbor Hope Cat Rescue. PO Box 2693, Gig Harbor. 253-858-6205. countyoffice.org/harbor-hope-cat-rescue-gig-harbor-wa-659
- Lakewood Animal Control. 6000 Main St, SW, Lakewood. 253-830-5010. cityoflakewood.us/police-homepage/animal-control-2.
- Lucky Paws Rescue. Dog rescue and adoption. Tacoma. luckypawsrescuewa.org
- Metro Animal Services. Serving Puyallup, Sumner, Algona, Bonney Lake, Edgewood, Milton, Pacific. 1200 39th Ave SE, Puyallup. 253-299-7387. metroanimalservices.org
- Mischief Maker's Rescue & Rehabilitation. Small animal, reptile, bird, and exotics rescue. 11806 200th Ave E, Bonney Lake. 775-400-5384. mischief-makers-rescue-rehab.business.site
- PAWS & Claws Animal Rescue. PO Box 732137, Puyallup. 253-531-8349. countyoffice.org/paws-claws-animal-rescue-puyallup-wa-49e
- Pierce County Animal Control. 2401 S 35th St, Tacoma. 253-798-7387. countyoffice.org/pierce-county-animal-control-tacoma-wa-6ab
- Puget Sound Rescue. 17206 SE 338th St, Auburn. 253-569-6983. pugetsoundrescue.org
- Puyallup Animal Control. 1200 39th Ave SE, Puyallup. 253-841-5595. countyoffice.org/puyallup-animal-control-puyallup-wa-8b2

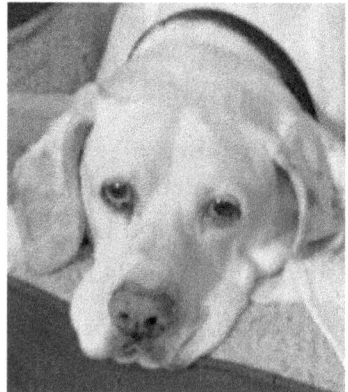

- Puyallup Animal Rescue. PO Box 814, Puyallup. 253-847-1243. adoptapet.com/shelter/67360-puyallup-animal-rescue-puyallup-washington

- The Humane Society for Tacoma & Pierce County. 2608 Center St, Tacoma. 253-383-2733, thehumanesociety.org

- The Zoo Society. Supports animal care at Defiance Point Zoo & Aquarium. 5400 N Pearl St, Tacoma. 253-404-3651. thezoosociety.org

- Today Sunny Sky's. 1102 E Main, Puyallup. 253-845-8866. sunnyskysshelter.org

Thurston County

- Angels Pet Rescue. 5148 Marian Dr NE, Olympia. countyoffice.org/angels-pet-rescue-olympia-wa-335

- Animal Rescue & Adopting. 8737 Whitewood Loop SE Yelm. 360-458-3281. countyoffice.org/animal-rescue-adopting-inc-yelm-wa-333

- Animal Services. 3120 Martin Way E, Olympia. 360-352-2510. countyoffice.org/animal-services-olympia-wa-334

- Concern For Animals. 1414 State Ave NE, Olympia. countyoffice.org/concern-for-animals-olympia-wa-90a

- Feline Friends. 6515 Sexton Dr NW, Olympia. 360-866-0599. countyoffice.org/feline-friends-olympia-wa-41e

- Foreclosure Pets. Animal shelter. Olympia. 360-349-2416. facebook.com/Foreclosurepetswa

- Rainier Animal Control. 600 Minnesota St, North Rainier. 360-446-2636. countyoffice.org/rainier-animal-control-rainier-wa-8bf

- Thurston County Humane Society. 3120 Martin Way E, Olympia. 360-866-8986. countyoffice.org/thurston-county-humane-society-olympia-wa-337

Horse and Large Animal Rescue, Rehabilitation

Kitsap and Mason Counties

- Happy Hooves Sanctuary. 12925 N Madison Ave NE, Bainbridge Island. 650-678-5378. happyhoovessanctuary.org

- Pony Up Rescue For Equines. 11619 Orchard Ave SE, Olalla. 206-900-1248. ponyuprescue.org

- Sunrise Equine Rescue. 401 E Mason Benson Rd, Grapeview. 360-275-2960. sunriseequinerescue.org

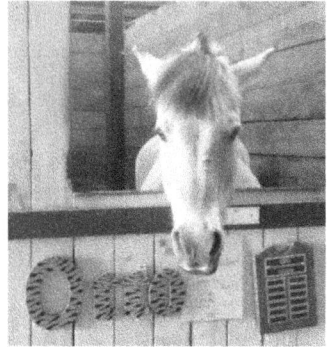

Pierce County

- Serenity Equine Rescue & Rehabilitation. 28818 SE 216th Way, Maple Valley. 425-432-9697. serenityequinerescue.com

- Thunder Mountain Farms Equine Rescue. 29609 SE 408th St, Enumclaw. 206-300-3732. thundermountainfarms.org

- Willow River Equine Rescue. 22020 286th Ave SE, Maple Valley. 206-454-9622. willowriverequinerescue.com

Thurston County

- Cross Creek Alpaca Rescue. Tenino. crosscreekalpacarescue.org

- Healing Hearts Ranch. 3500 85th Ln SW, Olympia. 360-701-6001. healingheartsrancholy.com

- Heartstrides Therapeutic Horsemanship. 3500 85th Ln SW. Olympia. 360-701-6001 heartstridestherapeutichorsemanship.com

- Hooved Animal Rescue of Thurston County. PO Box 711, East Olympia. harotc.org/home

- Rainier Equine Hoof Recovery Center. 12211 123rd Ave SE, Rainier. 360-790-4181. rainierhoofrehab.org

- Rainy Day Therapeutic Riding Center. 6118 Maple Meadows Lane NE, Olympia, 360-797-9102. rainydayranchtherapeutic.org

Zoo and Aquariums

- Point Defiance Zoo and Aquarium. 5400 North Pearl St, Tacoma. 253-404-3800. pdza.org

- Puget Sound Estuarian. Exhibits and programs that promote health of the unique estuary environment. 309 State Ave NE, Olympia. 360-918-8412. pugetsoundestuarium.org

TO THE NEW PACIFIC SEAS AQUARIUM

- SEA Discovery Center. Aquarium and marine education center. 18743 Front St NE, Poulsbo. 360-650-4905. sea.wwu.edu

- Seattle Aquarium. Resource for hands-on marine experiences and conservation education. 1483 Alaskan Way Pier 59, Seattle. 206-386-4300. seattleaquarium.org

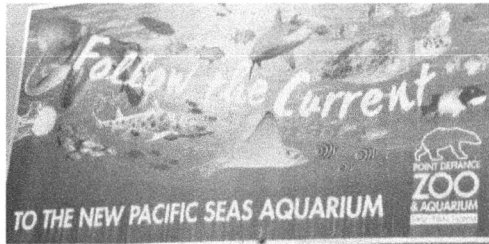

Wildlife Organizations

- Ecostudies Institute. Restoration of native species of birds, other wildlife, and their habitats and ecosystems.360-213-8829. Olympia. ecoinst.org

- South Puget Sound Salmon Enhancement Group. Protects and restores salmon populations and aquatic habitat. 6700 Martin Way E, Ste 112, Olympia. 360-412-0808. spsseg.org

- West Sound Wildlife Shelter. Provides injured, orphaned, and sick wildlife a second chance at life. Bainbridge Island. 206-855-9057. westsoundwildlife.org

- Wolf Haven. Wolf sanctuary and rescue. 3111 Offut Lake Rd SE, Tenino. 360-264-4695. wolfhaven.org

National Wildlife Organizations

- Audubon Society. Protects birds and their habitat. audubon.org

- Conservation International. Conservation and nature protection. conservation.org

- Jane Goodall Institute. Protection of chimpanzees and conservation of nature. janegoodall.org

- National Resources Defense Fund. Focus on protecting plants, animals, and the natural systems. nrdc.org

- National Wildlife Federation. Protects, restores wildlife habitats. nwf.org

- Nature Conservancy. Preserves and protects natural resources. nature.org

- Oceana. Focuses on protecting world's oceans. oceana.org

- Sierra Club. Grassroots advocates for environmental protection. sierraclub.org

- Wildlife Conservation Society. Global animal conservation program. wcs.org

- World Wildlife Fund. Nature conservation and protection. worldwildlife.org

- 4Ocean. International organization that works to clean oceans and coastlines and change plastic consumption habits. 4ocean.com

RESOURCES: ART, PHOTOGRAPHY, FILM

Visual Arts Spaces and Cultural Centers

The following are lists of art venues and spaces in or near King, Kitsap, Mason, Pierce, and Thurston counties. In these spaces you can engage in enriching and diverse art, film and photography experiences and discover interesting volunteer opportunities. Visit organization websites for more information.

King County

- Art Gallery North Seattle College. Exhibits that demonstrate cultural and artistic diversity. 9600 College Way North. Seattle. 206-528-4557. artgallery.northseattle.edu

- Auburn Arts Programs. Art classes and workshops, Arts Alley creative gathering place. auburnwa.gov

- Auburn Public Art Collection. Various locations. Also, the Downtown Sculpture Gallery, Art on Main Window Front Gallery, Mary Olson Farm Artist in Residence, Art Galleries of 2-and 3-dimensional art. 253-931-3043. auburnwa.gov

- Burke Museum. Focuses on Northwest Native art and cultural pieces, and natural history collections. University of Washington, 4303 Memorial Way NE, Seattle. 206-543-7907. burkemuseum.org

- Center on Contemporary Art. Contemporary exhibits and programs. 114 Third Ave S, Seattle. 206-728-1980. cocaseattle.org

- Chihuly Garden and Glass. Showcases the studio glass of Dale Chihuly. 305 Harrison St, Seattle. 206-753-4940. chihulygardenandglass.com

- College Gallery /Shoreline Community College. Continuing education/lifelong learning programs. 16101 Greenwood Ave N, Shoreline. 206-546-410. shoreline.edu/visual-arts-dept/gallery

- Daybreak Star Cultural Center. Native American art gallery and cultural center. 5011 Bernie Whitebear Way, Seattle. (Discovery Park). 206-285-4425. unitedindians.org

- Duwamish Longhouse and Cultural Center. Traditional longhouse, museum, art gallery. 705 W Marginal Way SW, Seattle. 206-431-1582. duwamishtribe.org

- Frye Art Museum. Painting and sculpture from 19th century to present. Free. 704 Terry Ave, Seattle. 206-622-9250. fryemuseum.org

- Helen S Smith Gallery. Green River Community College. 12401 SE 320th St, Auburn. 253-931-6542. greenriver.edu/community/art-gallery

- Henry Art Gallery. Contemporary art. Art museum of University of Washington. 15th Ave NE & NE 41st St, Seattle. 206-543-2280. henryart.org

- Kent Arts Commission Gallery. Diverse artists exhibit in solo or small groups. 400 W Gowe St, Kent. 253-856-5050. kentwa.gov

- Northwest Folklife. Showcases arts and culture of the Pacific Northwest. 305 Harrison St, Seattle. 206-684-7300. nwfolklife.org

- Olympic Sculpture Park. 9 acres of monumental artworks. 2901 Western Ave, Seattle. 206-654-3100. seattleartmuseum.org

- Seattle Art Museum. Collections and exhibits from around the world. 1300 First Ave, Seattle. 206-654-3100 seattleartmuseum.org

- Seattle Asian Art Museum. Extensive Asian art collection. 1400 E Prospect St, Seattle. 206-654-3210. seattleartmuseum.org

- Seattle Central College M. Rosetta Hunter Art Gallery. College gallery. 1701 Broadway, Seattle. 206-934-3800. artgallery.seattlecentral.edu

- Seattle University Galleries. Hedreen Gallery and Vachon Gallery; Lee Center for the Arts, 901 12th Ave. 206-296-5360. seattleu.edu

Kitsap and Mason Counties

- Arts & Humanities Bainbridge. Administers Bainbridge Creative District, promotes arts in Currents event calendar. 221 Winslow Way W, Ste 201, Bainbridge Island. 206-842-7901. ahbainbridge.org

- Aurora Valentinetti Puppet Museum. Showcases craftmanship of generations of puppet artists. Tours, workshops for all ages. 257 4th St, Bremerton. 360-728-2840. valentinettipuppetmuseum.com

- Bainbridge Arts & Crafts Gallery. Non-profit gallery of contemporary works by northwest artists. 151 Winslow Way E, Bainbridge Island. 206-842-3132. bacart.org

- Bainbridge Chinese Culture & Arts. Chinese natives teach Chinese language and culture through activities and events. 206-486-0826. bainbridgechinese.org

- Bainbridge Island Museum of Art. Contemporary art and craft of the Puget Sound region. 550 Winslow Way E, Bainbridge Island. 206-842-4451. biartmuseum.org

- Elandan Gardens. World-class bonsai collection, landscape artistry on the shores of Puget Sound. 3050 W State Hwy 16, Bremerton. 360-373-8260. elandangardens.com

- Kitsap Carvers. Workcarver group. Group session in Bremerton, Port Orchard, Poulsbo; lessons. kitsapcarvers.org

- Kitsap Peninsula Outdoor Art. Photos, maps of outdoor art on sidewalks, in parks, along waterfront, downtown districts. visitkitsap.com/outdoor-art

- Northwest Woodworkers Association. Woodworkers forum for all skill levels and interests. Seattle. nwwoodworkers.org

- Peninsula Art Association. Artists group that supports the arts, exchanges ideas, information, education, and instruction. sheltonarts.com

- Shelton Arts Commission, Civic Center Rotating Art Gallery. Shelton. 360-432-5106. sheltonwa.gov

- Sidney Art Gallery & Museum. Exhibits of northwest artists and photographers. 202 Sidney Ave, Port Orchard. 360- 876-3693. sidneymuseumandarts.com

Pierce County

- Arts & Culture Coalition of Pierce County. Group of arts, culture, and heritage organizations within the county. Member links of information on website. artsandculturecoalition.org

- Asia Pacific Cultural Center. Showcases Asia Pacific artists and their works. 851 South Tacoma Way, Tacoma. 253-383-3900. asiapacificculturalcenter.org

- Fred Oldfield Western Heritage & Art Center. History of Western lifestyle and advancing Western art. 9th Ave SW & 4th St SW, Puyallup. 253-267-5582. fredoldfieldcenter.org

- Gig Harbor Civic Art Collection. 253-851-8136. cityofgigharbor.net.

- Handforth Gallery, Tacoma Public Library. 102 Tacoma Ave S. 253-591-5688. tacomalibrary.org/handforth-gallery

- Kittredge (Hall) Gallery. University of Puget Sound, 1500 N Warner St, Tacoma. 253-879-2806. pugetsound.edu/kittredge-gallery

- Lakewold Gardens. Art exhibits, music, and literary events and festivals in the Gardens. 12317 Gravelly Lake Dr SW, Lakewood. 253-584-4106. lakewoldgardens.org

- Lakewood Public Art. Various art installations throughout city. 253-983-7887. cityoflakewood.us/art

- Maple Valley Creative Arts Council. 22024 SE 248th St, Maple Valley. 425-432-3470. mvcac.clubexpress.com

- Museum of Glass, 1801 Dock St, Tacoma. 253-284-4719. Premier contemporary art museum dedicated to glass and glass making. museumofglass.org

- Pacific Bonsai Museum. Amazing living art in outdoor setting of native trees 2515 S 336th St, Federal Way. 253-353-7345. pacificbonsaimuseum.org

- Peninsula Art League. Group of artists, art appreciators who share ideas, techniques, and take part in workshops and art shows. Gig Harbor. peninsulaartleague.org

- Puget Sound Sumi Artists. Studies in ink painting, calligraphy, flower arranging. Asia Pacific Cultural Center, 4851 S Tacoma Way, Tacoma. sumi.org

- Puyallup Outdoor Art Gallery. Self-guided digital or map tours, map at Public Library. artsdowntown.org/tours

- Tacoma Art Museum. Major museum for art of the Pacific Northwest and western region. 1701 Pacific Ave, Tacoma. 253-272-4258. tacomaartmuseum.org

- Tacoma Arts and Crafts Group. Members get together, make things, enjoy the variety of skills and talents, and have a good time. Tacoma. meetup.com/tacomaartsandcrafts

- Tacoma Community College. Offers a variety of free concerts, art exhibits. Creative writers. Artist and lecture series. 6501 S 19th St, Tacoma. 253-566-5000. tacomacc.edu/tcc-life/arts-culture

- Tacoma Public Art. City's Municipal Art Program. Map. Online Public Art Tour. 253-591-5000. cityoftacoma.org

Thurston County

- Arbutus Folk School. Year-round classes, workshops in ceramics, music, woodworking, blacksmithing, fiber arts, folk and traditional arts. 610 4th Ave, Olympia. 360-350-0187. arbutusfolkschool.org

- Art in Public Places. Washington's State Art Collection. 711 Capitol Way S, Ste 600, Olympia. 360-753-3860. arts.wa.gov/public-art

- Arts Washington, Creative Art Districts. State certified cultural and economic districts in Olympia and Tenino. 360-753-3860. arts.wa.gov

- Capitol Theater – Art in the Mezzanine. Local visual artists present their work in mezzanine, alcoves, and halls. 206 5th Ave SE, Olympia. 360-754-6670. olympiafilmsociety.org

- Evergreen Gallery. The Evergreen State College, Olympia. Art from diverse cultures, philosophies, discipline, and media. 2700 Evergreen Pkwy NW, Olympia. 360-867-6413. evergreen.edu

- Lacey Public Art. Website of public art locations. 360-491-3214. cityoflacey.org/publicart

- Monarch Contemporary Art Center and Sculpture Park. Art center and outdoor sculpture park. 8431 Waldrick Rd SE, Tenino. 360-264-2408. monarchsculpturepark.org

- Olympia Art League. Promotes visual arts and art happenings in South Puget Sound. Newsletter. Art education. Lacey Community Center, 6729 Pacific Ave SE, Olympia. olympiaartleague.com

- Olympia Arts & Heritage Alliance. Celebrating the arts, culture, and heritage of the South Sound region. 120 State Ave NE, Olympia. olyaha.org

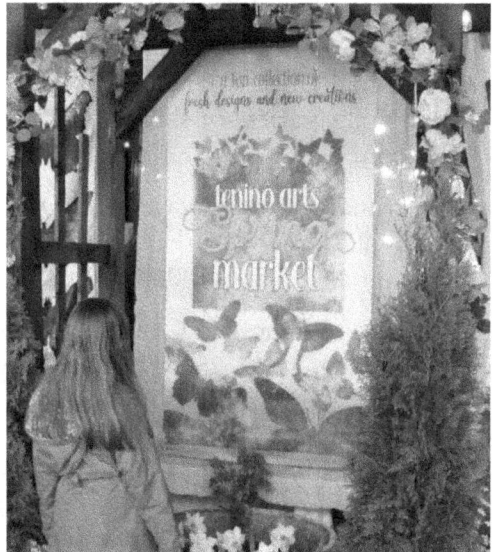

- Olympia Public Art. Variety of civic art projects to enjoy citywide. 360-709-2678. olympiawa.gov

- Olympia Weavers Guild. Members do fiber hand-weaving, knitting, paper art, embroidery, and related activities. olympiaweaversguild.org

- Tenino Arts. Community Arts Organization sponsoring events showcasing the creative arts locally. teninoarts.org

Art Walks, Festivals

The following is a list of area art walks and festivals in the South Sound which offer a casual, fresh-air way to stroll through art venues. Volunteers are always needed to help plan, promote, and set up events.

- Art in the Woods. Self-guided tour of North Kitsap Artists' studios. November. cafnw.org/art-in-the-woods

- Art on Echo Bay. Art, photography exhibit by local artists. Chapel on Echo Bay, 400 6th Ave, Fox Island. May. gigharborchamber.net

- Bainbridge Island First Friday Artwalk. Enjoy art at galleries along Winslow Way. bainbridgeisland.com/first-fridays-art-walk

- Bremerton First Fridays Art Walk. Downtown evening walk through galleries, shops, local eats. Businesses host arts, musicians, and more. bremertonfirstfriday.org

- Eatonville Lions Club Art Festival. Art, music. Glacier Park, Eatonville. August. eatonvilleartsandmusicfestival.com August

- Bainbridge Island Summer Studio Tour. August. Various studios around Brainbridge Island.

- Celebration of Western and Wildlife Art Show. Fairgrounds Expo, Puyallup. October. westernwildlifeartshow.org

- Gig Harbor Summer Arts Festival. Downtown, Gig Harbor. July. peninsulaartleague.org

- Olympia Arts Walk. Downtown festive arts experience. October. 360-753-8380. olympiawa.gov

- Poulsbo Arts Festival. Arts and local musicians. August. Waterfront Park. cafnw.org

- Proctor Arts Fest. Proctor and 26th. Autust. Tacoma. heproctordistrict.com

- Puyallup Art & Wine Walk. Puyallup Main Street Association. October. puyallupmainstreet.com

- Ruston Way Waterfront Walk. Walk along Commencement Bay shoreline commercial and cultural area. 5005 Ruston Way, Tacoma. metroparkstacoma.org

- Tacoma Art Trail. Free festival of light and sound downtown Tacoma. January. tacomalighttrail.org

- Tenino Arts Spring Market (and music). March. Tenino. teninoarts.org

- Third Thursday and Downtown Artwalk. Walk through museum district. Free or discounted admission at local museums. facebook.com/people/Tacoma-Third-Thursday-Art-Walk

- Seattle Neighborhood Art Walks. Venture north for neighborhood art works. 206-684-7171. seattle.gov/arts/experience/art-walks

Art Commissions, Alliances

The following are cultural organizations and city and county commissions that invite participation in planning and overseeing community art projects. They promote the growth of arts and culture through public art projects, grants, advocacy, and special events.

- Anderson Island Arts. Brings art, poetry, photography, film, music, to Anderson Island. 360 607-4462. andersonislandarts.com

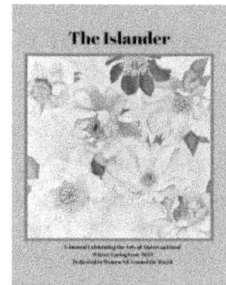

The Islander

- Arts & Culture Coalition of Pierce County. 26 arts, culture, and heritages organizations in Tacoma and Pierce County. artsandculturecoalition.org

- ArtsWA. Washington State Arts Commission. 711 Capitol Way S, Ste 600, Olympia. 360-753-3860. arts.wa.gov

- Auburn Arts Commission. 25 W Main St, Auburn. 253-931-3043. auburnwa.gov

- Bainbridge Island arts and Humanities Council. bainbridgecurrents.com

- Bonney Lake Arts Commission. Bonney Lake Justice & Municipal Center, 9002 Main St E, Bonney Lake. ci.bonney-lake.wa.us

- Cultural Arts Foundation Northwest. Supports arts and advancing creative potential. Poulsbo. 360-697-6342. cafnw.org

- Federal Way Arts Commission. 876 S. 333rd St., Federal Way. 253-835-6910. cityoffederalway.com

- Gig Harbor Arts Commission. City of Gig Harbor, 3510 Grandview St, Gig Harbor. 253-851-8136. cityofgigharbor.net

- Lakewood Arts Commission. City Hall, 6000 Main St, SW, Lakewood. 253-589-2489. cityoflakewood.us

- Maple Valley Public Arts Commission. City of Maple Valley, PO Box 320, Maple Valley. 425-432-9953. maplevalleywa.gov

- Olympia Arts Commission. Olympia City Hall, 601 4th Ave E, Olympia. 360-709-2678. olympiawa.gov

- Pierce County Arts Commission. 930 Tacoma Ave S., Tacoma. piercecountywa.gov

- Puyallup Arts Commission. Puyallup City Hall, 333 S Meridian, Puyallup. 253-841-4321

- Rainier Arts Commission, 102 Rochester St W, Rainier. 360-446-2265. cityofrainierwa.org

- Sidney Museum and Arts Association. 202 Sidney Ave, Port Orchard. 360-876-3693. sidneymuseumandarts.com

- Shelton Arts Commission, City of Shelton. 525 W. Cota St, Shelton. 360-426-4491. sheltonwa.gov

- Sumner Cultural Arts Commission. 1104 Maple St, Sumner, 253-863-8300. sumnerwa.gov/commissions

- Tacoma Arts Commission. City of Tacoma, 747 Market St, Tacoma. 25-591-5000. cityoftacoma.org

- Tenino, Recreation, Culture & History Commission. 149 Hodgden St S, Tenino. 360-264-2368. cityoftenino.us/city-govt

- Tumwater Cultural Arts Task Force. Tumwater. 360-754-4164. ci.tumwater.wa.us

- Yelm Arts Commission. 106 Second St SE, Yelm. 360-458-3244. yelmwa.gov

Youth Art Programs

The following are examples of organizations that offer volunteer opportunities in youth art programs. Organizations may require background checks.

- Island Arts, Anderson Island. Cultural arts center. Visual, literary, and performing arts. andersonislandarts.com

- Hilltop Artists. Youth development through tuition-free glass instruction, mentorship, and collaborative leadership opportunities. 253-571-7670. hilltopartists.org

- Fred Oldfield's West Heritage & Art Center. Art classes for students and adults. Red Gate, Washington State Fair, 9th Ave SW and 4th St SW, Puyallup. 253-752-9708. fredoldfieldcenter.org

- Pierce County Arts Connect. Classes in connection with Hilltop Arts in glass, photography, or other arts for girls in community supervision. 253-798-7900. piercecountywa.gov

- Peninsula Hands on Art. Art classes across all socioeconomic backgrounds. PO Box 2024, Gig Harbor. peninsulahandsonart.org

- Tacoma Creates. City-sponsored program to increase access to arts, culture, heritage, and science for underserved youth. Contact individual programs for volunteer opportunities. tacomacreates.org

- Two Waters Arts Alliance. Arts in School program. PO Box 868, Vaughn. twowaters.org

- Vashon Center for the Arts. 19600 Vashon Hwy. SW, Vashon. 206-463-5131. vashoncenterforthearts.org

Film, Video

The following is a list of organizations that focus on learning, enjoying, and practicing filmmaking and video in the South Sound.

- Arts First. Tacoma Creates. Filmmaking programs for youth, public programs. artsfirst.org

- Northwest Film Forum. Film and art center, presents festivals, community events, multidisciplinary performances, and workshops. 1515 12th Ave, Seattle. 206-329-2629. nwfilmforum.org

- Olympia Film Society. Maintains The Capitol Theater to present film, music, and art; preserves Capital Theater. 206 5th Ave SE, Olympia. 360-754-6670. olympiafilmsociety.org

- Olympia Film Collective. South Sound filmmakers who support creation of professional productions about the Northwest. 113 Thurston Ave NE, Olympia. 360-503-8381. olyfilm.com

- Tacoma Film Alliance. Supports and promote area film artists with resources, networking, and education. tacomafilmalliance.com

- The Grand Cinema. Learning programs built around filmmaking such as Science on Screen, short film competition, workshops at Tacoma Film Festival, youth camps and clubs. Grandcinema.com

Film Festivals

The following lists film festivals in and near Kitsap, Mason, Pierce, and Thurston counties. For a list of film festivals throughout the state, including those in Seattle, visit the Washington Filmworks website. washingtonfilmworks.org/faq/film-festivals-in-washington-state

- Anderston Island Film Festival. Diverse selection of films, merging storytelling and film. Many local. August. aifilmfestival.org

- Bainbridge Island Film Festival. Celebrates contemporary films and filmmakers. September. 147 Madrone Lane N, Bainbridge Island. 206-842-2982. bainbridgedowntown.org bifilmfest.eventive.org

- Gig Harbor Film Festival. Independent, feature length and shorts, narrative, documentaries, animated, foreign films. September. Galaxy Uptown Theatre, 4649 Fosdick Dr NW. gigharborfilm.org

- Northwest Flying Saucer Film Fest. Showcases short films exploring UFO genre. McFiler's Chehalis Theater. September. Chehalis. flyingsaucerparty.org/the-northwest-flying-saucer-film-fest-2

- Olympia Film Festival. 10 days of films, filmmakers, guests, discussion, workshops. May. Capitol Theater. 206 5th Ave SE, Olympia. olympiafilmsociety.org

- Poulsbo Film Festival. October. Historic Downtown Poulsbo. 360-731-5186. poulsbofilmfestival.com

- Shoreline Short Short Film Festival. Community College Theater. Shoreline.

- Tacoma Film Festival. October. 606 Fawcett Ave, Tacoma. 253-593-4474. tacomafilmfestival.com
- Tacoma Sister Cities International Film Festival. November. tacomasistercities.org/film-festival
- TCC Diversity Film Festival. Celebrates individual and cultural differences through film. April, May. The Grand Cinema. grandcinema.com/tcc-diversity-film-festival

Photo Clubs, Classes

The following includes clubs for photographers in the South Sound area and community colleges that offer photo classes.

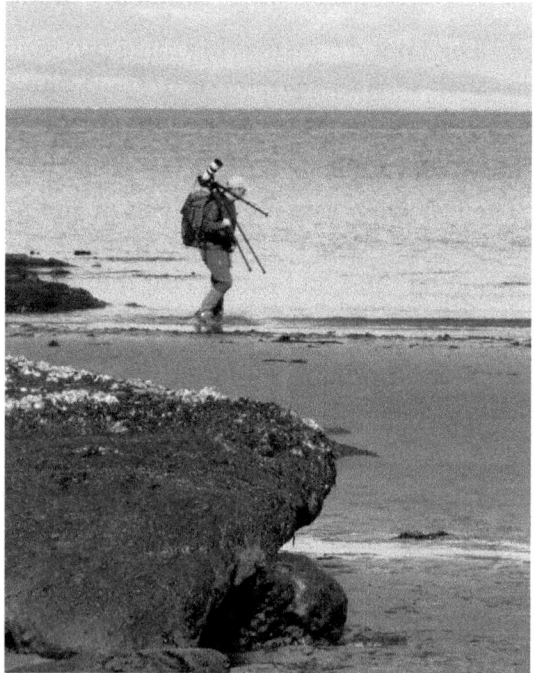

Photo Clubs

- Bainbridge Island Photo Club. Meetings, workshops, members photo sharing meetings. biphotoclub.org
- F:67 Camera Club. Bremerton. Meetings to learn, share, for and from others. f67cameraclub.org
- Kitsap Photography Guild. Learning and fellowship, themed learning opportunities. Silverdale. kitsapphotographyguild.com
- Northwest Council of Camera Clubs. Nonprofit association of camera clubs in western Washington State. nwcameraclubs.org
- Olympia Camera Club. Photographers of all skill levels learn through sharing, teaching, guest speakers. olympiacameraclub.org
- Olympia Photographers Group. Meetup Group for digital photographers. Olympia. meetup.com/olympia-photographers

- Tacoma Outdoor Photographers. Local photographers get together, take pictures, share work, practice photography skills. Tacoma. meetup.com/photography-meetup-tacoma

- Tacoma Photographic Society. Tacoma. Group that shares knowledge; holds group trips, classes, and outings. meetup.com/tacoma-photographic-society. tacomaphoto.org

- West Sound Photography Group, Silverdale. Includes camera clubs: Kitsap Photography Guild, F67 Camera Club, Olympic College Camera Club, Sound Exposure, Port Townsend Camera Club, Bainbridge Island Photo Club. meetup.com/westsoundphotographygroup

Community Colleges

- Evergreen State College. Photo classes, offers 60+ Tuition Waver Program. 2700 Evergreen Pky NW, Olympia. 360-867-6000. evergreen.edu

- Green River College Auburn. Art curriculum. Online and in-person classes. Helen S. Smith Gallery. Offers community education. 12401 SE 320th St, Auburn. 253-833-9111. greenriver.edu

- Olympic College. Shelton. 1600 Chester Ave., Bremerton. Poulsbo, Shelton campuses. 360-792-6050. olympic.edu

- Pierce College. Community and continuing education program. 1601 39th Ave SE Puyallup. 253-840-8452. pierce.ctc.edu/ce

- Sound Puget Sound Community College. Olympia campus: 2011 Mottman Rd SW. 360-596-5200; Lacey campus: 4220 6th Ave SE. 360-709-2000. spscc.edu/cce

- Tacoma Community College. Art classes, exhibits at The Art Gallery. Artist and lecture series. tacomacc.edu/tcc-life/arts-culture.

- University of Puget Sound. Tacoma. Various art programs. 1500 N Warner St, Tacoma. pugetsound.edu

RESOURCES: BUSINESS BUILDING

Many economic development and chamber organizations offer resources for startups resources for startup and existing businesses.

Economic Development, Chamber Organizations
Kitsap and Mason Counties

- Bainbridge Island Chamber of Commerce. 395 Winslow Way E, Bainbridge Island. 206-842-3700. bainbridgechamber.com

- Bremerton Community Development. 345 6th St, Ste 600, Bremerton. 360-473-5275. bremertonwa.gov

- Economic Development Council of Mason County. 628 W Alder St, Shelton. 360-426-2276. choosemason.com

- Greater Kingston Community Chamber of Commerce. 25923 Washington Blvd NE, Kingston. 360-860-2239. Kingstonchamber.com

- Greater Kitsap Chamber of Commerce. 409 Pacific Ave, Bremerton. 360-692-6800. 10315 Silverdale Way NW, Silverdale. 360-479-3579. greaterkitsapchamber.com

- Kitsap County. Links to resources for startups and established businesses. kitsapgov.com

- Kitsap Economic Development Alliance. Cavalon Place II, 2021 NW Myhre Road, Ste 100, Silverdale. 360-377-9499. kitsapeda.org

- Kitsap Regional Coordinating Council. Local governments in county collaborate on regional transportation, land use. 614 Division St, MS4, Port Orchard. 360-337-4960. kitsapregionalcouncil.org

- North Mason Chamber of Commerce. 30 NE Romance Hill Rd, Ste 103, Belfair. 360-275-4267. northmasonchamber.com

- Poulsbo Chamber of Commerce. 19168 Jensen Way, Ste 130, Poulsbo. 888-490-8545. poulsbochamber.com

- Puget Sound Regional Council. Planning for regional transportation, growth management, and economic development in King, Kitsap, Pierce and Snohomish Counties and other local entities. 1011 Western Ave, Ste 500, Seattle. 206-464-7090. psrc.org

- Shelton-Mason County Chamber of Commerce. 215 W Railroad Ave, Shelton. 360-426-2021. masonchamber.com

- South Kitsap Chamber of Commerce. 1014 Bay St, Port Orchard. 360-876-3505. skchamber.org

Pierce County

- Bonney Lake Chamber Collective. 424-262-3707. bonneylake.com/chamber

- Gig Harbor Chamber of Commerce. 3125 Judson St, Gig Harbor. 253-851-6865. gigharborchamber.net

- Lakewood Chamber of Commerce. 6310 Mt Tacoma Dr SW, Lakewood. 253-582-9400. lakewood-chamber.org

- Lakewood Economic Development. 6000 Main St SW, Lakewood. 253-983-7738. cityoflakewood.us/economic-development

- Pierce County Library System. mypcls.org/online-resources

- Puyallup Economic Development. Puyallup City Hall, 333 S Meridian, Puyallup. 253-841-5496. cityofpuyallup.org

- Puyallup Sumner Chamber of Commerce. 323 N. Meridian, Ste A, Puyallup. 253-845-6755. puyallupsumnerchamber.com

- Tacoma Community and Economic Development. Municipal Bldg, 747 Market St, 9th Floor, Tacoma. 253-591-5624. cityoftacoma.org

- Tacoma-Pierce County Chamber. 950 Pacific Ave Ste 300, Tacoma, 253-627-2175. tacomachamber.org

- Timberland Libraries. trl.org/small-business

- University Place Economic Development. 3609 Market Place West, Ste 200, University Place. 253-566-5656. cityofup.com

Thurston County

- Lacey Community & Economic Development. Lacey City Hall, 420 College St SE, Lacey. 360-491-5642. cityoflacey.org

- Lacey South Sound Chamber. 3925 8th Ave SE, Ste C, Lacey. 360-491-4141. laceysschamber.com

- Olympia Downtown Alliance. 115 State Ave, Ste 104, Olympia, 360-357-8948. downtownolympia.org

- Olympia Economic Development. 360-753-8591. olympiawa.gov

- Thurston County Chamber, Olympia, Lacey, and Tumwater. 809 Legion Way SE, 3rd Floor. 360-357-3362. thurstonchamber.com

- Timberland Libraries. trl.org/small-business

- Washington State. Requirements and resources for doing business in Washington State. 1-800-917-0043. wa.gov/businesses

- Washington State Department of Commerce. 1011 Plum St SE, Olympia. 360-725-4000.

- Washington State Small Business Guide. Information to get a business up and running in Washington State. business.wa.gov

Other Business Startup Resources

- Business Association of Washington Business. Statewide business association, also serves as state chamber of commerce and manufacturing and technology association. 1414 Cherry St SE, Olympia. 360-943-1600. awb.org

- SBA Learning Center. Digital learning platform to help start or expand a small business. sba.gov/sba-learning-platform

- Small Business Administration Seattle District. Provides help with SBA services, connections to SBA partner organizations. 2401 4th Ave, Ste 450, Seattle. 206-553-7310. sba.gov/district/seattle

- South Sound/Tacoma SCORE. Seasoned business professionals and entrepreneurs mentor business owners. Offers workshops and other resources in the South Sound region. score.org

- Washington Small Business Development Center. SBDC live and on-demand training for business owners in the state. 901 E 2nd Ave, Ste 210, Spokane. 833-492-7232. commerce.wa.gov

- Washington Center for Women in Business. Business counseling, resources, and programs for women-owned businesses in the state. 4220 6th Ave SE, Lacey. 1-888-821-6652. wcwb.org

- Washington PTAC. Washington Procurement Technical Assistance Center. Government contracting for Washington firms. Training and webinars. washingtonptac.org

RESOURCES: CARE FOR THE ENVIRONMENT

If you're passionate about sustaining and protecting our amazing environment, look into the organizations listed below to find the best places to join green teams in your area. Visit their websites for more information.

Outdoor Volunteering
Washington State

- National Parks Volunteering. Olympic, North Cascades, Rainier Parks. Build, maintain trails, historic sites, research, monitor wildlife, and more. nps.gov/getinvolved/volunteer

- Pacific Crest Trail Association. Backpackers hike along, and care for, the Pacific Crest Trail. 916-245-2543. pcta.org/volunteer

- Washington Department of Fish & Wildlife. Volunteers contribute to conservation of fish, wildlife, and habitat. 360-902-2256. wdfw.wa.gov/get-involved/volunteer

- Washington Department of Natural Resources. Work parties, campground host, Forest Watch volunteers. dnr.wa.gov/volunteer

- Washington State Parks and Recreation. Volunteers participate in community events, at beach cleanups, as park hosts and in other roles. 1111 Israel Road SW, Tumwater. 360-902-8844. parks.wa.gov

- Washington Trails Association. Volunteer work parties help maintain trails. Washington Trails Association. 705 2nd Ave, Ste 300, Seattle. 206-625-1367. wta.org/get-involved/volunteer

- Washington Wild. Focuses on protecting and restoring wildlands and waters through advocacy, education, civic engagement. 305 N 83rd St, Seattle. 206-633-1992. wawild.org/join-us/volunteer

- Wild Society. Volunteers support Wild Society guides and youth who learn in backcountry camps and weekend field study programs in Kitsap parks. Kingston. 360-347-6134. wildsociety.org/volunteer

Friends of Parks, Natural Areas

The following are parks and natural areas with Friends and volunteer groups in and near Kitsap, Mason, Pierce, and Thurston Counties.

Kitsap and Mason Counties

- Bainbridge Island Metro Park & Recreation District. Volunteer Trail Stewards maintain island trails, parks, and natural areas. Work parties. 206-842-2302. biparks.org/volunteers

- Bremerton Parks & Recreation. Friends of Kiwanis Park, Forest Ridge Park Stewardship, Lions Park Ad-A-Beach. 680 Lebo Blvd., Bremerton. 360-473-5305. bremertonwa.gov

- Kitsap County Parks Department. Park Stewards program help maintain parks and natural areas. 1195 NW Fairgrounds Rd, Bremerton. 360-337-5350. kitsapgov.com

- Mason County Parks. Trails Volunteering. Friends of Parks Program help maintain 10 parks; Park Hosts assist with visitor services. 411 N 5th St, Shelton. 360-427-9670. masoncountywa.gov/parks

- North Kitsap Trails Association. Involved with regional system of land and water trails connecting communities, parks, open space; promotes stewardship, enhanced livability. Maps, trails. northkitsaptrails.org

- Port Orchard Parks. 216 Prospect St, Port Orchard. 360-876-4407. portorchardwa.gov/port-orchard-parks

- Poulsbo Parks and Recreation. Maintenance of parks and trails; fish Park tasks. 19540 Front St NE, Poulsbo. 360-779-9898. cityofpoulsbo.com

- Shelton Parks & Recreation. Adopt-A-Park Program. Shelton Civic Center, 525 West Cota St. 360-432-5106 sheltonwa.gov

Pierce County

- Auburn City Parks and Trails. Adopt-a-Park program to help maintain, clean parks and open spaces. 25 W Main St, Auburn. 253-931-3000. auburnwa.gov

- Bonney Lake. Volunteers help with special outdoor events including Spring Clean-Up and Beautify Bonney Lake. 9002 Main St E, Bonney Lake. ci.bonney-lake.wa.us

- Dupont Parks & Recreation. Volunteers help care for parks and greenways, open spaces, or streetscapes. Project or ongoing. 1700 Civic, Dupont. 253-964-8121. dupontwa.gov

- Fircrest Parks and Recreation. Park volunteer events. 115 Ramsdell St, Fircrest. 253-564-8901. cityoffircrest.net

- Gig Harbor Parks. Day of service for companies, schools, or community service organizations. Parks Appreciation Day. 3510 Grandview St. 253-851-8136. cityofgigharbor.net

- Lakewood Parks & Recreation. Park volunteers pick up trash, clear invasive species; participate in Parks Appreciation Day. City Hall, 6000 Main St SW. 253-589-2489. cityoflakewood.us

- Metro Parks Tacoma. Several work parties, restoration projects at various parks, facilities, natural areas, and lakes. 4702 S 19th St, Tacoma. 253-305-1000. metroparkstacoma.org

- Pierce County Parks & Recreation. Parks, natural lands volunteers. One-time or ongoing projects. Pitch in for Parks program. 930 Tacoma Ave S, Tacoma. 253-798-4199. piercecountywa.gov

- Puyallup Parks and Recreation. Volunteers: Adopt-a-Trail Program to conserve and maintain parks, Trail Stewards maintain, monitor and work on trails. 808 Valley Ave NW. 253-841-5457. cityofpuyallup.org

Thurston County

- City of Lacey Parks & Trails. Adopt-a-Trail volunteers for several area parks. 420 College St SE, Lacey. 360-491-5644. cityoflacey.org

- City of Tumwater. Volunteers help maintain park spaces. Tumwater City Hall, 555 Israel Road SW, Tumwater. 360-754-5855. ci.tumwater.wa.us

- Friends of Nisqually NRWC. Volunteers help with education, guided walks, lectures, special events, gift shop. 100 Brown Farm Rd, Olympia. 360-753-9467. friendsofnisquallynwrc.org

- Olympia Parks, Arts & Recreation. Adopt-a-Park in neighborhoods, Park Stewards. Parks volunteers maintain trails, restore habitat. Olympia City Hall, 601 4th Ave E, Olympiaolympiawa.gov

Protecting Ecological Areas

The following are organizations dedicated to preserving ecological areas in and near Kitsap, Mason, Pierce, and Thurston Counties. Visit their websites for more information.

Kitsap and Mason Counties

- Bainbridge Island Native Food Forest. Restores old ecosystems for native species through regenerative farming. 250 Madrona Way NE, Ste 110B, Bainbridge Island. 206-842-5537. friendsofthefarms.org

- Great Peninsula Conservancy. Nonprofit land trust, dedicated to protecting natural habitats, landscapes, open spaces of region. 423 Pacific Ave, Ste 300, Bremerton. 360-373-3500. greatpeninsula.org

- Illahee Forest Preserve. Heritage Park with 570 acres, preserving the natural character of forest lands. 5474 Almira Dr NE, Bremerton. 360- 479-1049. Bremerton.

- Kitsap Community Foundation. Nonprofit Directory lists area nonprofit environmental organizations. kcf.fcsuite.com/erp/donate/list/directory

- Kitsap Environmental Coalition. Focuses on healthy lands, water, and habitat in Kitsap Peninsula. kitsapenvironmentalcoalition.org

- Mason Conservation District. Works with landowners to efficiently manage their land and associated natural resources. 50 W Business Park Rd, Shelton. 360-427-9436. masoncd.org

- Olympic Forest Coalition. Promotes protection, conservation, and restoration of natural forest ecosystems on the Olympic Peninsula. Quilcene. olympicforest.org

- The Salmon Center. Salmon research and education. Volunteers collect fish trap data, restore habitat, support education, raise funds. 600 NE Roessel Rd, Belfair. 360-275-3575. pnwsalmoncenter.org

- Sustainable Bainbridge. Various projects to help the community deal with climate change. 221 Winslow Way W, Ste 101, Bainbridge Island. sustainablebainbridge.org

- Wild Olympics. Coalition to protect wild forest and river watersheds on the Olympic Peninsula. Quilcene. wildolympics.org

Pierce County/South King County

- Center for Responsible Forestry. Advocates to preserve old growth forests in Puget Sound Region. Tacoma. c4rf.org

- Citizens for a Healthy Bay. 535 Dock St, Ste 213, Tacoma. 253-383-2429. healthybay.org

- Communities for a Healthy Bay. Engages people to clean up, restore and protect Commencement Bay and surrounding water, habitats. 535 Dock St, Ste 213, Tacoma. 253-383-2429. healthybay.org

- Environmental Education in Pierce County. Provides free and low-cost classes and programs to increase awareness, knowledge of environmental issues. piercecountywa.gov

- Environmental Science Center. Environmental education for all ages, outdoor classes, public programs, events. 2220 SW Seahurst Park Rd, Burien. 206-248-4266. envsciencecenter.org

- Friends of Pierce County. Focused on environmental protection and sustainable land use. friendsofpiercecounty.org

- Harbor Wildwatch. Focused on stewardship for Puget Sound, greater Salish Sea. Operates Skansie Interpretive Center. 3207 Harborview Dr, Gig Harbor. 253-514-0187. harborwildwatch.org

- National Audubon Society. 2917 Morrison Road W, Tacoma. 253-565-9278. eastsideaudubon.org

- Pierce Conservation District. Works with landowners to efficiently manage their land and associated natural resources. 308 W Stewart, Puyallup. 253-845-9770. piercecd.org

- Puget Sound WildCare. Wildlife rehabilitation, environmental education, and wildlife conservation. 2817 216th Ave SE, Kent. 360-886-8000. pugetsoundwildcare.org

- Puget Soundkeeper Alliance. Protects, preserve waters of Puget sound. 130 Nickerson St, Ste 107, Seattle. 206-297-7002. pugetsoundkeeper.org

- Puyallup Watershed Initiative. Works to improve health, environmental condition of the watershed and its communities. 3025 Harborview Dr, Gig Harbor. 253-858-5050. trff.org

- South Sound Water Restoration. Addresses pollution issues due to population growth in Budd Inlet. 253-241-1803. sswrp.org

- Washington's National Park Fund. Philanthropic partner to Mt. Rainer, North Cascades, Olympic National Parks. Volunteering, fundraising. 1904 3rd Ave #400, Seattle. 206-623-2063. wnpf.org/get-involved/events

- Washington Water Trails Association. Promotes public access to waterways, shorelines, marine trails for human-powered watercraft. 4649 Sunnyside Ave N #307, Seattle. 206-545-9161. wta.org

- Washington Wildlife Rehabilitation Association. Advances professional wildlife rehabilitation through education and community-building. Shoreline. wwrawildlife.org

Thurston County

- Ecostudies Institute. Restoration of native bird species, other wildlife, habitats, ecosystems. 360-213-8829. Olympia. ecoinst.org

- Billy Frank Jr. Nisqually National Wildlife Refuge. Refuge of diverse wildlife. Education and visitor Center. 100 Brown Farm Rd, Olympia. 360-753-9467. fws.gov/refuge/billy-frank-jr-nisqually

- Black Hills Audubon Society. PO Box 2524, Olympia. 360-352-7299. blackhills-audubon.org

- Capitol Lake Improvement and Protection Association. Provides public input for management of Capitol Lake. savecapitollake.org

- Capitol Land Trust. Ecological conservation in south Puget Sound and Chehalis Basin Watersheds. 4405 7th Ave SE, Ste 306. 360-943-3012. capitollandtrust.org

- Deschutes Estuary Restoration Team (DERT). Dedicated to restoring the urban estuary in downtown Olympia. deschutesestuary.org

- Nature Conservancy Washington. Caring for the lands and waters of Washington. 120 Union Ave SE, Olympia. 360-956-9445. nature.org

- Nisqually Land Trust. Stewards of water, fish, wildlife of the Nisqually River Watershed. 100 Brown Farm Rd NE, Olympia. 360-489-3400. nisquallylandtrust.org

- Nisqually Reach Nature Center. Environmental education. Visitor Center. 4949 D'Milluhr Dr NE, Olympia. 360-459-0387.

- OlyEcosystems. Olympia coalition for urban ecosystems preservation. olyecosystems.org

- Puget Sound Estuarium. Exhibits, programs promote the health ofarea's unique estuary environment. 309 State Ave NE, Olympia. 360-918-8412. pugetsoundestuarium.org

- Salmon Defense. Protects, defends Pacific Northwest salmon and salmon habitat. 6700 Martin Way E, Ste 114, Olympia. Olympiasalmondefense.org

- South Puget Sound Salmon Enhancement Group. Protects and restores salmon populations and aquatic habitat. 6700 Martin Way E, Ste 112, Olympia. 360-412-0808. spsseg.org

- South Sound Green. Community education on watershed protection. Thurston Conservation District, 2918 Ferguson St SW, Ste A, Tumwater. (360) 754-3588 x108. southsoundgreen.org

- Thurston Conservation District. Works with landowners to efficiently manage their land and associated natural resources. 2918 Ferguson St, SW, Tumwater. 360-754-3588. thurstoncd.com

- Thurston ECO Network. Ecology resources for education, communication, and outreach projects. Neighborhood work parties. Thurston County Public Health. thurstoneconetwork.org

- US Fish & Wildlife Department Service. 510 Desmond Dr SE, #102, Lacey. 360-753-9440. fws.gov

RESOURCES: COMMUNITY SERVICE ORGANIZATIONS

The following organizations provide services or information about services to people experiencing challenges with a disability, housing, food, and other human issues in and near Kitsap, Mason, Pierce, and Thurston Counties. Visit their websites for more information about volunteering. Programs may require background checks of volunteers.

Disability Services

The following are nonprofits and government agencies within or near Mason, Kitsap, Pierce, and Thurston Counties that provide services to disabled individuals.

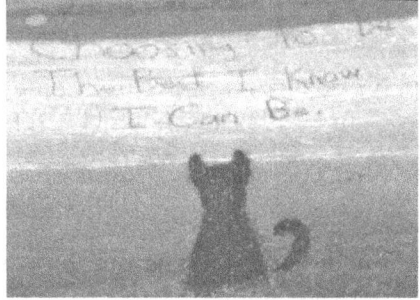

Statewide

- Ashley House. Home to children, teens, young adults who cope with the challenges of a catastrophic injury, serious illness, or a congenital birth defect. 33811 9th Ave S, Federal Way. 253-5339-050. ah-nw.org

- Camp Beausite Northwest. Residential camp and weekend respite during summer for children and adults with special needs. 510 Beausite Lake Rd, Chimacum. 360-732-7222. campbeausitenw.org

- Catholic Community Services. Provides quality, integrated services and housing for those struggling with poverty. Mason, Thurston Counties. 360-753-3340. ccsww.org

- Spina Bifida Advocates of Washington State. Accessible Trails in Washington. 8404 83rd Ave SW Lakewood. sbaws.org/resources

- Washington Autism Alliance. Provides resources for people with autism spectrum disorders and their families. Various volunteer roles. 425-894-7231. washingtonautismalliance.org

Kitsap and Mason Counties

- Bainbridge Island Visually Impaired Persons Support Group. Education, support, and encouragement to blind and low-vision persons. Bainbridge Island. 206-780-2835.

- Catholic Communities Services. Volunteers assist elderly and disabled adults with household tasks, transportation, shopping, minor home repairs, etc. 1323 S. Yakima Ave, Tacoma. 253-502-2741. ccsww.org/volunteer-services-volunteer-kitsap-county

- Exceptional Foresters. Mason, Thurston counties. Provides residential, vocation opportunities for people with disabilities. 2009 W Railroad Ave, Shelton. 360-426-0077. team-efi.org

- Kitsap County Aging and Long-Term Care. Volunteers assist seniors and those in need of long-term care; serve on County Area Agency on Aging, and as Long-Term Care Ombudsman. 614 Division St, MS-4, Port Orchard. 360-337-4650. kitsapgov.com

- Lewis-Mason-Thurston Area Agency on Aging. Provides information on services to seniors and adults with disabilities. 2008 Olympic Hwy N, Shelton. 360-664-2168. lmtaaa.org

- Stephens House. Activities to help guide individuals with intellectual disabilities towards meaningful community relationships. Bainbridge Island. 206-780-1211. bispecialneedsfoundation.org

- Vitalize Kitsap. Community engagement, personal growth programs for teens and adults with I/DD. Bainbridge Island. 206-842-5594. vitalizekitsap.org

Pierce County

- Catholic Community Services -Volunteer Services. Provides Shelter and homeless services, housing, services for people with disabilities. Mason, Thurston, Piece Counties. 360-753-3340. ccsww.org

- Center for Independence. Resource for individuals with disabilities to fully participate in the community and live independently. Thurston, Pierce counties. 7801 Bridgeport Way W #200, Lakewood. cfi-wa.org

- Children's Therapy Center. Pediatric therapy. Pierce, King Counties. 6419 Lakewood Dr W, University Place. 253-531-8873; 29020 216th Ave SE, Black Diamond, 253-854-5660. ctckids.org

- Down Syndrome Community of Puget Sound. Supports children with Down Syndrome and their families. Kitsap, King, Pierce Counties. 4746 11th Ave NE, Ste 102, Seattle. 206-257-7191. dscpugetsound.org

- L'Arche Tahoma Hope Community. A community of people, with and without disabilities, who live and work together. 12302 Vickery Ave E, Tacoma. 253-535-3178. larchetahomahope.org

- Pierce County Human Services. Volunteer service on various Human Services organizations advisory boards and committees. Tacoma. piercecountywa.gov

- Pierce County Coalition for Developmental Disabilities. (PC2). Resources about services and programs for people with disabilities. 3716 Pacific Ave, Ste A, Tacoma. 253-564-0707. pc2online.org

- Pierce County Human Services - Aging & Disability Resources. Provides assistance to developmentally disabled children and adults. 3602 Pacific Ave, Tacoma. 253-798-4500. piercecountywa.gov

- Special Olympics Washington. Opportunities for inclusive sports, health, and community building for children and adults with intellectual disabilities. 2815 2nd Ave, Ste 37, Seattle. 206-362-4949. specialolympicswashington.org

Thurston county

- Catholic Community Services. Volunteers assist elderly and disabled adults with household tasks, transportation, shopping, minor home repairs, etc. 3545 7th Ave SW, Olympia. 844-851-9380. ccsww.org/volunteer-services-volunteer-thurston-county

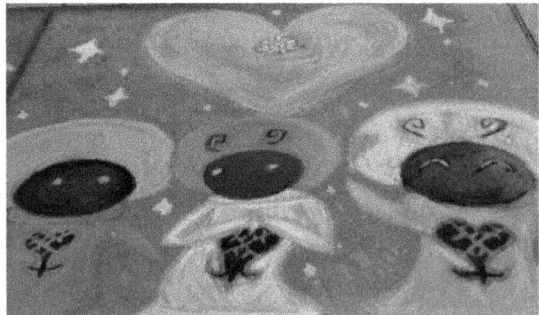

- Office of the Deaf and Hard of Hearing. Offers programs and services for Deaf, DeafBind and other hearing disabled. 4450 10th Ave. SE, Lacey. 360-725-3450. dshs.wa.gov/altsa/odhh

- Thurston County Development Disabilities. Serves people with developmental disabilities through community partners, many offer volunteer opportunities. thurstoncountywa.gov

- Thurston County Inclusion. Brings year-round peer engagement activities for youth with and without intellectual disabilities. Tumwater. 360-329-2795. thurstoncountyinclusion.org/volunteer

Emergency and Family Services

The following are resources for those interested in volunteering at homeless shelters, food banks, and other services to families and individuals in need. Programs may require background checks.

Kitsap and Mason Counties

- Bainbridge Island Resource Directory. Directory of nonprofits that provide services to help people, including families and seniors, respond to life's challenges. Bainbridge Island Senior Center, 370 Brien Dr SE, Bainbridge Island. 206-842-1616. resourcedirectorybi.org

- Bremerton Homeless Shelters. Contact shelters listed directly for volunteer information. shelterlist.com/city/wa-bremerton 0085. hoodcanalfoodbank.org

- Care Net Pregnancy Resource Center of Mason County. Educates, supports women and couples facing unplanned pregnancies. 360-427-9171. sheltoncarenet.org

- Community Lifeline of Mason County. Provides meals, showers, emergency shelter; connects those in need to resources. 218 N 3rd, Shelton. 360-462-4439. sheltonlifeline.org

- Crossroads Housing. Emergency Shelter. Crossroads Housing. 71 Sargison Loop, Shelton. 360-427-6919 crossroads-housing.net

- Crazy Love Ministries. 110 S. First St, Shelton. Street ministry takes food, clothing, support, and relief services directly to those in need through the Mason County Warming Center. 110 S. First St, Shelton. 360-358-3355. crazyloveministries.org

- Family Education & Support Services. Provides family support services for healthy child development. 709 E Johns Prairie Rd, Ste A, Shelton. 360-545-2060. familyess.org

- Habitat for Humanity of Mason County. Builds affordable housing for needy families with donations of materials and time. Volunteers build housing, operate stores. 1826 Olympic Hwy N, Shelton, 22653 NE State Rte 3, Belfair. habitatmasonwa.org

- Habitat for Humanity of Kitsap County. Builds affordable housing for needy families with donations of materials and time. Volunteers build housing, operate stores. 3581 Wheaton Way, Bremerton. 360-479-3853. kitsaphabitat.org

- Helpline House. Provides food, housing and utility assistance, counseling, child, and senior services. 282 Knecthel Way NE, Bainbridge Island. 206-842-9867. helplinehouse.org/

- Kitsap County Housing and Homelessness Division. Volunteers apply for various opportunities through Kitsap County Dept of Emergency Management. kitsapdem.com/programs/volunteer

- Kitsap Rescue Mission. Kitsap Fairgrounds Pavilion, 1200 Fairgrounds Rd NW, Bremerton. 360-373-3428. kitsaprescue.org

- Love In the Name of Christ of Mason County. Links church ministries and volunteers to people in need. 109 S. 2nd St, Shelton. 360-462-5683. loveincofmasoncounty.org

- Martha Reed Foundation. Volunteers support community with various projects, events. 360-790-5732. facebook.com/MarthaReedFoundation

- Mason County H.O.S.T. Housing options for homeless youth. 807 W Pine St, Shelton. 360-426-7664. mason-co-host.org

- Mason County Public Health. Provides information about homeless housing and shelter, food banks, and other services for families and individuals. masoncountywa.gov/health

- North Mason Food Bank. 22471 NE State Rt 3, Belfair. 360-275-4615. northmasonfoodbank.org

- Shelton Homeless Shelters. Contact shelters listed directly for volunteer information. shelterlist.com/city/wa-shelton

- The Saint's Pantry Food Bank. 205 W Cota St, Shelton. 360-427-8847. thesaintspantry.org

- Turning Pointe Survivor Advocacy Center. Provides safety, support for sexual and domestic abuse survivors. Shelton and Belfair. 360-432-1212. piercecountywa.gov/3715/Homeless-Programs

Pierce County

- Auburn Homeless Shelters. Contact shelters listed directly for information. shelterlist.com/city/wa-auburn

- City of Tacoma. List of shelters and resources. Contact shelters listed directly for volunteer information. cityoftacoma.org

- Eloise's Cooking Pot Food Bank. Serves east, south Tacoma. 3543 E McKinley Ave. 253-426-1994. themadf.org/eloises-cooking-pot

- Tacoma/Pierce County Habitat for Humanity. Builds affordable housing for needy families. Volunteers build housing, operate stores. 4824 S Tacoma Way, Tacoma. 253-627-5626. tpc-habitat.org

- Human Services Homeless Programs. Supports coordinated entry systems for families and individuals experiencing homelessness. Visit website of listed organizations for volunteering information. piercecountywa.gov/3715/Homeless-Programs

- Nourish Pierce County. Operates 6 food banks and 14 mobile sites. Contact sites listed directly for volunteer information. nourishpc.org

- Pierce County. List of food banks. Volunteer through Volunteer Portal. piercecountywa.gov/454/Food-Bank

- Pierce County Emergency Shelters. Online links to emergency shelters and services. To volunteer, contact each listed shelter individually. piercecountywa.gov/430/Emergency-Shelters

- Pierce County Overnight Shelters. Area shelts list. Contact shelters for volunteer information. pchomeless.org/Facilities/Shelters

- Puget Sound Pet Food Bank. 608 S. Washington St, Tacoma. 21006 Mountain Hwy E, Spanaway. 253-250-5078. pugetsoundpetfoodbank.org

- St, Leo Food Connection. 1323 S Yakima Ave, Tacoma. 253-383-5048. foodconnection.org

- Tacoma City Association of Colored Women's Clubs. Provides a variety of charitable, cultural, and educational services. 2316 Yakima Ave, Tacoma. 253-627-9777. tcacwc.org

Thurston County

- Community Youth Services. Provides services to help youth; those in foster care, safe housing, finishing school, finding work and more. 711 State Ave NE, Olympia. 360-943-078. communityyouthservices.org

- GRUB (Garden-Raised Bounty) Focus on growing, preparing good food. Works with marginalized young people, low income, seniors experiencing hunger, tribal communities, and veterans. 2016 Elliott Ave NW, Olympia. 360-753-5522 goodgrub.org

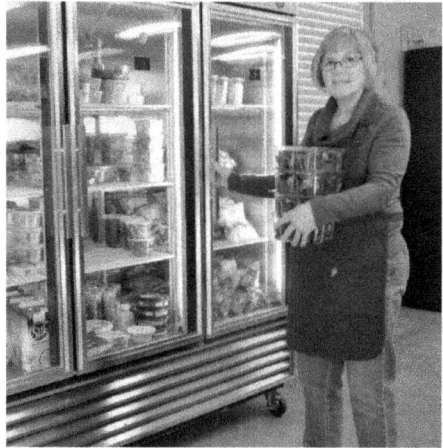

- Interfaith Works Shelter. Olympia. Contact shelter directly for volunteer information. interfaith-works.org

- Olympia. Community homeless information. Contact shelters listed for volunteer information. olympiawa.gov

- Olympia Homeless Shelters. Contact shelters listed directly for volunteer information. shelterlist.com/city/wa-olympia

- Olympia Homeless Shelters. Contact shelters listed directly for volunteer information. shelterlistings.org/city/olympia-wa.

- Olympia Salvation Army. 1505 4th Ave E. 360-352-8596. olympia.salvationarmy.org

- Rainier Emergency Food Center. Valley Heart Assembly of God. 11318 Vail Cutoff Rd SE, Rainier. 360-280-7326. rainierfoodbank.weebly.com

- Rebuilding Together Thurston County. Volunteers provide free home repairs and handicap modifications for low-income homeowners and nonprofit facilities. 809 Legion Way, Ste 306, Olympia. 360-539-7830. rebuildingtogethertc.org

- South Puget Sound Habitat for Humanity. Builds affordable housing for needy families with donations of materials and time. Volunteers build housing, operate stores. 1216 2nd Ave SW, Tumwater; 400 Cooper Point Rd SW, Olympia; 207 Yelm Ave E, Yelm. 360-956-3456; pshabitat.org

- Tenino Food Bank Plus. 224 Sussex Ave E, Tenino. 360-264-5505. teninocsc.org

- Thurston County Food Banks. 220 Thurston Ave NE, Olympia. 7027 Martin Way E, Olympia. 940 Israel Rd SW, Tumwater. 360-352-8597. thurstoncountyfoodbank.org

- Thurston County StandUp for Kids. Volunteers connect homeless youth with services. standupforkids.org/thurston-county

- Thurston County Washington. Community Resources. Online list, links to homeless services. Contact organizations directly for volunteer information. thurstoncountywa.gov

- Women's Shelters in Lacey, Washington. Contact shelters directly for volunteer information. womenshelters.org/cit/wa-lacey

- Yelm Food Bank. 624 Crystal Springs St NW, Yelm. 360-458-7000. yelmcommunityservices.com

RESOURCES: EXPLORING THE SOUTH SOUND

The following are websites that focus on visitor and travel information within and near Kitsap, Mason, Pierce, and Thurston Counties. The list is organized by geographic area: county/city/major geographic destinations.

Websites provide detailed information on things to do and see, including cultural attractions, events, outdoor destinations, and activities, lodging, entertainment, facilities, event calendars, and more.

For more about outdoor destinations and activities, see *RESOURCES: HIKING AND WALKING* information on page 226.

Have fun exploring…

Washington State

Two excellent starting points for discovering exploring options are State of Washington Tourism website stateofwatourism.com and the Visitor pages of wa.gov. You'll find visitor and travel information by region, city, geographic area, type of activities and attractions. Order free maps, guidebooks, and other resources for exploring the state.

Kitsap and Mason Counties

Bainbridge Island

- Bainbridge Island Chamber of Commerce. 395 Winslow Way E, Bainbridge Island. 206-842-3700. bainbridgechamber.com

- Bainbridge Island. City visitor Information. 280 Madison Ave N, Bainbridge Island. 206-842-7633. bainbridgewa.gov

- Bainbridge Island Downtown Association. Visitor information, cultural and other events, walking guide. 147 Madrone Lane N, Bainbridge Island. 206-842-2982. bainbridgedowntown.org

- Discover Bainbridge Island. Visitor information website. bainbridgeisland.com

- Visit Bainbridge Island. Visitor information website. visitbainbridgeisland.org

Bremerton

- Discover Bremerton. City-provided information about activities, events, and facilities. 345 6th St, Ste 600. 360-473-5275. bremertonwa.gov/31/Discover-Bremerton

- Greater Kitsap Chamber of Commerce. 409 Pacific Ave, Bremerton. 360-692-6800. 10315 Silverdale Way NW, Silverdale. 360-479-3579. greaterkitsapchamber.com

- Greater Kitsap Visitor Center Bremerton. 4th and Pacific Ave, Bremerton. 360-479-3579. business.greaterkitsapchamber.com

Kitsap County/Kitsap Peninsula

- Greater Kingston Community Chamber of Commerce. 25923 Washington Blvd NE, Kingston. 360-860-2239. kingstonchamber.com

- Greater Kitsap Chamber of Commerce. 409 Pacific Ave, Bremerton. 360-692-6800. 10315 Silverdale Way NW, Silverdale. 360- 479-3579. greaterkitsapchamber.com

- Kitsap Economic Development Alliance. Cavalon Place II, 2021 NW Myhre Rd, Ste 100, Silverdale. 360-377-9499.

- South Kitsap Chamber of Commerce. Visitor resources. 1014 Bay St, Port Orchard. 360-876-3505. skchamber.org

- Visit Kitsap Peninsula. Extensive visitor information for cities/towns/communities including Bainbridge Island, Bremerton, Gig Harbor, Port Gamble, Port Orchard, Poulsbo, and other communities in the county. 800-337-0580. visitkitsap.com

Mason County

- Economic Development Council of Mason County. Resources for visitors. 628 W Alder St, Shelton. 360-426-2276. choosemason.com

- Mason County Community. Website of resources for visitors. masoncounty.community/resources/tourism

- North Mason Chamber of Commerce. Resources for visitors. 30 NE Romance Hill Rd, Ste 103, Belfair. 360-275-4267. northmasonchamber.com

Port Gamble

- Port Gamble. City-provided visitor information. 360-297-8074. portgamble.com

Port Orchard

- Port Orchard Visitors. City-provided visitor information. portorchardwa.gov/visitors

- South Kitsap Chamber of Commerce. Visitor resources. 1014 Bay St, Port Orchard. 360-876-3505. skchamber.org

Poulsbo

- Poulsbo Chamber of Commerce. Visitor resources. 19168 Jensen Way, Ste 130, Poulsbo. 888-490-8545. poulsbochamber.com

- Visit Poulsbo. Visitor information website. visitpoulsbo.com

Shelton

- Shelton Caboose Visitor Center. 230 W Railroad Ave, Shelton. 360-426-2021. masonchamber.com

- Shelton Visitors. City-provided visitor and community information. 525 W Cota St, Shelton. 360-426-4491. sheltonwa.gov/visitors

Mt. Rainier National Park

- Mt. Rainier Business Alliance. Guide to activities near Nisqually River Valley entrance. Ashland. 360-569-2211. mt-rainier.com

- Mount Rainier National Park. National Park Service, extensive information on enjoying the Mount Rainier area. nps.gov/mora

- Mt. Rainier Visitor Center. Henry M Jackson Memorial Visitor Center. 52807 Paradise Rd. E, Ashford. 360-569-6571. visitrainier.com/the-basics/visitor-info-centers

- Mt. Rainier Visitor Center. Longmire Wilderness Information Center. Hwy 706, Ashford. 360-569-6650. visitrainier.com/the-basics/visitor-info-centers

- Mt. Rainier Visitor Center-Sunrise Visitor Center. Sunrise Park Rd, Ashford. 360-663-2425. visitrainier.com/sunrise-visitor-center

- Mt. Rainier Visitor Center-White River Wilderness Information Center. 360-569-6670. visitrainier.com/white-river-wilderness-information-center

- Travel Tacoma Mt. Rainier Visitor Center. 1516 Commerce St, Tacoma. 253-284-3254. traveltacoma.com

- Visit Rainier. Website of information on exploring the expansive national park. visitrainier.com/the-trailhead

Olympic Peninsula

- Explore Hood Canal. Describes events, things to do, and travel information activities around Hood Canal. explorehoodcanal.com

- Olympia Peninsula. Information for travelers about exploring cities, towns, parks, forests in the Olympic Peninsula. Outdoor activities, maps, visitor centers, events. olympicpeninsula.org

- Olympic Peninsula-Hoodsport Visitor Information Center. 150 N Lake Cushman Rd, Hwy 101, Hoodsport. olympicpeninsula.org/visitor-centers-and-chambers-of-commerce

- Olympic Peninsula-Kamilche Visitor Information Center, Squaxin Nation. 91 W State Rte 108, Shelton. 360-432-0921. olympicpeninsula.org/visitor-centers-and-chambers-of-commerce

- Olympia Peninsula-Union Visitor Information Center. Hunter Farms, 1921 WA-106, Shelton. olympicpeninsula.org/visitor-centers-and-chambers-of-commerce

Pierce County

Bonney Lake

- Bonney Lake Visitors. City-provided information about area recreation, events, and parks and trails. 9002 Main St E, Bonney Lake. ci.bonney-lake.wa.us/visitors/play

Gig Harbor

- Gig Harbor Chamber of Commerce. 3125 Judson St, Gig Harbor. 253-851-6865. gigharborchamber.net

- Visit Gig Harbor. City-provided visitor information. 3510 Grandview St, Gig Harbor. visitgigharborwa.com

Lakewood/Steilacoom

- Explore Steilacoom. City-provided visitor and community information, includes city parks, museums, attractions. 1030 Roe St, Steilacoom. 253-581-1912. townofsteilacoom

- Lakewood Chamber of Commerce. 6310 Mt. Tacoma Dr SW, Lakewood. 253-582-9400. lakewood-chamber.org

- Lakewood Visitor Information Center. 6310 Mt. Tacoma Dr SW, Ste B, Lakewood. 253-582-9400. lakewood-wa.com

Pierce County

- Pierce County. County's website includes extensive tourism and visitor information covering mountain, natural areas and shoreline activities, cultural, and recreational opportunities. piercecountywa.gov

- Pierce County Events Calendar. Events in cities throughout the county including Tacoma, Puyallup, Lakewood and beyond. southsoundtalk.com/tacoma-events-calendar

- Tacoma-Pierce County Chamber. 950 Pacific Ave. Ste 300, Tacoma. 253-627-2175. tacomachamber.org

Puyallup

- Puyallup Economic Development. Puyallup City Hall, 333 S. Meridian, Puyallup. 253-841-5496. cityofpuyallup.org

- Puyallup Sumner Chamber of Commerce. 323 N. Meridian, Ste A, Puyallup. 253-845-6755. puyallupsumnerchamber.com

Tacoma

- Point Defiance Visitor Center. 5715 Roberts Garden Dr, Tacoma. 253-305-1000. metroparkstacoma.org

- Tacoma. City-provided visitor and community information; activities, museums, performing arts, attractions, special events, tourism. cityoftacoma.org/visitors

- Tacoma Community and Economic Development. Municipal Bldg, 9th Floor, 747 Market St, Tacoma. 253-591-5624. cityoftacoma.org

- Tacoma Event Calendar. Events Calendar for Tacoma, Pierce Co, including Tacoma, Gig Harbor, Fife, Lakewood, Puyallup, Sumner, Dupont, and Mt. Rainier. traveltacoma.com/things-to-do/events

- Travel Tacoma. Tacoma Regional Convention and Visitor's Bureau. Information on travel and sports; parks, attractions, activities, and many other things to do and see in Pierce County, Tacoma, Mt. Rainier, Crystal Mountain, Puyallup, Gig Harbor, Lakewood, Sumner, DuPont, Fife, and University Place. traveltacoma.com

University Place

- University Place Economic Development. 3609 Market Place West, Ste 200, University Place. 253-566-5656. cityofup.com

- University Place Visitors. City-provided visitor information on outdoor and city attractions, events, and activities. 3609 Market Place West, Ste 200, University Place. 253-566-5656. cityofup.com

Thurston County

Lacey

- Discover Lacey. Visitor information website. discoverlacey.com

- Experience Olympia and Beyond. Website includes visitor and community information on Lacey. experienceolympia.com

- Lacey Community & Economic Development. Lacey City Hall, 420 College St SE, Lacey. 360-491-5642. cityoflacey.org

- Lacey Parks, Culture & Recreation. City-provided community recreation information. laceyparks.org

- Lacey South Sound Chamber. 3925 8th Ave SE, Ste C, Lacey. 360-491-4141. laceysschamber.com

- Lacey South Sound Chamber & Visitors Center. 3925 8th Ave SE, Ste C, Lacey. 360-491-4141. laceysschamber.com

Olympia

- Experience Olympia. Visitor and community information on the Olympia area. Newsletter, travel guide. experienceolympia.com

- Olympia. City-provided visitor and community information. Parks, arts and culture, events, attractions. olympiawa.gov

- Olympia Downtown Alliance. Visitor information. 115 State Ave, Ste 104, Olympia, 360-357-8948. downtownolympia.org

- Olympia Economic Development. Visitor and information 360-753-8591. olympiawa.gov

Thurston County

- Experience Olympia and Beyond. Visitor and community information on Olympia, Lacey, Tumwater, Yelm, Tenino, Rainier, Bucoda, Rochester, and Grand Mound. experienceolympia.com

- Grand Mound Rochester Chamber of Commerce. Visitor resources and information. 9917 Hwy 12 SW, Rochester. 360-858-7362. grandmoundrochesterchamber.com

- Thurston County. Provides information on county-owned and other area parks, trails and open spaces, and fairground event calendar. thurstoncountywa.gov

- Thurston County Chamber, Olympia, Lacey, and Tumwater. Visitor information. 809 Legion Way SE, 3rd Floor. 360-357-3362. thurstonchamber.com

- Yelm Area Chamber of Commerce. Visitor information. 138 Prairie Park Lane, Yelm. 360-458-6608. yelmchamber.com

Other Visitor Websites

Among many, many other travel sites you can find online, are:

- Go Northwest! Travel guide to destinations, activities, attractions, lodging, etc. in Washington State. gonorthwest.com

- Seattle. City's extensive website of community information. Parks, recreation, event schedules, urban activities. seattle.gov

- Seattle Visitor Center. 700 Pike St, Ste 800, Seattle. 260-461-5800. Visitseattle.org

- Small Town Washington. Travel blog that focuses on exploring Washington's small towns, national parks, and weekend getaways. smalltownwashington.com

- Visit Seattle. Extensive travel and tourism site. visitseattle.org

Water, Land Transit

The following provides information on the transit systems serving the Puget Sound area. For information bicycle routes, see *RESOURCES: FITNESS, Cycling Clubs, Maps*, on page 199.

- Intercity Transit. Thurston County's transportation system of bus, vanpool and Dial-A-Lift Services connecting Lacey, Olympia, Tumwater, The Nisqually Indian Community, and Yelm; connects to routes in Lakewood (Pierce County). intercitytransit.com

- King County Metro. King County's extensive transportation system of buses, express buses, streetcars, water taxis, and transit centers in and around Seattle and the county. kingcounty.gov

- Kitsap Transit. The county's transportation system of bus, vans, vanpools, and ferries throughout the peninsula and connections to other South Sound transportation systems. kitsaptransit.com

- Mason Transit Authority. The county's transportation system of bus, Dial-A-Ride within the county, and to connections to other South Sound systems. masontransit.org

- Pierce Transit. The county's extensive transportation system of bus, vanpools, trolly, park and ride locations. piercetransit.org

- Seattle Transit. Seattle's streetcar system; city works closely with network of other area transportation systems. seattle.gov/transportation/getting-around/transit

- Sound Transit. System of light rail, train, buses, and transit centers connecting various locations in the Tacoma and Seattle areas. soundtransit.org

- Washington Ferry Schedule. Find Washington ferry connections by route all around Puget Sound. 855-362-4232. wsdot.com/ferries

Festivals and Events

The following is a list of many popular community festivals in the South Sound. Art, film, and music festivals are listed separately. Visit festival websites for current information.

For Art Festivals, see *RESOURCES: ART, PHOTOGRAPHY, FILM, Art Walks, Festivals* on page 155. For film festivals see *RESOURCES: ART, PHOTOGRAPHY, FILM, Film Festivals* on page 159, and for music festivals see *RESOURCES: MUSIC ORGANIZATIONS, Music Festivals, Events* on page 263.

March

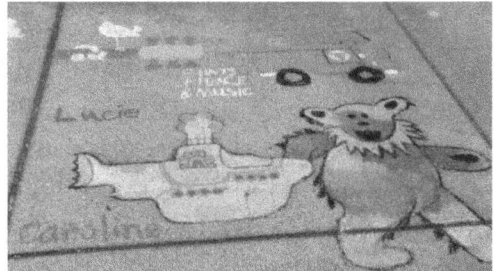

- Flower Power Kneeland Park. Shelton.

- Lacey's Cultural Celebration. Lacey. St, Martin's University. cityoflacey.org/events_list/lacey-cultural-celebration

- Luck of the Irish Festival. Freighthouse Square, Tacoma.

- Olympia Dance Festival. Features a variety of dance groups from Western Washington. Washington Center for the Performing Arts. washingtoncenter.org

April

- Daffodil Festival & Parade. Orting. cityoforting.org

- Gray Sky Blues Festival. Downtown Tacoma. wablues.org

- Nisqually Valley Home & Garden Show. Yelm. yelmchamber.com

- Pierce County Daffodil Festival. Multiple locations, Tacoma.

- Port Gamble Cruise Nights. Thursdays, April-September. portgamble.com/upcoming-events

- Spring Fair. Washington State Fair Events Center. Puyallup. thefair.com

May

- Cinco de Mayo. Street Fair. Garfield & C Tacoma.
- Gig Harbor Beer Festival. Uptown Gig Harbor. gigharborbeerfestival.com
- Lacey Spring Fun Fair. St, Martin's University. laceyparks.org/funfair
- Olympia Wooden Boat Fair. Percival Landing Park. Olympia. olywoodenboat.org
- Peninsula Home and Garden Expo. Kitsap Fairgrounds. Bremerton. members.northmasonchamber.com
- Petpalooza. Game Farm Park, Auburn.
- Tacoma Ocean Fest: Free festival of arts, sciences and water fun.

June

- Alls Faire. Thurston County Fairgrounds, Lacey. allsfaire.org
- Auburn's Kidsday. Les Gove Park, Auburn.
- Keyfest. Festival and carnival. Gateway Park, Gig Harbor. keyfair.org
- Kitsap Medieval Faire. Kitsap County Fairgrounds. Bremerton. kitsapmedievalfaire.org
- Maple Valley Days. Lake Wilderness Park, Maple Valley. maplevalleydays.com
- Maritime Gig Festival. Parade, festival. Visitor Center, Gig Harbor. gigharborchamber.net
- Mason County Forest Festival. Shelton. chamber.masonchamber.com
- Meeker Days Festival. Car show, music. N Meridan, Puyallup.
- Prairie Days and Parade. Downtown, Yelm.
- Summer Splash! Festival of Fun. Various events, sand sculptors. June-August. https://www.hocm.org/events-programs
- Tacoma Highland Games. Frontier Park, Graham. tacomagames.org
- Tacoma Ocean Fest. Foss Waterway Seaport. tacomaoceanfest.org

- Tacoma Water Lantern Festival. Spanaway. June.
- Taste of Tacoma. Point Definance Park, Tacoma. thefair.com/the-taste-nw
- Washington Midsummer Renaissance Faire. 19401 Sumner-Buckley Highway, Bonney Lake. washingtonfaire.com

July

- Auburn 4th of July Festival. Arts, car show. auburnwa.gov
- Auburn's Fourth of July Festival. Les Gov Park. Auburn. auburnwa.gov
- Enumclaw Rotary St, Fair. Downtown. Enumclaw
- Expo & Bite of Mason County Street Fair. Shelton. masonchamber.com/eventscalendar
- Goodguys Packific Northwest Nationals. Washington State Fairground, Puyallup.
- King Couty Fair. Expo Center. Enumclaw.
- Kitsap Arts and Crafts Festival. Village Green Park, Kingston.
- Lakewood SummerFest. Forst Steilacoom Park, Lakewood. cityoflakewood.us/summerfest
- Mosaic. Tacoma's Arts & Culture Festival. Wright Park, Tacoma.
- Mt. Rainier Wine Festival. Alpine Inn, Crystal Mountain. visitrainier.com/events
- Nisqually Valley BBQ Rally. Yelm. yelmchamber.com
- Pacific Northwest Scottish Highland Games. Clan Gathering. Expo Center, Enumclaw. sshga.org/the-games
- Steilacoom Fourth of July Celebration. Downtown, Steilacoom. steilacoomchamber.co
- Sumner Rhubarb Days. Downtown, Sumner. sumnermainstreet.com
- Tacoma Freedom Fair. Ruston Way Waterfront. Tacoma.
- Taste of Tacoma. Point Definance Park, Tacoma. thefair.com/the-taste-nw
- Tenino Oregon trail Days. Downtown, Tenino. teninoacc.org
- Thurston County Fair. Fairgrounds. Lacey. thurstoncountywa.gov

August

- BREW FIVE THREE: Tacoma's Beer & Music Festival. Broadway & 9th St, Tacoma. August. tacomaartslive.org
- Chalk the Walks. Write uplifting messages on sidewalks, parks. Shelton. chamber.masonchamber.com/events
- Classic Car & Truck Show. Spanaway Park. piercecountywa.gov
- Classic Car Show. Spanaway Park. Tacoma. August. piercecountywa.gov
- Fort Nisqually Brigade Encampment. Ft. Nisqually Living History Museum. Tacoma. August. metroparkstacoma.org
- Freedom Fair Fly-In. Bremerton National Airport. Car show, airplanes on display. portofbremerton.org/freedom-fair-fly-in
- Garfield St, Fair and Car Show. C St & Park Ave. Tacoma. discoverparkland.org
- Kitsap County Fair. NW Fairgrounds Road. Bremerton. kitsapfair.org
- Kitsap Wine Festival at Harborside Fountain Park. Bremerton.
- Music & Heart in Wright Park. Tacoma. musicandheart.org
- Olympia Brew Fest. Port Plaza, Olympia. olybrewfest.com
- Olympia Pet Parade. Downtown. Olympia.
- Orting Summerfest. Orting City Park, Orting.
- Pierce County Fair. Frontier Park, Graham. piercecountyfair.com
- Port Gamble Summer Faire. Live music, raptor Rhapsody. portgamble.com/upcoming-events
- Sumner Classy Chassis Car Show. Downtown, Sumner. sumnermainstreet.com/events
- The Cruz Car Show. Downtown Port Orchard.
- Washington Midsummer Renaissance Faire. 19401 Sumner-Buckley Hwy, Bonney Lake. August. washingtonfaire.com

September

- Bremerton Blackberry Festival. Waterfront. blackberryfestival.org
- Gig Harbor Cider Swig. LeMay – America's Car Museum, Tacoma. ciderswig.org September.

- Olympia Harbor Days Festival. Olympia. harbordays.com
- Roy Pioneer Rodeo. 8710 Higgins Greig Rd, Roy. royrodeo.com
- Tacoma Water Lantern Festival. Spanaway Lake Park, Spanaway. waterlanternfestival.com
- Washington State Fair. 902 Meridian, Puyallup. thefair.com

October

- City of Fife Harvest Festival. Dacca Park, Fife. cityoffife.org
- Lake Sylvia State Park Fall Festival. Lake Sylvia, Montasano. facebook.com/LakeSylviaStateParkFallFestival
- Orting Red Hat Days. Multiple locations. Orting. facebook.com/redhatdays
- Skookum Rotary OysterFest. Shelton. oysterfest.org/cms
- Washington OysterFest. Sanderson Field, Shelton. oysterfest.org

November

- Art in the Woods. Tours into North Kitsap working studios. November. cafnw.org
- Auburn's Veterans Day Parade. Main St, Auburn.
- Christmas at Meeker Mansion. 312 Spring St, Puyallup. facebook.com/meekermansion
- Fantasy Lights at Spanaway Park. Spanaway.
- Holiday Gift & Food Fair. Kitsap County Fairgrounds. Bremerton. holidaygiftfair.com
- Point Defiance ZooLights. Point Defiance Zoo. Tacoma. pdza.org
- Port Gamble Ghost Conference. Paranormal in Port Gamble. portgamble.com/upcoming-events
- TAM Día de los Muertos Free Community Festival. Tacoma Art Museum. Tacoma. tacomaartmuseum.org

RESOURCES: FITNESS, HEALTHY LIVING

The following includes lists of fitness resources and information within and near Mason, Kitsap, Pierce, and Thurston Counties. Resources include lists of outdoor organizations, cycling resources, pickleball resources, and other providers of fitness opportunities and classes including parks and recreation, YMCA and community college programs and classes.

Outdoor Fitness Clubs

Below is a list of a variety of outdoor clubs for cycling, hiking, and walking, skiing, and other outdoor adventures. For more information on hiking and walking, see *CHAPTER 15: HIKING AND WALKING* on page 97 and *RESOURCES: HIKING AND WALKING* on page 226.

Statewide and Seattle

- Evergreen State Walking Club. Association of volkssport clubs in the state. Clubs sponsor neighborhood walks; promotes walking and safe, convenient, and attractive walk areas. Area groups include:

- Emerald City Wanderers. Group walks of varied distances and mapped walks in and around Greater Seattle. emeraldcitywanderers.org

- Fit Fun and Friendly Olympians. Holds hikes, walks, cross-country skiing, snowshoeing, trail running, and social activities. All levels. Olympia. meetup.com/fit-fun-and-friendly-olympians

- Interlaken Trailblazers Walking Club. Group walks, varied distances mapped walks in and around Greater Seattle. interlakentrailblazers.org

- Outdoor Adventure and Recreation Group. Social group of people who enjoy new seeing places and exploring. meetup.com/hiking-235

- REI Classes and Events. Sponsors outdoor classes, guided day trips and virtual events. Search by location. rei.com/events

- Sound Steppers. Group walks of varied distances and mapped walks in areas north of Seattle. Soundsteppers.org

- The Mountaineers. Outdoor trips, courses, books, and events for all ages and experience levels in Pacific Northwest. See seasonal catalog. 7700 Sand Point Way NE, Seattle. 206-521-6000. mountaineers.org

- Walking Volkssport NW. Group walks of varied distances and mapped walks in northwest Seattle area. meetup.com/walkers-574

- Washington Outdoor Women. Teaches traditional outdoor skills to women and girls through a variety of classes and workshops. Belleview. 425-455-1986. washingtonoutdoorwomen.org

- Washington Trails Association. A group of hikers who like to explore and maintain public lands. Website includes maps and information about hiking in Washington state. 705 2nd Ave, Ste 300 Seattle. 206)-625-1367. wta.org

Mason and Kitsap Counties

- Black Hills Audubon Society. Chapter of National Audubon Society representing Lewis, Mason, and Thurston counties. Olympia. 360-352-7299. blackhills-audubon.org

- Easy Outdoor Buddies of North Kitsap. Group gatherings for easy outdoor activities such as forest hiking, biking, kayaking, swimming. meetup.com/easyoutdoorbuddies

- Kitsap Outdoors. Organizes introductory and advanced hikes, snow travel, camping, backpacking and bikes. Silverdale. meetup.com/kitsap-outdoors

- Key Peninsular Kayakers. Lakebay. All ages and levels exploring local waterways in Kitsap area. meetup.com/key-peninsula-kayakers

- Mason County Parks and Trails Maps. Links to maps available on the county website. Locations and descriptions of parks

and trails and recreation areas. Mason County's Parks. Includes maps of Oakland Bay Park, Mason County Recreation North and South biking, kayaking, and diving, Hood Canal, Shelton, West Mason, Olympics. masoncountywa.gov/forms/parks/trails_map.pdf

- Kitsap County Parks Trail Maps. Includes maps of Anderson Landing, Banner Forest, Guillemot Cove, Hansville Greenway, Illahee Preserve Heritage Park, Newberry Hill Heritage Park, North Kitsap Heritage Park, Port Gamble Trail, South Kitsap Regional Park Forester. kitsapgov.com/parks/Pages/TrailMaps

Pierce County

- Birding and More with the Tahoma Audubon Society. Tacoma. meetup.com/birding-with-the-tahoma-audubon-society

- Early Bird Adventures. Hiking and camping year-round in Washington forests and other activities. Puyallup. meetup.com/early-bird-adventures

- Pathfinders. Hikes on Pacific Northwest Trails to enjoy nature and build friendships. Tacoma. tacoma-hiking-meetup-group

- Tahoma Audubon Society. Advocates for the protection of wildlife through education and activities. University Place. Adriana Hess Audubon Center, 2917 Morrison Rd W, University Place. 253-565-9278. tahomaaudubon.org

- Tacoma Outdoors Adventures. Sponsors outdoor activities such as biking, hiking, camping, snowshoeing, and social events. All levels. Lakewood. meetup.com/tacomaoutdoors

- Tacoma Pierce County Physical Activity Resources. Website of resources (listed below) for physical activity. tpchd.org/healthy-people/physical-activity

  o Tacoma-Pierce County Walking Guide—Information and details about many local parks and trails. Also includes tips on how to start a walking program. tpchd.org/healthy-people/physical-activity/walking-guide

  o City of Puyallup Walking Map. Area walking routes, walk tips.

  o Pierce County Parks and Recreation. Local resources for recreation activities.

- o Community Walkability. Resources to improve your neighborhood's walkability.

- o Pierce county Bike Map. piercecountywa.gov/2219/Bike-Map

- Tacoma Runners. Social running club, running workouts, fun runs. facebook.com/groups/tacomarunners. tacomarunners.com

- Tacoma Unlikely Walkers & Hikers. Supportive and welcoming for all walkers and hikers. Tacoma. meetup.com/tacoma-unlikely-hiker

Thurston County

- Club Oly Runners. Sponsors group runs, fun runs, speed workouts, endurance runs, and social events. All levels. Olympia. meetup.com/olympia-running

- Outdoor Adventure and Recreation Group. Social outdoor group, hiking, other outdoor activities. Olympia. meetup.com/hiking-235

- Olympia Dragon Boating Meetup. Dragon boating for all backgrounds and fitness levels. Coaching and equipment provided. meetup.com/olympia-dragon-boating-meetup

- Olympia Outdoor and Fun Time Adventurers. Outdoor/fitness events: walking/hiking, fishing, camping, kayaking, snowshoeing, biking. Olympia. meetup.com/olympia-outdoor-adventurers-oofta

- Olympia Walking Map. Includes trails, landmarks, public art and more. 360-956-7575. trpc.org

- South Sound Birders. Sponsors field trips, wildlife classes, lectures, and other events, many in connection with Black Hills Audubon Society. meetup.com/south-sound-birders

- South Sound Walkers Meetup. Group walks in and around Thurston county. Distance, locations vary. meetup.com/South-Sound-Walkers

- Thurston Regional Planning Council. Walking maps. 2411 Chandler Court SW, Olympia. trpc.org/938/Walking-Recreation

Cycling Clubs, Maps

The following are lists of area cycling places and other resources including clubs and Meetups. Visit their websites for more information.

- Cascade Bicycle Club. Serves bike riders of all ages, races, genders, income levels, and abilities throughout the state. Cascade Bicycling Center, 7787 62nd Ave NE, Seattle. 206-522-3222. cascade.org

- Easy Outdoor Buddies of North Kitsap. Group gatherings for easy outdoor activities such as forest hiking, biking, kayaking, swimming. meetup.com/easyoutdoorbuddies

- League of American Bicyclists. Represents, advocates for cyclists nationwide. Local and state information. bikeleague.org

- Mason County Parks and Trails Maps. Links to maps available on the county website. Locations and descriptions of parks and trails and recreation areas. Mason County's Parks. Includes maps of Oakland Bay Park, Mason County Recreation North and South biking, kayaking, and diving, Hood Canal, Shelton, West Mason, Olympics. masoncountywa.gov/forms/parks/trails_map.pdf

- Kitsap County Parks Trail Maps. Includes maps of Anderson Landing, Banner Forest, Guillemot Cove, Hansville Greenway, Illahee Preserve Heritage Park, Newberry Hill Heritage Park, North Kitsap Heritage Park, Port Gamble Trail, South Kitsap Regional Park Forester. kitsapgov.com/parks/Pages/TrailMaps

- Olympia Outdoor and Fun Time Adventurers. Sponsors outdoor/fitness events including walking/hiking, fishing, camping, kayaking, snowshoeing, biking. Olympia. meetup.com/olympia-outdoor-adventurers-oofta

- Pierce County Bike Map. Guide for cyclists traveling to major centers, attractions, and other key destinations. Download. piercecountywa.gov

- RIDE Thurston County. Guide map to urban and rural bicycling routes for transportation and recreation. Thurston Regional Planning Council. Olympia. 360-956-7575. thurstonbikemap.com

- Tacoma Outdoors Adventures. Sponsors outdoor activities such as biking, hiking, camping, snowshoeing; and social events. All levels. Lakewood. meetup.com/tacomaoutdoors

- Tacoma Pierce County Physical Activity Resources. Pierce county Bike Map. piercecountywa.gov/2219/Bike-Map

- Tacoma Washington Bicycle Club. Club rides and joint events with other clubs. twbc.org

- West Sound Cycling Club. Socially paced rides including pauses at points of interests, museums, or cafes. Silverdale. meetup.com/silverdale-road-cycling-meetup

- Washington Bicycle Maps. Website provides alphabetical listing of state and local bike and trails maps for the state. wabikes.org

- West Sound Cycling Club. Socially paced rides including pauses at points of interests, museums, or cafes. Silverdale. meetup.com/silverdale-road-cycling-meetup

- Washington Bikes. Cycling advocates; provides resources for cyclists in Washington. 7787 62nd Ave NE, Seattle. 206-522-3222. wabikes.org

- Washington State Bicycle Association. Governing body of competitive bicycling in Washington, Oregon, and North Idaho. Information, calendar of events, contacts. wsbaracing.org

Pickleball Clubs

The following is a list of area pickleball clubs and places where you can learn and play pickleball in your city or county. Visit their websites for more information.

Also visit the website of your city or county's parks and recreation programs. See *RESOURCES: FITNESS, HEALTHY LIVING, Parks and Rec, YMCAs* on page 204.

Pickleball Clubs

- Grit City Gherkins. Supports open play sessions and pickleball events throughout Tacomametroparkstacoma.org/activities-and-sports/about-pickleball

- MetroParks Pickleball. Sponsors leagues, classes, tournaments. Tacoma. metroparkstacoma.org

- South Sound Pickleball Club. Gig Harbor. Schedules and discussion. facebook.com/groups/167007723639205

- Thurston County Pickleball Club. Club for pickleball crazies. Retail discounts, tournaments, workshops, resources. tcpcwa.com

Pickleball Courts

Kitsap and Mason Counties

- Bainbridge High School Lower Gym. 4 indoor and 6 outdoor courts. 9530 High School Rd, Bainbridge Island. 206-842-2306. bisd303.org

- Battle Point Park. 6 courts. 11299 Arrow Point Dr NE, Bainbridge Island. 206-842-2306. biparks.org

- Bremerton High School Tennis Courts. 1298 High Ave. Bremerton.

- Bremerton Lions Park. 4 courts. 251 Lebo Blvd, Bremerton.

- Central Kitsap High School. 2 courts. 10140 Frontier Pl NW, Silverdale.

- Chief Kitsap Academy Gym. 3 indoor courts. Club. 15838 Sandy Hook Rd NE, Poulsbo.

- Courthouse Park. 2 courts. 1820 Jefferson St, Port Townsend.

- East Bremerton Community Gym. 9 indoor courts. 2810 Spruce Ave. Bremerton.

- Kingston Tennis Courts. 4 indoor courts. 26159 Dulay Rd NE, Kingston.

- Kitsap Tennis and Athletic Center. 6 indoor/outdoor courts. 1909 NE John Carlson Rd, Bremerton.

- Lakewood Community Center. 9112 Lakewood Dr SW, Ste 121, Lakewood.

- Lions Park. 2 courts. 585 NE Matson St, Poulsbo. 360-779-9898.

- Manette Park. 4 courts. 1125 Vandalia Ave, Bemerton.
- Mountain View Courts. 1925 Blaine St, Port Townsend.
- Mullenix Rd Court. 1 court. 6419 SE Mulleni Rd, Port Orchard
- Port Townsend High School. Blaine St, Port Townsend.
- Poulsbo Lions Park. 2 courts. 585 NE Matson St, Poulsbo.
- Seabeck Community Center.4 courts. 15565 Seabeck Hey NW, Seabeck.
- Shelton Transit-Community Center. 601 Franklin St, Shelton.
- Sheridan Park Rec Center. 3 courts. 680 Lebo Blvd, Bremerton.
- Strawberry Field Park. 2 courts. 7666 High School Rd NW, Bainbridge Island. 206-842-2306. Biparks.org
- VanZee Memorial Park. 4 courts. 300 Tremont St, Port Orchard.
- Village Green Inside Courts. 2 courts. 261 Dulay Rd NE, Kingston.
- Williams-Olson Park. 1 outdoor court. 6200 NE Williams Lane, Bainbridge Island. Biparks.org

Pierce County

- Canterwood Golf & Country Club. 2 indoor courts. Club. 12606 54th Ave NW, Gig Harbor. 253-851-1845.
- Hales Pass Park. 2 courts. 3507 Nash Dr NW, Gig Harbor. 253-307-4313. penmetparks.org
- Meeker Middle School. 4402 Nassau Ave NE, Tacoma. 253-571-6500. 6 courts.
- Metro Parks Tacoma. Clubs, clinics, leagues, tournaments, other resources. metroparkstacoma.org/activities-and-sports/about-pickleball. Location of pickleball courts maintained by Metro Parks. Community Centers, Tacoma.

  o Center at Norpoint. 3 indoor courts.4818 Nassau Ave NE, Tacoma. 205-404-3900.

  o People's Community Center. 3 indoor courts. 1602 Martin Luther Kind Jr Way, Tacoma. 253-404-3915.

  o Eastside Community Center. 3 indoor courts. 1721 E 56th Str, Tacoma. 253-303-3990.

o Hope/Schatz (next to STAR Center). 3 indoor courts.

o Browns Point Playfield. 2 courts. 4915 La Hal Da Lane NE. 253-305-1000

o Jefferson Park, Outdoor. Outdoor. 801 N Mason Ave, Tacoma.

o Jenks Park. 2 courts. 5301 W Tapps Dr E, Bonney Lake. 243-677-8947.

o Point Defiance Park, 5400 N Pearl St, Tacoma.

o STAR Center. Outdoor. 3873 S 66th St, Tacoma.

o Stewart Heights Park. 4 courts. 5715 Reginald Gutierrez Ln, Tacoma.

o Vassault Park. 2 courts. 6100 N 37th St, Tacoma.

- Sehmel Homestead Park. 10123 78th Ave NW, Gig Harbor. 253-858-3400. penmetparks.org

- Sprinkler Recreation Center. 4 courts. 14824 C St S, Tacoma. 253-531-6300. piercecountywa.gov

- The Drop Pickleball Club. 2360 S. Fawcett Ave, Tacoma. 1 indoor and 8 indoor courts.

- Tom Taylor Family YMCA. 4 indoor courts. 10550 Harbor Hill Dr, Gig Harbor. 253-853-9622. ymcapkc.org

Thurston County

- 23 Kitchens. 6 indoor, 5 outdoor courts, recreation complex. 2440 Marvin Rd NE, Lacey. 360-615-2323. 23kitchens.com

- Barclift Park. 690 Barclift Ln SE, Tumwater. 1 court.

- Briggs YMCA. Club. 1530 Yelm Hwy SE, Olympia.

- Jim Brown Park. 535 Bates ST SW, Tumwater. 1 court.

- LBA Park. 3333 Morse-Merryman RD SE, Olympia.

- Olympia Center. 222 Columba St NW, Olympia.

- Rainier Vista Park. 5475 45th Ave SW, Lacey.

- Stevens Field. 300 24th Ave SE, Olympia.

- Steamboat Tennis & Athletic Club. 3505 Steamboat Island Rd NW, Olympia.

- Woodruff Park. 4 courts. 1500 Harrison Ave NW, Olympia.

Parks and Rec, YMCAs

The following is a
listing of parks and
recreation programs
and YMCAs that offer
fitness programs
within or near Kitsap,
Mason, Pierce, and
Thurston Counties.
Visit their websites for
more information.

Kitsap and Mason Counties

- Bainbridge Island Metro Park & Recreation District. Fitness activities and programs, adult walks. 206-842-2302. biparks.org

- Bremerton Family YMCA. 2261 Homer Jones Dr. 360-377-3741. ymcapkc.org/locations/bremerton-family-ymca

- Bremerton Parks & Recreation. Senior fitness programs and classes. 680 Lebo Blvd., Bremerton. 360-473-5305. bremertonwa.gov

- Haselwood Family YMCA. 3909 Randall Way, Silverdale. 360-698-9622. ymcapkc.org/locations/haselwood-family-ymca

- Kitsap County Parks. Parks, outdoor facilities. 1195 NW Fairgrounds Rd, Bremerton. 360-337-5350. kitsapgov.com/parks

- Mason County Parks. Parks information. 411 N 5th St, Shelton. 360-427-9670. masoncountywa.gov/parks

- Port Orchard Parks. Parks information. 216 Prospect St, Port Orchard. 360-876-4407. portorchardwa.gov/port-orchard-parks

- Poulsbo Parks and Recreation. Fitness activities and classes. 19540 Front St, NE, Poulsbo. 360-779-9898. cityofpoulsbo.com

- Shelton Parks & Recreation. Shelton Civic Center. Fitness programs and activities. 525 West Cota St, 360-432-5106 sheltonwa.gov

- Shelton Family YMCA. 3101 N Shelton Springs Rd, Shelton. 360-753-6576. southsoundymca.org/shelton-ymca

Pierce County

- Auburn Parks, Arts & Recreation. Senior health programs, classes, activities, trips. 25 W Main St, Auburn. 253-931-3000. auburnwa.gov

- Bonney Lake. Classes and recreation activities. 9002 Main St E, Bonney Lake. ci.bonney-lake.wa.us

- Dupont Parks & Recreation. Senior programs, events, and activities. 1700 Civic 98327. 253-964-8121. dupontwa.gov

- Fircrest Parks and Recreation. Classes and active adult programs. 115 Ramsdell St, Fircrest. 253-564-8901. cityoffircrest.net

- Gig Harbor Parks. Information about city parks and facilities. 3510 Grandview St, 253-851-8136. cityofgigharbor.net

- Gordon Family YMCA. 16101 64th St East, Sumner. 253-826-9622. ymcapkc.org/locations/gordon-family-ymca

- Lakewood Family YMCA. 7515 Lakewood Dr SW. 253-584-9622. ymcapkc.org/locations/lakewood-family-ymca

- Lakewood Parks & Recreation. Senior activity center holds exercise classes. City Hall, 6000 Main St SW. 253-589-2489. cityoflakewood.us

- Mel Korum Family YMCA. 302 43rd Ave SE, Puyallup 253-841-9622. ymcapkc.org/locations/mel-korum-family-ymca

- Metro Parks Tacoma. A wide variety of senior programs, exercise, and sports. 4702 S 19th St, Tacoma. 4702 S. 19th St, Tacoma, 253-305-1000. metroparkstacoma.org

- Morgan Family YMCA. 1002 S Pearl St, Tacoma. 253-564-9622. ymcapkc.org/locations/morgan-family-ymca

- PenMet Parks. Senior educational, fitness and recreation programs. 5717 Wollochet Dr NW #3, Gig Harbor. 253-858-3400. penmetparks.org

- Pierce County Parks & Recreation. A wide variety of recreation and sports programs. 930 Tacoma Ave S, Tacoma. 253-798-4199. piercecountywa.gov

- Puyallup Parks and Recreation. Classes and senior programs. 808 Valley Ave NW. 253-841-5457. cityofpuyallup.org

- Tacoma Center YMCA. 1144 Market St, Tacoma. 253-597-6444. ymcapkc.org/locations/tacoma-center-ymca

- Tom Taylor Family YMCA. 10550 Harbor Hill Dr, Gig Harbor. 253-853-9622.

Thurston County

- Briggs Community YMCA. 1530 Yelm Hwy SE, Olympia. 360-753-6576. southsoundymca.org

- City of Lacey Culture and Recreation. Variety of health, fitness programs. 420 College St SE, Lacey. 360-491-5644. laceyparks.org

- City of Tumwater. Parks and Recreation. Adult health and fitness programs. 360-754-5855. ci.tumwater.wa.us

- Olympia Parks, Arts & Recreation. Adult health and fitness classes. Olympia City Hall, 601 4th Ave E, Olympiaolympiawa.gov

- PARC & Recreation. Parks, Arts, Recreation and Culture organization. 149 Hodgden St S, Tenino. 360-264-2368. cityoftenino.us/parks-recreation

- Plum Street YMCA. 505 Plum St SW, Olympia. 360-357-6609. ymca.org/locations/plum-street-ymca-branch

RESOURCES: GARDENING

The following are lists of resources within or near Kitsap, Mason, Pierce, and Thurston Counties for area gardeners.

Public and Demonstration Gardens

The following contains listings of public and demonstration gardens for those interested in visiting, volunteering, and learning about all things gardening in the northwest.

King County

- Bellevue Botanical Garden. Free. 53 acres of display gardens, woodlands, meadows, wetlands; diverse selection of native plants. 12001 Main St, Bellevue. 425-452-2750. bellevuebotanical.org

- Carl S. English Jr. Botanical Garden at the Ballard Locks. English landscape style. 1,500 varieties from around the world, local natives. 3015 NW 54th St, Seattle. 206-789-2622 x375.

- Covington Water District Waterwise Demonstration Garden. showcases WaterWise gardening. Drought tolerant natives. 18631 SE 300th Pl, Covington. 253-631-0565. covingtonwater.com

- Dunn Gardens. Woodland gardens, perennial borders, sweeps of lawn. Range of sizes, new and old, diminutive to towering. 13533 Northshire Rd NW, Seattle. 206-362-0933. dunngardens.org

- Erna Gunther Ethnobotanical Garden at the Burke Museum of Natural History. Displays most useful northwest plants and traditional uses. 17th Ave NE and NE 45th, Seattle.

- Ethnobotanical Garden at Daybreak Star Cultural Center. Learning garden of over 60 species of native plants. 3801 W Government Way, Seattle. 206-285-4425. unitedindians.org

- Highline Botanical Garden. Free. 11-acre heritage garden. 13735 24th Ave S, SeaTac. 206-391-4003. highlinegarden.org

- Highline Community College. Native plant habitat garden divided into 4 regions of state: eastern, coastal, NW forest and subalpine. S 240th St & Pacific Highway S, Des Moines. 206-878-3710.

- King County. County-provided, earth-friendly information, guides, books, links to sites about gardening and yard care. kingcounty.gov

- Kruckeberg Botanic Garden. Four-acre blend of native plants and unusual exotics in naturalistic wooded setting. 20312 15th Ave NW, Shoreline. 206-546-128. kruckeberg.org

- Kubota Garden. Free. 20-acre Japanese garden in the Rainier Beach neighborhood of Seattle. 9817 55th Ave S, Seattle. 206-725-5060. kubotagarden.org

- Lake Wilderness Arboretum. Several gardens and natural areas. 22520 SE 248th St, Maple Valley. 253-293-5103. lakewildernessarboretum.org

- Pacific Bonsai Museum. Connects people to nature through living art of bonsai. 2515 S 336th St, Federal Way. 253-353-7345. pacificbonsaimuseum.org

- Seattle Chinese Garden. Sichuan-style Chinese Garden. Donation. Showcases rich heritage of Chinese arts and culture. South Seattle College, 5640 16th Ave SW. seattlechinesegarden.org

- Seattle Japanese Garden. 3.5-acre stroll style garden within Washington Park Arboretum. Varied natural landscapes. 1075 Lake Washington Blvd E, Seattle. 206-684-4725. seattlejapanesegarden.org

- Washington Park Arboretum. University of Washington, 2300 Arboretum Dr E, Seattle. 206-543-8800. botanicgardens.uw.edu

- UW Botanic Gardens. Many distinct gardens at Center for Urban Horticulture, 3501 NE 41st St, and Washington Park Arboretum, 2300 Arboretum Dr E. 206-543-8616. botanicgardens.uw.edu

Kitsap and Mason Counties

- Albers Vista Gardens. World class garden to be inspired, motivated, and educated about creating sustainable landscapes. 124 E 31st St, Bremerton. 206-779-3172. albersvistagardens.org

- Bloedel Reserve. A variety of unique garden spaces. 7571 NE Dolphin Dr, Bainbridge Island. 206-842-7631. bloedelreserve.org

- Catalyst Park Demonstration Garden. Includes 12,000 square feet including food bank donations of fresh vegetables, learning garden, community gardens. Managed by WSU Master Gardener volunteers. 8th and Harvard, Shelton. 360-427-9670. extension.wsu.edu/mason

- Elandan Gardens. Bonsai museum is set among ponds, waterfalls, sculptures, and lush gardens on the shores of Puget Sound. 3050 State, Hwy 16 W, Bremerton. 360-373-8260. elandangardens.com

- Heronswood Garden. A vast array of plants from around the world, over 8,000 different varieties, six distinct yet integrated gardens. Showcase for S'Klallam tribal culture. 7530 NE 288th St, Kingston. 360-297-9620. heronswoodgarden.org

Pierce County

- Galluci Learning Garden. Cooperative community of people who learn/teach gardening skills, grow, sell, and share food. Hilltop neighborhood. Tacoma. gallucilearninggarden.org

- Lake Wilderness Arboretum. Free. Several gardens and natural areas. 22520 SE 248th St, Maple Valley. lakewildernessarboretum.org

- Lakewold Gardens. Estate gardens of various gardening styles; pathways of rocks, streams, woodland, mature trees. 12317 Gravelly Lake Drive SW, Lakewood. 253-584-4106. lakewoldgardens.org

- Lavender Hill Farm. Organic lavender farm. 10425 SW 238th St, Vashon. 206-463-2322. lavenderhillvashon.com

- Northwest Native Plant Garden. Displays native flora of the Pacific Northwest on paths through 1½ acre garden. Point Defiance Park. metroparkstacoma.org

- Old Goat Farm Garden and Nursery. Display garden, specialty nursery and animal rescue. Woodlands, gardens, pasture. 20021 Orting Kapowsin Hwy. E. Graham. 360-893-1261. oldgoatfarm.com

- Point Defiance Park Gardens. Various gardens near the Zoo and Aquarium. metroparkstacoma.org/point-defiance-park-gardens

- Powells Wood Garden. Pacific Northwest forest blended with an English style garden. Seven garden areas. 430 S Dash Point Rd, Federal Way. 253-529-1620. powellswood.org

- Rhododendron Species Botanical Garden. 22-acre woodland garden, home to world's largest collection of Rhododendron species. 2525 S 336th St, Federal Way. 253-838-4646. rhodygarden.org

- Tacoma Chinese Reconciliation Park. Preserves historical memory of tragic expulsion of Chinese people from Tacoma in 1885. 1741 N. Schuster Pky, Tacoma. 253-330-8828. tacomachinesepark.org

- University Place Community Garden. 7102 40th St W, University Place. universityplacecommunitygarden.org

- W.W. Seymour Conservatory. Exotic tropical plants and seasonal floral displays in historic glass conservatory. 316 South G St, Tacoma. 253-591-5330. metroparkstacoma.org

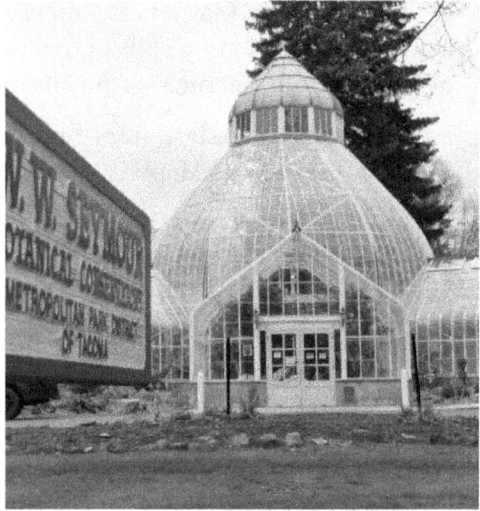

- Wright Park. Community Center, 27-acre arboretum, collection of more than 600 trees. 501 S I St, Tacoma. 253-591-5297. metroparkstacoma.org

Thurston County

- Capitol Sunken Garden. Perennial flowers. West Capitol Campus Grounds. 415 12th Ave SW, Olympia. extension.wsu.edu

- Centennial Rose Garden. 230 bushes, 63 varieties. Schmidt House and Tumwater Falls Park. 110 Deschutes Way SW, Tumwater. 360-943-2550. olytumfoundation.org/centennial-rose-garden

- Closed Loop Park. Demonstration, ornamental garden on former landfill site. Variety of plants, shrubs, and trees. Inside Thurston Co Waste and Recovery Center, Hogum Bay Rd. extension.wsu.edu

- Dirt Works Demonstration Garden – Composting Demo – Plant Nursery – Food Bank Garden. On Olympia's west side within Yauger Park. 530 Alta St SW, Olympia. Olympia.gov

- Evergreen Teaching Gardens. Learning gardens around campus of Evergreen State College. blogs.evergreen.edu/teachinggardens

- Monarch Sculpture Park. Contemporary outdoor sculpture park and center for the arts Walks in or bike in. 8431 Waldrick Road SE, Tenino. monarchsculpturepark.org

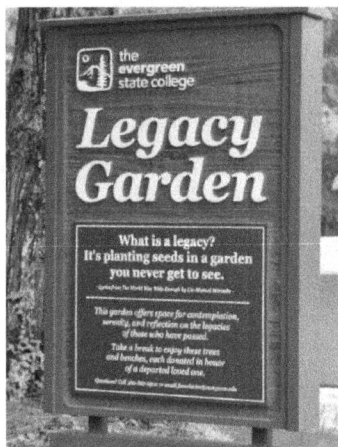

- Olympia Farmers Market Garden. Demonstrates use of small spaces for maximum efficiency in gardening and composting. East end of market. extension.wsu.edu

- Partner Gardens. Three gardens. Echo Garden, The Pollinator Garden, WSU Extension Office Garden. Thurston County Fairgrounds. 3054 Carpenter Road SE, Lacey. extension.wsu.edu

- Samarkand Rose Garden and Olympia Memorial Garden. Free. Squaxin Park. 2600 East Bay Drive NE, Olympia. 360-753-8380.

- The Ethnobotanical Gifts Garden. Consists of several ethnobotanically-oriented habitat and theme areas. Longhouse Education and Cultural Center, Evergreen State College. 360-867-6413 evergreen.edu/longhouse/ethnobotanical-gifts-garden

- Yashiro Japanese Garden. Free. Picnic areas; public art. 1010 Plum St SE, Olympia. 360.753.8380 olympiawa.gov

Garden Clubs, Groups

The following is a list of South sound Garden Clubs by location.

- Black Hills District of Garden Clubs. Thurston County, Mason County south of Union, Lewis County, southern part of Grays Harbor County and Pacific County. blackhillsdistrict.com
  - o Black Hills Flower Designers Club
  - o Friendly Flowers Garden Club
  - o Friendly Neighbor Garden Club Illahee GC
  - o Olympia Garden Club. olympiagardenclub.org
  - o Chinook District, South King County. chinookgc.org

- o Auburn Garden Club
- o Des Moines Garden Club
- o Enumclaw Garden Club
- o Maple Trails Garden Club
- o Marine Hills Garden Club. marinehillsgardenclub.blogspot.com
- o O'Brien Garden Club. obriengardenclub.org
- o Parkside Garden Club. sites.google.com/site/parksidegardenclub
- o Southgate Garden Club
- o Sunset View Garden Club
- Cross Sound District. Kitsap County, eastern Mason County north of Union, Bainbridge Island. wagardenclubs.com/clubs-membership
  - o Central Valley Garden Club
  - o Evergreen Garden Club facebook.com/EvergreenGardenClubBelfair
  - o Long Lake Garden Club
  - o Poulsbo Garden Club. facebook.com/poulsbogardenclub
- Hill and Dale District. Pierce County. hillanddaledistrict.weebly.com
  - o Aster Nots Garden Club, Tacoma, University Place.
  - o Country Gardeners Garden Club, Spanaway, Parkland. hillanddaledistrict.weebly.com
  - o Dogwood Garden Club of Eatonville. dogwoodgardenclub.com
  - o Garden Hour Garden Club of Edgewood, Milton, Auburn.
  - o Glove & Trowel Garden Club of Puyallup, South Hill, Tacoma.
  - o Happy Thymes Garden Club of Sumner, Orting.
  - o Interlaaken Garden Club of Lakewood, Steilacoom.
  - o Root & Bloom Garden Club of Puyallup, South Hill, Graham. www.rootandbloomgardenclub.weebly.com

Other Gardening Groups and Resources

- American Rhododendron Society. Chapters in Olympia, Gig Harbor, Shelton, Tacoma, and Seattle. Rhodendron.org

- GRUB (Garden-Raised Bounty) Focuses on growing and preparing good food. Works with marginalized young people, low income, seniors experiencing hunger, tribal communities, and veterans. 2016 Elliott Ave NW, Olympia. 360-753-5522 goodgrub.org

- King County Native Plant Resources for Pacific Northwest. Provides resources including native plant guides, books, publications, websites, native plant sales and nurseries. kingcounty.gov/services/environment

- Kitsap County Dahlia Society. Members raise, show, and cultivate dahlias; maintain community gardens in Bremerton, Silverton, Port Gamble. Poulsbo. kitsapdahlias.org

- Kitsap Peninsular Mycological Society. Members who enjoy all things wild mushrooms. Bremerton. kitsapmushrooms.org

- Master Gardeners of King County. Provides a resource for home gardening including classes, workshops, speakers, tip sheets, email clinic. Operates several demonstration gardens in Greater Seattle. 206-543-0943. extension.wsu.edu

- Master Gardener Foundation Kitsap County. Master Gardeners group that supports learning gardens, public seminars, and delivery of organic produce to food banks. Silverdale. kitsapgardens.org

213

- Master Gardener Foundation of Thurston County. Master Gardeners group that supports learning gardens, public seminars, and classes. 3054 Carpenter Rd SE, Olympia. mgftc.org

- Pierce Conservation District. Harvest Pierce County connects community members with volunteer gardeners. Provides Community garden maps and tools to start one. Works with WSU Master Gardeners, City of Tacoma. piercecd.org

- Thurston County Community Gardens. Information about community gardens that are collaborative, shared, open space available to resident gardeners. co.thurston.wa.us

- Washington State Federation of Garden Clubs. Coordinates the interests of garden clubs in Washington State. wagardenclubs.com

- Washington Native Plant Society. Promotes conservation of native plants and habitats through study, education, and advocacy. Chapters, activities, resources throughout the state. wnps.org

- WSU Community Gardens. Provides, maintains community gardens, demonstration gardens in Pierce County. Volunteers teach, demonstrate and support garden engagement. extension.wsu.edu/pierce/community-gardens

- WSU Extension Mason County. Provides educations programs and other resources to residents through 4-H, Master Gardener Program, food safety resources, and other resources. 303 N 4th St, Shelton, 360-427-9670. extension.wsu.edu/mason

- WSU Extension Thurston County. Conducts Master Gardener Program, 4-H Program, Master Recycler Composter Program, and other resources. extension.wsu.edu/thurston

- WSU Master Gardener Program. Provides community resources, events, training, education for home gardening and horticulture. Maintains several demonstration gardens. extension.wsu.edu

Classes, Workshops

The following are types of organizations and places that offer free and inexpensive gardening classes, events, and workshops. (See also the list of area Garden Clubs on page 211; many also offer gardening classes.

- AARP Gardening & Nature Events. Interactive online events and classes. local.aarp.org/virtual-community-center/gardening-nature

- Community College classes and programs. For a list of community colleges, see *RESOURCES: LEARNING PLACES, Colleges, Universities* on page 233.

- Demonstration gardens and botanical gardens. For a list of area gardens, see *RESOURCES: GARDENING, Public and Demonstration Gardens* on page 207.

- Library program. For a listing of area libraries see *RESOURCES: LEARNING PLACES, Libraries* on page 235.

- University of Washington Botanic Gardens. Youth and adult programs and workshops, tours, speakers. 2300 Arboretum Drive E, Seattle. botanicgardens.uw.edu

- Washington State University. Master gardener programs. Resources and research-based garden help. Free publications on gardening. Local extension offices. mastergardener.wsu.edu/resources.

  o King County. extension.wsu.edu/king/gardening

  o Kitsap County. extension.wsu.edu/kitsap/gardening

  o Mason County. extension.wsu.edu/mason/master-gardener

  o Pierce County. extension.wsu.edu/pierce/mg

  o Thurston County. extension.wsu.edu/thurston/gardening

- Virtual gardening classes and events. See online sources such as youtube.com.

RESOURCES: GOVERNMENT SERVICE

The following provides descriptions and contact information for those interested in an advisory or other volunteer role in South Sound city, county, or regional government.

City Government

Citizen volunteers serve on boards and commissions much like those of counties. For information, visit the citizen involvement pages of your city's website.

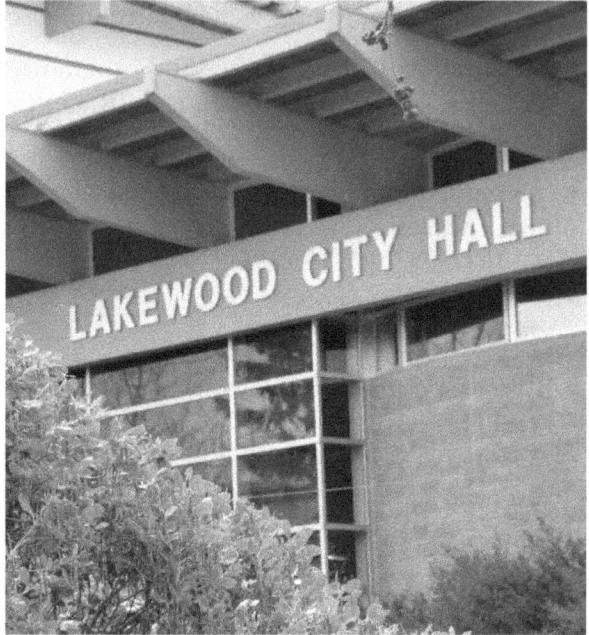

- Anderson Island, Parkland, Spanaway. Citizens Advisory Board reports to Pierce City Council. 930 Tacoma Ave S, Tacoma. piercecountywa.gov

- Bonney Lake. Volunteers serve on various boards and commission including arts, planning, civic service, and salary. 9002 Main St, E, Bonney Lake. 253-862-8602. ci.bonney-lake.wa.us

- Dupont. Advisory roles in Municipal Commissions for cultural, planning, recreation, taxes, transportation. 1700 Civic Drive, DuPont. 253-964-8121. dupontwa.gov

- Gig Harbor. Advisory Boards volunteers. Arts, Civil Service, Design Review, Parks, Planning, Salary Commissions; Lodging Tax Advisory Committee. 3510 Grandview St, Gig Harbor. 253-851-8136. cityofgigharbor.net

- Lacey. Community representatives serve on boards and commissions on land use, zoning social services, parks, library services, historical matters, diversity, equity, and inclusion. Lacey City Hall, 420 College St SE, Lacey. 360-491-3214. cityoflacey.org

- Lakewood. Community representatives serve on boards and commissions on arts, community services, landmarks and heritage, lodging tax, parks and recreation, planning, public safety, salaries. City Hall, 6000 Main St SW, Lakewood. 253-589-2489. cityoflakewood.us

- Olympia. Community representatives serve on boards and commissions related to arts and culture, heritage, disabilities, planning, utilities, safety, planning, and equity. 601 4th Ave E, Olympia. olympiawa.gov

- Rainier. Various citizen advisory boards and committees. 102 Rochester St W, Rainier. 360-446-2265. cityofrainierwa.org

- Shelton. City Council. 525 W Cota St, Shelton. 360-426-4491 sheltonwa.gov

- Steilacoom. Boards and commissions. 1030 Roe St, Steilacoom. 253-581-1912. townofsteilacoom.org

- Sumner. Various commissions related to city services. 253-863-8300. 1104 Maple St, Sumner. sumnerwa.gov/commissions.

- Tacoma. Volunteer committees, boards and commissions related to city services such as arts, building, police, contracting, community engagement, public facilities, and other services and initiatives. 747 Market St, Tacoma. 253-591-5000. cityoftacoma.org

- Tenino. City Council. 149 Hodgden St S, Tenino. 360-264-2368. cityoftenino.us

- Tumwater. A variety of advisory boards related to city services and initiatives. 555 Israel Road SW, Tumwater. 360-754-5855. ci.tumwater.wa.us

- University Place. City Council advisory commissions. 3609 Market Place West, Ste 200, University Place. 253-566-5656. cityofup.com

- Yelm. Advisory Boards, Commissions for historic preservation, planning, arts, library, salary, parks, trees, lodging, and law enforcement. 106 2nd St SE, Yelm. 360-458-3244. ci.yelm.wa.us

County Government

Citizen volunteers in county government take active roles in shaping policies, programs, and decisions supporting specific county activities and goals. For information, visit the boards and committees pages of your county website.

- Kitsap County. Volunteer positions on various advisory boards, councils, commissions, and committees. 619 Division St, 4th Floor, Port Orchard. 360-337-7080. kitsapgov.com

- Mason County. Volunteer positions on various advisory boards for county services. 411 N 5th St, Shelton. 360-427-9670. masoncountywa.gov

- Pierce County. Volunteer positions on various boards and commissions for arts and culture, recreation, county services; advisory commissions for communities of Anderson Island, Frederickson, Gig Harbor, Graham, Key Peninsula, Parkland-Spanaway-Midway Island. 930 Tacoma Ave S, Tacoma. piercecountywa.gov

- Thurston County. Volunteer positions on various boards and commissions for arts and culture, recreation, county services. 3000 Pacific Ave SE, Olympia. 360-786-5440. thurstoncountywa.gov

State Government

Visit the State of Washington website (wa.gov/how-to-guides/volunteer-or-give-charity) for links to and information about:

- Volunteer work with state agencies, ranging from administration to hands-on efforts in the field.

- Volunteer work outside at state parks, DNR-managed lands, activities that benefit fish, wildlife, and natural habits, and for Washington Conservation Corps.

- Volunteer work during disasters to help during states of emergency and disasters, or work with Medical Reserve Corps or the Disaster Reservist Program.

- Volunteering work at a food bank.

RESOURCES: HEALTHCARE VOLUNTEERING

South Sound retirees with an interest in healthcare volunteering, the following lists facilities, and organizations to check out within or near Kitsap, Mason, Pierce, and Thurston Counties. Programs may require background checks of volunteers.

Healthcare Organizations

South Sound healthcare providers range from large, multi-hospital and medical care systems to community healthcare organizations that offer free or income-based services.

Kitsap and Mason Counties

- Mason General Hospital, Mason Clinic. Multiple family clinics offering specialty services to all patients. Volunteers extend care in serving the patients, the community, and the staff. 1701 N 13th St, Shelton. 360-426-2653. masongeneral.com

- Peninsula Community Health Services. Services to all regardless of ability to pay at locations listed below. Medical, non-medical, dental volunteer roles. 360-377-3776. pchsweb.org/volunteer

  o Agape Behavioral Health Clinic. 4841 Auto Center Way, Ste 203, Bremerton.

  o Almira Medical and Dental Clinics. 5455 Almira Dr. NE, 5453 Primary Care Dental Clinic Bldg D, Bremerton.

  o Belfair Medical and Dental Clinics. 31 NE State Route 300, Ste 200, Belfair.

  o Clare Ave Medical and Dental Clinics. 2720 Clare Ave, Bremerton.

  o Franklin St Clinic. 727 Franklin St, Shelton.

  o Key Peninsula Medical and Dental Clinics. 11901 137th Ave NW Unit A, Gig Harbor.

  o Kingston Medical and Dental Clinics. 25989 Barber Cut Off Road, Kingston.

  o Mobile Behavioral Health Clinic. Mobile Dental Clinic. Various Kitsap County sites.

  o Mobile Medical and Dental Clinics. Various Kitsap County sites.

- ○ Pendleton Place Medical Clinic. 5454 Kitsap Way, Room 343, Bremerton.
- ○ Port Orchard Medical and Dental Clinics. 320 South Kitsap Blvd, Port Orchard.
- ○ Poulsbo Medical and Dental Clinics. 9705 Viking Ave NW, Ste 201, Poulsbo.
- ○ Quick Response Team. Responses related to substance abuse disorder. 360-801-2020. Mason County.
- ○ Salvation Army Behavioral Health Services. 832 6th St, Stand By Me Room, Bremerton.
- ○ Silverdale Medical Clinic. 3100 Northwest Bucklin Hill Rd, Ste 202, Silverdale. 360-377-3776
- ○ School Based Health Center. North Mason School District. North Mason Community Gym. 300 E. Campus Dr, Belfair.
- ○ School Based Health Centers, Bremerton: Barker Creek. 1400 NE McWilliams Rd, Room 141/143; Bremerton High School, 1500 13th St, Room 114; Esquire Hills Elementary School, 2650 NE John Carlson Rd; Fairview Middle School, 8107 Central Valley Rd NE, Main Office; Mountain View Middle School, 2442 Perry Ave., 6th Grade Bldg, Olympic High School. 7077 Stampede Blvd. NW, Portable H14.
- ○ School Based Health Center. Madrona Heights, 2150 Fircrest Dr SE, Room G-1. Port Orchard.
- ○ School Based Health Center, Silverdale: Klahowya. 7607 NW Newberry Hill Rd, Clinic Room.
- ○ Silverdale Medical and Dental Clinics. 3100 NW Bucklin Hill Rd, Ste 202, Silverdale.
- ○ Sixth St, Medical and Dental Clinics. 616 Sixth St, Bremerton.
- St, Michael Medical Center. 1800 NW Myhre Rd, Silverdale, 360-744-8800. Apply to volunteer at Virginia Mason Franciscan Health. vmfh.org/our-foundations/volunteering
- Virginia Mason Bainbridge Island Medical Center. 1344 Wintergreen Lane NE, Bainbridge Island. 206-842-5632. vmfh.org/find-a-location

Pierce County

- Christ Community Free Clinic. Provides free urgent medical and dental care for uninsured and underinsured. 1 A St NW, Auburn. 253-736-2634. christfreeclinic.org

- Kaiser Permanente Medical Centers. Major Washington healthcare provider. Volunteers staff information desk, transport patients, run errands, help at hospice facilities, many other roles. 206-326-2225. Email: VolunteersKPWA@kp.org.

- Mdc Homeless Service Center. Behavioral health services for economically disadvantaged and homeless people are provided on a sliding scale. 2342 Tacoma Ave. S., Tacoma. 253-597-4194

- Community Health Care. Provides medical, behavioral, and dental healthcare, six locations. Sliding scale. commhealth.org
  - Hilltop Regional Health Center. 1202 Martin Luther King Jr. Way, Tacoma.
  - Kimi & George Tanbara, MD Healthcare Center. 1708 E 44th St, Tacoma.
  - Lakewood Healthcare Center. 10510 Gravelly Lake Dr SW.
  - Parkland Medical Center. 11225 Pacific Ave, Tacoma.
  - Spanaway Healthcare Center. 134 188th St South.
  - Key Medical Center. 15610 89th St Ct NW, Lakebay.

- MultiCare. Major health care organization with 12 hospitals. Volunteers serve in a variety of roles throughout the system. Contact individual facilities. multicare.org/volunteers
  - Mary Bridge Children's Hospital. 317 Martin Luther King Jr. Way, Tacoma. 253-403-1400. marybridge.org/locations/mary-bridge-childrens-hospital
  - MultiCare Allenmore Hospital. 1901 S Union Ave, Tacoma. 253-459-6200. multicare.org/location/allenmore-hospital
  - MultiCare Auburn Medical Center. 202 N Division St, Auburn. 253-833-7711. multicare.org/location/auburn-medical-center
  - MultiCare Covington Medical Center. 17700 SE 272nd St, Covington. 253-372-6500. multicare.org/location/covington-medical-center

- o MultiCare Good Samaritan Hospital. 401 15th Ave SE, Puyallup. 253-697-4000. multicare.org/location/good-samaritan-hospital
- o MultiCare Tacoma General Hospital. 315 Martin Luther King Jr Way, Tacoma. 253-403-1000. multicare.org/location/tacoma-general-hospital

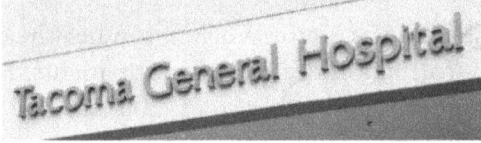

  • Neighborhood Clinic. Provides healthcare to those who cannot afford or access healthcare. Volunteers serve in clinic. 1323 S Yakima Ave, Tacoma. 253-627-6353. neighborhoodclinictacoma.org

- Peninsula Community Health Services. Services to all. Locations in Pierce and Kitsap counties, regardless of ability to pay. Medical, non-medical, dental volunteer roles. 360-377-3776. pchsweb.org/volunteer

- Key Peninsula Medical and Dental Clinics. 11901 137th Ave NW Unit A, Gig Harbor. 360-377-3776. pchsweb.org

- Sea Mar Community Health Center. Provides healthcare to diverse communities in Lakewood, Puyallup, Spanaway, and Tacoma, specializing in service to Latinos. Volunteers serve in a variety of roles. seamar.org/services-pierce. seamar.org/volunteer-program

- Tacoma-Pierce County Health Department. Public health volunteers in administrative services, environmental health, communicable disease control, strengthening families. 3629 South D St, Tacoma. 253-649-1500. tpchd.org/i-want-to-/jobs/volunteer

- Trinity Neighborhood Health Clinic. Volunteer doctors and nurses provide free healthcare in Hilltop Neighborhood. 1615 6th Ave, Tacoma. 253-272-8819. tpctacoma.org/neighborhood-clinic

- Virginia Mason Franciscan Health. Leading health system in state with 10 hospitals and 300 care sites. Apply to volunteer at specific location. See website list. vmfh.org/our-foundations/volunteering

- St. Anthony Hospital. 11567 Canterwood Boulevard NW, Gig Harbor. 253-530-2000
  - o St Clare Hospital. 11315 Bridgeport Way SW, Lakewood. 253-985-1711
  - o St. Joseph Med Center. 1717 South J St, Tacoma. 253-426-4101

o Women's Health Clinic. 1213 S. 11th St, Tacoma. 253-597-4163

Thurston County

- MultiCare Capital Medical Center. 3900 Capital Mall Drive SW, Olympia. 360-754-5858. Volunteers fill a variety of roles throughout the organization. multicare.org/volunteers

- Olympia Free Clinic. Volunteer-based medical clinic for underserved communities. 520 Lilly Rd NE, Bldg 3, Olympia. 360-890-4074 x 3 theolympiafreeclinic.org/volunteer

- Olympia Union Gospel Mission Health Resource Center - Olympia Free Clinic. Volunteers are dental, vision professionals. 309 Washington St, NE, Olympia. 360-943-6400. ougm.org

- Sea Mar Community Health Center. Provides healthcare to diverse communities in Lacey, Olympia, Tumwater, and Yelm. Volunteers serve in a variety of roles. seamar.org/services-thurston

- St. Peter Hospital, Providence. A variety of volunteer positions within many departments. 413 Lilly Rd NE, Olympia. 360-491-9480. 360-493-7482. providence.org

Health-Based Organizations

The following is partial list health-based organizations – those that advance cures and treatment of a specific condition or disease.

- ALS Association Evergreen Chapter. Services and education for people with ALS, their families, caregivers, and healthcare professionals. Volunteers work in office, at outreach, educational and fundraising events. Kent. 425-656-1650. webwa.alsa.org

- Alzheimer's Association Washington State. Involved in research, care, support, education to reduce dementia risk. 19031 33rd Ave West, Ste 301. Lynnwood. 206-363-5500. alz.org/alzwa

- American Cancer Society Washington. Dedicated to eliminating cancer as a major health problem through research, education, advocacy, and service. Seattle. 800-227-2345. cancer.org

- American Diabetes Association Alaska & Washington. Dedicated to diabetes prevention, cure, improving the lives of all people affected by diabetes. 206-282-4616. diabetes.org

- American Heart Association Puget Sound. Dedicated to building healthier lives, free of cardiovascular diseases and stroke. 601 Union St, Ste 2420, Seattle. 206-336-7200. heart.org

- American Stroke Association. 1142 Broadway Ste 120, Tacoma. 253-240-3310. heart.org

- Community Alternatives for People with Autism. Employment support services for people with autism. 12001 Pacific Ave #201, Tacoma. 253-536-2339. capaautism.org

- Diabetes Association of Pierce County. PO Box 110427, Tacoma, 253-272-5134.

- Easter Seals Washington. Provides services for children, adults with autism, other disabilities or special needs. 200 W Mercer St, Ste. 210E, Seattle. 206-281-5700. easterseals.com/washington

- Greater Northwest MS Society. Works to improve quality of life for those with MS and their families. 180 Nickerson St, Ste 100, Seattle. 206-284-4236. nationalmssociety.org/Chapters/WAS

- Kara Lynn Foundation. Supports children and families facing adversity due to various neurological challenges. 230 East Fairfield Court, Shelton. karalynnfoundation.com

- Muscular Dystrophy Association. Dedicated to finding treatments and cures for muscular dystrophy, (ALS) and other neuromuscular diseases. 21905 64th Ave W, Mountlake Terrace, 206-283-2183; 14432 SE Eastgate Way, Bellevue, 425-641-3200. Mda.org

- Parkinson's Foundation Pacific Northwest. Research, support services. 702-847-6603. parkinson.org/PacificNW

Hospice and End-of-Life-Care

The following are hospice organizations in Kitsap, Mason, Pierce, and Thurston Counties. Background checks of volunteers may be required.

- Assured Hospice. 2102 Carriage St SW, Ste D, Olympia. 360-236-9204. lhcgroup.com

- Envision Hospice, Washington. 1818 S Union St, Ste 1A, Tacoma. 206-452-0058; 801 SW 150th St, Ste 102, Burien, 206-452-0058; 181 South 333rd St, Ste C120, Federal Way, 360-350-4875; 7191 Wagner Way NW, Ste 201, Gig Harbor, 360-350-4875. envhh.com

- Franciscan Hospice and Palliative Care. 2901 Bridgeport Way W, University Place. 253-534-7000.

- Hospice Without Borders. Provides palliative care street outreach. 1713 State Ave NE, Olympia. hospicewithoutborders.com

- Kaiser Permanente Home Health and Hospice Services. 206-326-4444. wa-provider.kaiserpermanente.org

- Kindred at Home. Tacoma, 4020 S 56th St #101, 253-475-6862. Puyallup, 2913 NE 5th Ave #202, 253-435-9953.

- MultiCare Home Health & Hospice. 3901 S Fife St, Tacoma. 253-301-6400. multicare.org

- Olympic Adult Family Home and Hospice. 1955 H St, SE, Auburn. 253-545-0259. olympicadultfamilyhomeandhospice.business.site

- Providence Hospice of Seattle. 2811 S 102nd St, Ste 200, Tukwila. 206-320-4000. providence.org/locations/wa/hospice-of-seattle

- Providence SoundHomeCare and Hospice. 4200 6th Ave SE, Ste 201, Lacey. 360-459-8311. providence.org

- Puget Sound Home Health and Hospice. 111 Tumwater Blvd SE Ste A302, Tumwater. 360-839-2122. pugetsoundhh.com

- Puget Sound Home Health and Hospice. 4002 Tacoma Mall Blvd Ste 204, Tacoma. 253-581-9410. pugetsoundhh.com

- Virginia Mason Franciscan Health. 2901 Bridgeport Way W, University Place. 253-534-7000. vmfh.org

RESOURCES: HIKING AND WALKING

Listed below are sources of information about areas to hike and walk in and near communities in Kitsap, Mason, Pierce, and Thurston Counties. Visit their websites for more information.

Find Hikes in Natural, Wildlife and Scenic Areas

Kitsap and Mason Counties

- Bremerton Parks & Recreation. Parks system map and guide. bremertonwa.gov

- Explore Hood Canal. Describes trails to beaches, islands, creeks, primeval forests, lakes, historic sites, and more. explorehoodcanal.com/thingstodo/hiking

- Kitsap County. Provides links to trail maps, public parks and trails, national water trails, and outdoor recreation. visitkitsap.com

- Kitsap Trail Guide. Full size hiking and mountain bike trails maps and descriptions of the area. kitsaptrailguide.com/parks-and-trails.

- Kitsap County Parks Trail Maps. Includes maps of Anderson Landing, Banner Forest, Guillemot Cove, Hansville Greenway, Illahee Preserve Heritage Park, Newberry Hill Heritage Park, North Kitsap Heritage Park, Port Gamble Trail, South Kitsap Regional Park Forester. kitsapgov.com/parks/Pages/TrailMaps

- Kitsap Outdoors. Organizes introductory and advanced hikes, snow travel, camping, backpacking and bikes. Silverdale. meetup.com/kitsap-outdoors

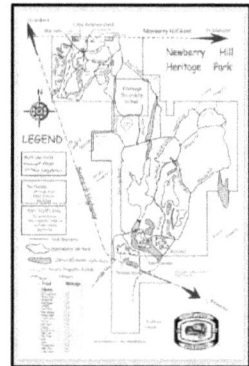

- Kitsap Trail Guide. Guide to hiking trails, walking paths, and mountain bike routes in and around Bremerton, Silverdale, and Port Orchard. kitsaptrailguide.com

- Mason County Parks and Trails. Descriptions and maps of area trails. masoncountywa.gov/parks

- Mason County Parks and Trails Maps. Links to maps are available on the county website. Locations and descriptions of parks and trails and recreation areas. Mason County's Parks. Includes maps of Oakland Bay Park, Mason County Recreation North and South biking, kayaking, and diving, Hood Canal, Shelton, West Mason, Olympics. masoncountywa.gov/forms/parks/trails_map.pdf

- North Kitsap Trails Association. Involved in regional system of land and water trails connecting communities, parks & open space, promotes stewardship and enhance livability. Maps and trails. northkitsaptrails.org

Pierce County

- City of Tacoma. Hiking and Biking Trails. Descriptions of trails in Metro parks, Pierce County, and Tacoma. cityoftacoma.org/visitors

- Pierce County Trails. Links to parks, trails throughout the county. piercecountywa.gov

- National Park Service. Descriptions, regulations, and maps of wilderness camping and hiking at Mount Rainier. nps.gov/mora

- PenMet Parks. Information and details about many local parks and trails. 5717 Wollochet Dr NW #3, Gig Harbor. 253-858-3400. penmetparks.org

- Tacoma-Pierce County Walking Guide. Information and details about many local parks and trails. Also includes tips on how to start a walking program. tpchd.org/healthy-people/physical-activity/walking-guide
  - o City of Puyallup Walking Map. Various walking routes, walk tips.
  - o Pierce County Parks and Recreation. Local resources for recreation activities.
  - o Community Walkability. Resources to improve your neighborhood's walkability.

- Walk Tacoma. Free in-person or self-guided walking tours around Tacoma. downtownonthego.com/go
- Washington's National Park Fund. Mt. Rainier National Park. Hiking maps and descriptions of trails in Mt. Rainier National Park.

Thurston County

- City of Lacey. Walking and Biking Trails. Parks and trails maps. laceyparks.org/parks-trails/trails
- City of Tumwater. Parks & Trails Map. ci.tumwater.wa.us/departments/parks-recreation
- City of Olympia. Great Places to Walk. Walking maps of city, trails, neighborhoods, waterfront. olympiawa.gov/community
- Thurston County. Lists and describes walking, hiking trails within county-owned, city-owned, and other areas. thurstoncountywa.gov
- Thurston Regional Planning Council. Walking maps. 2411 Chandler Court SW, Olympia. Olympia Walking Map. Includes trails, landmarks, public art and more. 360-956-7575. trpc.org
- Walk Olympia. Descriptions and maps of loop trails through the beaches, woods, and prairies near Olympia. walkolympia.com

Other Resources

- All Trails. Search online for hiking and walking trails in the US by city, park, or trail name. alltrails.com
- Washington's National Park Fund. Official philanthropic partner to Mount Rainer, North Cascades, and Olympic National Parks. Includes information about national parks. wnpf.org
- Washington Trails Association. Information about hiking trails written by local hiking experts. Search for hikes by name, region, features, and rating. wta.org/go-outside/hikes

Outdoor Hiking, Walking, Snow Sports Groups

A variety of walking and hiking groups, including Meetup groups, throughout the South Sound offer options for walkers and hikers of all abilities and levels. Find current meetup descriptions and schedules at Meetup.com. Search by city, then by interest such as fitness, exercise, walking, hiking, etc. Sign up, show up.

Washington State

- Evergreen State Walking Club. Association of volkssport clubs in the state. Clubs sponsor neighborhood walks; promotes walking and safe, convenient, and attractive walking areas. Area groups include:
  - o Emerald City Wanderers. Group walks of varied distances and mapped walks in and around Greater Seattle. emeraldcitywanderers.org
  - o Interlaken Trailblazers Walking Club. Group walks of varied distances and mapped walks in and around Greater Seattle. interlakentrailblazers.org
- Northwest Nature Hikes, Workshops, Camps & Classes. Activities in north and central Washington. Renton. meetup.com/northwest-nature-hikes-seattle-area-cascades-and-olympics
- REI Classes and Events. Sponsors outdoor classes, guided day trips and virtual events. Search by location. rei.com/events
- Sound Steppers. Group walks of varied distances and mapped walks in areas north of Seattle. Soundsteppers.org
- The Mountaineers. Offers outdoor trips, courses, books, and events for all ages and experience levels in Pacific Northwest. Seasonal catalog. 7700 Sand Point Way NE, Seattle. 206-521-6000. mountaineers.org
- Walking Volkssport NW. Group walks of varied distances and mapped walks in northwest Seattle area. meetup.com/walkers-574
- Washington Outdoor Women. Teaches traditional outdoor skills to women and girls through a variety of classes and workshops. Belleview. 425-455-1986. washingtonoutdoorwomen.org
- Washington Trails Association. A group of hikers who like to explore and maintain public lands. Website includes maps and information about hiking in Washington state. 705 2nd Ave, Ste 300 Seattle. 206)-625-1367. wta.org

Kitsap and Mason Counties

- Easy Outdoor Buddies of North Kitsap. Group gatherings for easy outdoor activities such as forest hiking, biking, kayaking, swimming. meetup.com/easyoutdoorbuddies

- Kitsap Outdoors. Meetup activities include hiking, snow travel, camping, backpacking, and biking. meetup.com/Kitsap-Outdoors

- North Kitsap Trails Association. Involved in regional system of land and water trails connecting communities, parks and open space, promotes stewardship and enhances livability. Maps and trails. northkitsaptrails.org

- Olympic and Kitsap Peninsula Walking/Hiking. Meetup group Fitness walking group doing 10K and longer/shorter hikes. Port Angeles. meetup.com/meetup-group-xevtilbx

- Peninsula Wilderness Club. Active outdoor pursuits: hiking, biking, backpacking, climbing, kayaking, skiing. Bremerton. pwckitsap.org

Pierce County

- Birding and More with the Tahoma Audubon Society. Tacoma. meetup.com/birding-with-the-tahoma-audubon-society

- Creaky Knees. Hikes, weekends away, longer trips for those who prefer a slower pace. Milton. meetup.com/creaky-knees-meetup

- Early Bird Adventures. Hiking and camping year-round in Washington forests and other activities. Puyallup. meetup.com/early-bird-adventures

- Pathfinders. Hikes on Pacific Northwest Trails to enjoy nature and build friendships. Tacoma. tacoma-hiking-meetup-group

- Tahoma Audubon Society. Advocates for the protection of wildlife through education and activities. University Place. Adriana Hess Audubon Center, 2917 Morrison Rd W, University Place. 253-565-9278. tahomaaudubon.org

- Tacoma Outdoors Adventures. Sponsors outdoor activities such as biking, hiking, camping, snowshoeing, and social events. All levels. Lakewood. meetup.com/tacomaoutdoors

- Tacoma Pierce County Physical Activity Resources. Website of resources (listed below) for physical activity. tpchd.org/healthy-people/physical-activity

- Tacoma Unlikely Walkers & Hikers. Supportive, welcoming walking, hiking activities. Tacoma. meetup.com/tacoma-unlikely-hiker

Thurston County

- Black Hills Audubon Society. Chapter of National Audubon Society representing Lewis, Mason, and Thurston counties. Olympia. 360-352-7299. blackhills-audubon.org

- Fit Fun and Friendly Olympians. Holds hikes, walks, cross-country skiing, snowshoeing, trail running, and social activities. All levels. Olympia. meetup.com/fit-fun-and-friendly-olympians

- Olympia Outdoor and Fun Time Adventurers. Sponsors outdoor/fitness events including walking/hiking, fishing, camping, kayaking, snowshoeing, biking. Olympia. meetup.com/olympia-outdoor-adventurers-oofta

- Olympia Dragon Boating Meetup. Dragon boating for all backgrounds and fitness levels. Coaching and equipment provided. meetup.com/olympia-dragon-boating-meetup

- Outdoor Adventure and Recreation Group. Social group, people who enjoy new places, exploring. Olympia. meetup.com/hiking-235

- South Sound Birders. Sponsors field trips, wildlife classes, lectures, and other events, many in connection with Black Hills Audubon Society. meetup.com/south-sound-birders

- South Sound Walkers Meetup. Group walks of varied distances and locations in and around Thurston county. meetup.com/South-Sound-Walkers

Townie Walks, Historical Walks

Walk and learn about your city, town, or historical area in self-guided, mapped routes found in several communities.

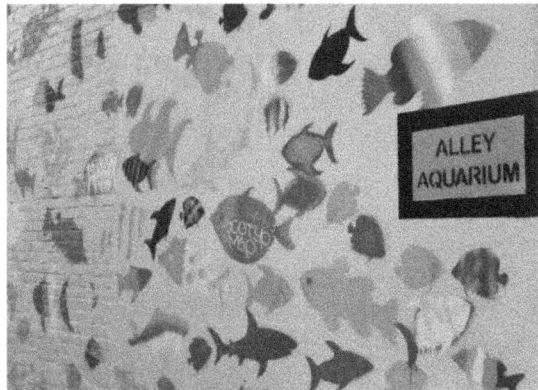

- Bainbridge Island Self-Guided Tours. Maps to explore downtown Winslow and other areas. bainbridgehistory.org/visit/plan-a-visit

- Bremerton Historic Sites Walking Tour. Kitsap History Museum. 280 4th St, Bremerton. 360-479-6226. kitsapmuseum.org

- Downtown on the Go. Various walking, biking, and other transportation activities around Tacoma. downtownonthego.com

- Evergreen State Walking Club. Association of volkssport clubs in the state. Clubs sponsor neighborhood walks; promotes walking and safe, convenient, and attractive walking areas. See the *Outdoor Hike, Walk, Snow Sports Groups* section above to find local groups.

- Family Nature Walks. Naturalist-led walks explore various Tacoma parks. metroparkstacoma.org/activities-and-sports

- History Walking Tours. Self-Guided Tours in historical areas of Tacoma. Sponsored by Office of Historic Preservation. cityoftacoma.org

- Historical Touring Map of Lakewood. Map and description of historical sites in Lakewood. cityoflakewood.us

- History Link's Walking Tours. Self-guided walking tours of Seattle and other areas of historic interest. historylink.tours

- Olympia's Hidden Histories. A series of self-guided walking tours created by Evergreen State College. Search online for Olympia's Hidden Histories Walking Tour.

- Olympia Historic Walking Tours. Download descriptions and maps of historic walking tours around Olympia. olympiawa.gov

- Olympia Historical Society Walking Tours. Walking tours of areas of historic interest. Links to other historic maps, walks. olympiahistory.org

- Tacoma Nature Center Interpretive Walks. Self-guided Wetland Walk, History Walk, Forest Walk.

- Port Orchard Walking Map. Of historic homes, museums, art gallery, theater. portorchardwa.gov/port-orchard-walking-map

- Poulsbo Historical Society. Historical walks of Poulsbo. 360-516-3975. poulsbohistory.com

- Visit Kitsap Peninsula. Descriptions of urban trails. visitkitsap.com/bridgetobridge

RESOURCES: LEARNING PLACES

This section includes lists of a variety of types of learning places where you can attend classes and lectures and learn from others, such as colleges and universities, libraries, adult enrichment programs, parks programs, and senior and community centers.

Colleges, Universities

The following is a list of credit and non-credit community colleges and universities. Many also offer a variety of classes through community education programs.

- Belleview College.
  Community education. TELOS Retiree programs. Online classes.
  3000 Landerholm Cir SE, Bellevue. 425-564-1000.
  bellevuecollege.edu

- Central Washington University. Pierce County. Also offers a continuing education program. 9401 Farwest Dr SW, Lakewood. 253-964-6636. cwu.edu/pierce-county

- Clover Park Technical College. 4500 Steilacoom Blvd SW, Lakewood. 253-589-5800; 17214 110th Ave. E, Puyallup, 253-583-8904. cptc.edu

- Edmonds College Continuing Education. Offers Creative Retirement Institute classes for retirees. Online and in-person classes. 425-640-1459 edmonds.edu

- Evergreen State College. Offers 60+ Tuition Waver Program. 2700 Evergreen Parkway NW, Olympia. 360-867-6000. evergreen.edu

- Green River College. Offers Prime Time program for adult learners and continuing and community education. Online and in-person classes. 12401 SE 320th St, Auburn. 253-833-9111. greenriver.edu

- Lifetime Learning Center. Workshops, lectures, and events for older adults. 3841 NE 123rd St, Seattle. 206-949-8882. lifetimelearningcenter.org

- North Seattle College. Continuing and community education. 9600 College Way North. Seattle. 206-934-3600

- Northwest Indian College. 12501 Yelm Hwy SE, Olympia. 360-456-5221. nwic.edu/about-nwic

- Olympic College, Shelton. Also offers community education. 937 W Alpine Way, Shelton. 360-432-5400. olympic.edu

- Osher Lifelong Learning Institute at the University of Washington. Courses, lectures, study groups, special events for adults over age 50. In-person and Zoom courses. Seattle. osher.uw.edu/programs

- Pacific Lutheran University. Also offers continuing education. 12180 Park Ave S, Tacoma. 253-535-7411. Tacoma. plu.edu.

- Pierce College. Community and continuing education program.1601 39th Ave SE Puyallup. 253-840-8452. pierce.ctc.edu/ce

- Saint Martin's University. Community programs. 5000 Abbey Way SE, Lacey. 360-491-4700. stmartin.edu

- Seattle Central College. Continuing and community education program. Offers Broadway Hill Club: Classes for Seniors. Online and in-person classes. 701 Broadway Ave, Seattle. 206-934-3800. seattlecentral.edu

- Shoreline Community College. Continuing education/lifelong learning programs. 16101 Greenwood Ave N, Shoreline. 206-546-410. shoreline.edu

- South Puget Sound Community College. Offers continuing education program. Olympia, 2011 Mottman Rd SW. 360-596-5200; Lacey, 4220 6th Ave SE. 360-709-2000. spscc.edu

- South Seattle College. Senior adult education classes with reduced credit price. 6000 16th Ave SW, Seattle. 206-934-3800. southseattle.edu

- Tacoma Community College. Offers continuing education and a personal interests program. 6501 South 19th St, Tacoma. 3993 Hunt St NW, Gig Harbor. 253-566-5000. tacomacc.edu

- University of Puget Sound. Also offers a Senior University program. 1500 N Warner St, Tacoma. pugetsound.edu/senior-university.

- University of Washington. Tacoma. Offers continuing education program. 1900 Commerce St, Tacoma. 253-692-4742. tacoma.uw.edu

Libraries

Below are listings of libraries and library systems where you can browse schedules of classes, lectures, events, historical talks, and many other types of programs.

Kitsap and Mason Counties

- Kitsap Regional Library Foundation. Serves Kitsap residents through nine locations, online access to library materials and services, and home delivery to individuals with barriers to using their Library location. krl.org/about-kitsap-regional-library.

    o Bainbridge Island. 1270 Madison Ave N, 206-451-5050. krl.org/bainbridge-island

    o Downtown Bremerton. 612 5th St, 360-447-5420. krl.org/downtown-bremerton

    o Kingston. 26159 Dulay Rd NE, 360-860-5070. krl.org/kingston

    o Little Boston. 31980 Little Boston Road NE. 360-860-5080. krl.org/little-boston

    o Manchester. 8067 E Main St, 360-447-5430. krl.org/manchester

    o Port Orchard. 87 Sidney Ave, 360-447-5440. krl.org/port-orchard

    o Poulsbo. 700 NE Lincoln Road, 360) 447-5450. krl.org/poulsbo

    o Silverdale. 3650 NW Anderson Hill Rd, Ste 101, 360-447-5470. krl.org/silverdale

    o Sylvan Way. 1301 Sylvan Way, 360-447-5480. krl.org/sylvan-way

- Kitsap Regional Library Friends Groups. Holds fundraising events such as book sales to raise money for items not in a library's budget.

Also sponsors other library programs and events. Libraries with friends groups include (contact library for information):

- o Bainbridge Island Friends of the Library
- o East Bremerton Friends of the Library
- o Kingston Friends of the Library
- o Manchester Friends of the Library
- o Port Orchard Friends of the Library
- o Poulsbo Friends of the Library
- o Silverdale Friends of the Library

- Hoodsport Timberland Library. 40 N Schoolhouse Hill Rd, Hoodsport. 360-877-9339. trl.org/locations/hoodsport

- North Mason. 23081 NE State Rte 3, Belfair. 360-275-3232. trl.org/locations/north-mason

- Shelton Timberland Library. 710 Alder St, Shelton. 360-426-1362. trl.org/locations/Shelton

Pierce County

- Pierce County Library System. piercecountylibrary.org

  - o Administrative Center and Library. 3005 112th St E, Tacoma, 253-548-3300

  - o Bonney Lake. 18501 90th St E, 253-548-3308.

  - o Buckley. 123 S. River Ave, 253-548-3310 or 360-829-0300.

  - o Eatonville. 205 Center St W, 253-548-3311 or 360-832-6011.

  - o Fife. 6622 20th St E, 253-548-3323.

  - o Gig Harbor. 4424 Point Fosdick Dr NW, 253- 548-3305.

  - o Graham. 9202 224th St E, 253-548-3322.

  - o Lakewood, 6300 Wildaire Rd SW, 253-548-3302. Tillicum, 14916 Washington Ave SW, 253-548-3314.

  - o Orting. 202 Washington Ave S, 253-548-3312.

  - o Parkland/Spanaway. 13718 Pacific Ave S, Tacoma, 253-548-3304

- o South Hill. 15420 Meridian E, 253-548-3303
- o Summit. 5107 112th St E, Tacoma, 253-548-3321
- Tacoma Public Library. Locations: Main-1102 Tacoma Ave. South, 253-280-2800; 3411 S 56th St, 253-280-2960; 215 S 56th St, 280-2930; 3523 E G St, 253-280-2950; 7001 6th Ave, 253-280-2970; 3772 N 26th St, 253-280-2980; 765 S 84th St, 253-280-2910; 215 S 56th St, 253-280-2930; 212 Browns Point Blvd., 253-280-2920; 1721 E 56th St, 253-404-3990.

Thurston County

- Hawks Prairie Timberland Library. 8205 Martin Way Ste B, Lacey. 360-252-9658. trl.org/locations/hawks-prairie

- Lacey Timberland Library. 500 College St SE, Lacey 360-491-3860. trl.org/locations/lacey

- Olympia Timberland Library. 313 8th Ave SE, Olympia. 360-352-0595. trl.org/locations/olympia

- The Mountaineers. Olympia. Outdoor resources. Open to members. mountaineers.org

- Tenino Timberland Library. 172 Central Ave W, Tenino. 360-539-3329. trl.org/locations/tenino

- Tumwater Timberland Library. 7023 New Market St, Tumwater. 360-943-7790. trl.org/locations/Tumwater

- Washington State Law Library. 243 Israel Road SE, Tumwater. 360-357-2136. courts.wa.gov/library

- Yelm Timberland Library. 210 Prairie Park St, Yelm. 360-539-3330. trl.org/locations/yelm

Parks and Recreation

Below are listings of parks and recreation programs in or near Kitsap, Mason, Pierce, and Thurston Counties. Check the websites and activity calendars of parks and recreation programs for adult group classes and activities such as creative arts, crafts, music, dance, outdoor activities, games, history, and more.

Kitsap and Mason Counties

- Bainbridge Island Metro Park & Recreation District. Fitness, arts, music, and hobby classes. 11700 NE Meadowmeer Circle, Bainbridge Island. 206-842-2302. biparks.org

- Bremerton Parks & Recreation. 680 Lebo Blvd, Bremerton. 360-473-5305. bremertonwa.gov

- Kitsap County Parks Department. 1195 NW Fairgrounds Rd, Bremerton. 360-337-5350. kitsapgov.com

- Mason County Parks. 411 N 5th St, Shelton. 360-427-9670. masoncountywa.gov/parks

- Poulsbo Parks and Recreation. Fitness and classes. 19540 Front St, NE, Poulsbo. 360-779-9898. cityofpoulsbo.com

- Shelton Parks & Recreation. Shelton Civic Center, 525 West Cota St, 360-432-5106. sheltonwa.gov

Pierce County

- Dupont Parks & Recreation. Classes, senior programs. 1700 Civic 98327. 253-964-8121. dupontwa.gov

- Fircrest Parks and Recreation. Classes and active adult program. 115 Ramsdell St, Fircrest, 253-564-8901. cityoffircrest.net

- Lakewood Parks & Recreation. Classes and senior programs. Activity center. City Hall, 6000 Main St SW. 253-589-2489. cityoflakewood.us

- Metro Parks Tacoma. Wide variety of arts, culture, music, fitness, and other classes. 4702 S 19th St, Tacoma. 4702 S. 19th St, Tacoma, 253-305-1000. metroparkstacoma.org

- PenMet Parks. Senior educational and recreational programs. 5717 Wollochet Dr NW #3, Gig Harbor. 253-858-3400. penmetparks.org

- Pierce County Parks & Recreation. Wide variety of fitness and recreation classes. 930 Tacoma Ave S, Tacoma. (253) 798-4199. piercecountywa.gov

- Puyallup Parks and Recreation. Puyallup Recreation Center. Classes and senior Programs. 808 Valley Ave NW. 253-841-5457. cityofpuyallup.org

- University Place Parks Department. 3609 Market Place West, Ste 200, University Place. 253-566-5656. cityofup.com

Thurston County

- Lacey Parks, Culture & Recreation. A variety of cultural and fitness programs. 420 College St SE, Lacey. 360-491-0857. laceyparks.org

- Olympia Parks, Arts & Recreation. Arts and fitness classes. 222 Columbia St NW, Olympia. 360-753-8380. olympiawa.gov

- Tumwater Parks and Recreation. A variety of adult fitness and enrichment classes, senior programs and activities. 555 Israel Rd SW, Tumwater. 360-754-5855. ci.tumwater.wa.us/departments/parks-recreation-department

Senior and Community Centers

Area Community and senior and adult community centers offer classes, programs, and other learning opportunities on many topics. For a listing of area community centers, see *RESOURCES: SENIOR SERVICES, Senior and Community Centers*, on page 267.

Healthcare Centers and Hospitals

Many medical centers offer free and inexpensive classes on a variety of healthy living topics. See *RESOURCES: HEALTHCARE VOLUNTEERING, Healthcare Organizations* on page 219 for a list of area medical facilities. Visit their websites and search for classes.

City, County, State Government

Various departments of city, county, or state governments may offer classes and learning events related to their services such as gardening, safety, outdoor topics, and more. For a list of government websites, see *RESOURCES: GOVERNMENT SERVICE* on page 216.

RESOURCES: LITERARY ARTS: WHERE TO READ, WRITE

The following literary arts organizations provide resources for readers, writers, and authors over a wide variety of genres, interests, and media.

Bookstores

Looking for your next read and other book lovers? Book clubs pop up everywhere. Good places to check are your local bookstores, many with book and author events; many can also direct you to book clubs in other places. Bookstores in Kitsap, Mason, Pierce, and Thurston Counties include:

- A Good Book Café. Quirky local bookstore. 1014 Main St, Sumner. 235-891-9682. agoodbooksumner.com

- A Novel Bookstore. Events, book clubs. 305 1st St S, Yelm. 360-458-4722. yelmsnovelbookstore.com

- Ballast Book Company. Book clubs, author/book events. 409 Pacific Ave Unit 202, Bremerton. 360-626-3430. ballastbookco.com

- Barnes & Noble Booksellers. Author/book events. 5711 Main St SW, Lakewood, 253-983-0852; 31530 Black Lake Blvd SW, Olympia. 360-534-0388. stores.barnesandnoble

- Browsers Bookshop. Independent bookstore. Author/book events, 107 Capitol Way N, Olympia. 360-357-7462. browsersolympia.com

- Elliott Bay Book Company. Hosts author events. 1521 10th Ave, Seattle. 206-624-6600. elliottbaybook.com

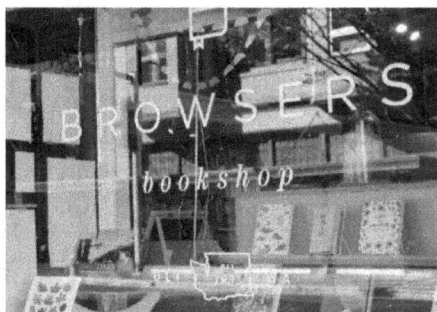

- Gig Harbor Book Company. Used books. 3226 Harborview Dr, Gig Harbor. 253-970-9899.

- Invitation Bookshop. Book club. Events. 5125 Olympic Dr, Ste 1-4, Gig Harbor. 253-432-4566. invitationbookshop.com

- King's Books. Community oriented bookstore. Book/author events, several book clubs, community gatherings. 218 St. Helens Ave, Tacoma. 253-272-8801. Tacoma. kingsbookstore.com

- Last Word Books. Independent bookstore. 501 4th Ave, East Olympia. 360-786-9673. lastwordbooks.org

- No Dearth of Books. Book and reading events. Family-owned. Nautical, Pacific Northwest titles. 7803 Pioneer Way, Gig Harbor. 253-853-3355. nodearthofbooks.com

- OrcaBooks Co-op. Member-owned, worker-run cooperative. Book and reading events. 315 5th Ave SE, Olympia. 360-352-0123. orcabooks.com

Libraries

Libraries and library systems offer a variety of book clubs, author/book events and other reading activities. For a list of libraries, see *RESOURCES: LEARNING PLACES, Libraries* on page 235.

Community Colleges, Parks and Rec

A variety of writing programs and classes are offered at area community colleges and parks programs. For more information, visit their websites, browse their seasonal catalogs, and search for writing programs and classes. See *RESOURCES: LEARNING PLACES, Colleges, Universities* on page 233 and *Parks and Recreation* on page 237.

Writing Groups, Conferences

Many area writing groups offer opportunities to write, learn, and publish for all writing genres. The following is a list of writers groups resources in and near Kitsap, Mason, Pierce, and Thurston Counties.

- Bainbridge Artisan Resource Network (BARN). Studio home for writers, other creatives disciplines. 8890 Three Tree Lane NE, Bainbridge Island. 206-842-4475. bainbridgebarn.org

- Cascadia Poetics Lab. Poetry community sponsors workshops, festivals, and other opportunities for poets. Hosts the Cascadia Poetry Festival in October. Seattle. cascadiapoeticslab.org

- Clarion West. Provides writers of all backgrounds with instruction to bring speculative fiction in various genres to light. Seattle. 206-322-9083. clarionwest.org/about/mission-vision

- Chuckanut Writers Conference. June. Village Books and Paper Dreams. Bellingham. 360-671-2626. chuckanutwritersconference.com

- Edmonds College. Classes through Creative Retirement Institute. 20000 68th Ave W, Lynnwood. 425-640-1459. edmonds.edu

- Emerald City Romance Writers. Provides growth, support, inspiration, and education; helps writers in the romance genre get published. Seattle/Puget Sound. emeraldcityromancewriters.org

- Greater Gig Harbor Literary Society. Coordinate events for authors at local venues. facebook.com/groups/910909713115967

- Hedgebrook is a global community of women writers and people seeking extraordinary books, poetry, plays, films, music by women. Retreats. Annual conference. Whidbey Island. hedgebrook.org

- Hugo House. Literary arts organization for all levels of writers and readers. Classes, events, coaching, and consultation in many genres. 1634 11th Ave, Seattle. 206-322-7030. hugohouse.org

- Imprint Bookstore Workshops. Workshops and classes for writers. 820 Water St, Port Townsend. 360-379-2617. imprintbookstore.com

- Kitsap Literary Arts and Writers. Group of writers who discuss publishing (both traditional and e-pub), platforming. facebook.com/KLAWteam

- Mystery Writers Northwest. Organization for writers, readers, and professionals in the mystery and crime-writing fields. mysterywritersnorthwest.org

- North Seattle College. Continuing education writing classes. 9600 College Way N, Seattle. 206-934-3705. conted.northseattle.edu

- Pacific Northwest Writers Association. Community of writers provides education, accessibility to publishing industry. Workshops, magazine, annual conference. Issaquah. 425-673-2665 pnwa.org

- Pierce College. Community and continuing education program. 1601 39th Ave SE Puyallup. 253-840-8452. pierce.ctc.edu/ce

- Puget Sound Writers Guild. Meets primarily as a critique group. 500 College Street NE, Lacey. 360-438-1771. pugetsoundwritersguild.org

- The Writer's Workshop. Offers a variety of online writing classes, travel writing, online writing. Creative writing classes. thewritersworkshop.net

- Timberland Regional Libraries. Library system sponsors a number of book clubs at libraries in Mason and Thurston Counties. trl.org/

- Sciworthy. Resources, courses for science writers. learn.sciworthy.com

- SCRiB Lab. Free online classes, events for writers, all genres. spl.org

- Seattle Arts & Lecture Series. Literary series features a lineup of authors. Online and in-person. lectures.org

- Seattle Central College. Continuing education classes in writing. 1701 Broadway, Seattle. 206-934-5448 ce.seattlecentral.edu

- Seattle Writing Workshop. May. One day workshop on various writing, publishing topics.theseattlewritingworkshop.com

- Society of Children's Book Writers and Illustrators of Western Washington. Programs, retreats, and conference for adults writing for children and teens. penandstory.com

- University of Washington Continuing Education. Variety of fiction, nonfiction and editing programs. 4311 11th Ave NE, Seattle. 206-543-2310. pce.uw.eduv

- Whatcom Community College Continuing Education. 237 W Kellog Rd, Bellingham. 360-383-3200. whatcom.edu

- Willamette Writers. August. Community of writers, all genres, screenwriters; chapter meetings, annual conference. 5331 S Macadam Ave, Ste 258, PMB 215, Portland, OR. 971-200-5385. willamettewriters.org

- Write in the Harbor Writer's Conference. November. Tacoma Community College, 3393 Hunt St NW, Gig Harbor. 253-566-5000. tacomacc.edu

- Write on the Sound Conference. October. Annual writing conference focused on the craft of writing. 700 Main St, Edmonds. 425-771-0228. edmondswa.gov

- Writers Connection. Provides resources, referrals, and information for all writers. Newsletter. writersconnection.org

RESOURCES: MUSEUMS, HISTORICAL SITES, SOCIETIES

Below are listings of museums and historical sites in and near King, Kitsap, Mason, Pierce, and Thurston Counties.

For more information about location, hours, special events, programs, and lectures, as well as volunteer opportunities, visit the organization's website.

State of Washington

Washington Department of Archaeology & Historic Preservation. *Visit Historic Places* provides a listing of must-see historic places in Washington State. Advocates for preservation of historic buildings, structures, sites, objects, and districts. 1110 S Capitol Way, Ste 30, Olympia. 360-586-3065. dahp.wa.gov

King County

- Art Gallery North Seattle College. Exhibits that demonstrate cultural and artistic diversity. 9600 College Way N Seattle. 206-528-4557. artgallery.northseattle.edu

- Burke Museum. Focus on Northwest Native art and cultural pieces, and natural history collections. University of Washington, 4303 Memorial Way NE, Seattle. 206-543-7907. burkemuseum.org

- Ballard Historical Society. Preserves culture and history of Ballard neighborhood. www.ballardhistory.org

- Ballard Locks Museum/Visitor Center. Busiest locking system in the US. 3015 NW 54th St, Ballard. 206-783-7059. ballardlocks.org

- Belleview Arts Museum. Art museum of supporting diverse experiences and engagement in arts, craft, and design. 510 Bellevue Way NE, Bellevue. 425-519-0770. bellevuearts.org

- Bill & Melinda Gates Foundation Discovery Center. 440 5th Ave N, Seattle. Interactive exhibition/global health innovations. Free. discovergates.org

- Black Diamond Museum of History. Black Diamond Historical Society. Restored railroad depot/museum 32527 Railroad Ave, Black Diamond. 360-886-2142. blackdiamondmuseum.org

- Black Heritage Society. Preserves the history and art of Black people in Washington State. 206-324-1126 x190. bhswa.org/wordpress

- Burke Museum of Natural History and Culture. Official state museum of natural and cultural collections. 4300 15th Ave NE, Seattle. 206-543-7907. burkemuseum.org

- Center for Wooden Boats. Historic wooden sailboats, rowboats, and others. 1010 Valley St, Seattle. 206-382-2628. cwb.org

- Center on Contemporary Art. Contemporary exhibits and programs. 114 Third Ave S, Seattle. 206-728-1980. cocaseattle.org

- Chihuly Garden and Glass. Showcases the studio glass of Dale Chihuly. 305 Harrison St, Seattle. 206-753-4940. chihulygardenandglass.com

- Coast Guard Museum Northwest. U.S. Coast Guard ship models, uniforms, photos, and artifacts. Pier 36, 1519 Alaskan Way S, Seattle. 206-217-6993. rexmwess.com/cgpatchs/cogardmuseum

- College Gallery/Shoreline Community College. Continuing education/lifelong learning programs. 16101 Greenwood Ave N, Shoreline. 206-546-410. shoreline.edu/visual-arts-dept/gallery

- Des Moines Historical Society Museum. Free. Exhibits of artifacts, images, and monographs of Des Moines (WA) history. 730 South 225th St, Des Moines. 206-824-5226. dmhs.org

- Duwamish Longhouse and Cultural Center. Traditional longhouse, museum, art gallery. 705 West Marginal Way SW, Seattle. 206-431-1582. duwamishtribe.org

- Eastside Heritage Center. Preserves the history and stories of the people of Seattle's Eastside neighborhoods. 11660 Main St, Bellevue. 425-450-1049. eastsideheritagecenter.org

- Edmonds Historical Museum. Free. Edmonds history told through exhibits and artifacts. 118 5th Ave N, Edmonds. 425-774-0900. historicedmonds.org

- Frye Art Museum. Paintings, sculpture from 19th century to present. Free. 704 Terry Ave, Seattle. 206-622-9250. fryemuseum.org

- Georgetown Steam Plant. Steam engines in the former power plant. Georgetown Steam Plant. 6605 13th Ave S, Seattle 206-763-2542. seattle.gov/city-light

- Giant Shoe Museum. Collection of giant shoes. Pike Place Market, Seattle. 206-623-2870. wasgs.org

- Greater Kent Historical Society Museum. Operates the Kent Museum of local history. 855 E Smith St, Kent. 253-854-4330. kenthistoricalmuseum.org/

- Henry Art Gallery. Art museum of University of Washington. 15th Ave NE & NE 41st St, Seattle. 206-543-2280. Contemporary art. henryart.org

- Hydroplane & Race Boat Museum. Museum devoted to powerboat racing. 5917 South 196th St, Kent. 206-764-9453. thunderboats.org

- Jack Straw New Media Gallery. Combines sound, digital media, and other genres. 4261 Roosevelt Way NE. Seattle. 206-634-0919. jackstraw.org

- Japanese Cultural & Community Center. Operates Northwest Nikkei Museum. Cultural events and activities. 1414 S. Weller St, Seattle. 206-568-7114. jcccw.org

- Kent Arts Commission Gallery. Exhibits by diverse artists in solo or small groups. 400 W Gowe St, Kent. 253-856-5050. kentwa.gov

- KidsQuest Children's Museum. Offers a variety of kids learning opportunities.1116 108th Ave NE, Bellevue. 425-637-8100. kidsquestmuseum.org

- Kirkland Arts Center. Community education, art studios, exhibitions. 620 Market St, Kirkland. 425-822-7161. kirklandartscenter.org

- Kirkland Heritage Society and Museum. Historical artifacts and stories of Kirkland history. 203 Market St, Kirkland. kirklandheritage.com

- Korean American Historical Society. Heritage of Koreans living in the U.S. and abroad. Society's collection housed at Wing Luke Museum of the Asian Pacific American Experience. 719 S King St, Seattle. 253-235-9393. kahs.org

- Last Resort Fire Department Museum. Free. Vintage fire trucks, equipment, uniforms. 1433 NW 51st St, Ballard. 206-783-4474. lastresortfd.org

- Log House Museum. 3003 61 Ave SW, Seattle. Local history, operated by SW Seattle Historical Society. 206-350-0999. loghousemuseum.org

- Maple Valley Historical Fire Engine Museum. Two museums operated by Maple Valley Historical Society. 22012 SE 248th St, Maple Valley. 425-432-3470. maplevalleyhistorical.com

- Mercer Island Historical Society. Collects, preserves the history of Mercer Island. City Hall, 611 SE 36th, Mercer Island. mercerislandhistory.org

- Museum of Communications. Historic telephone equipment. 700 E Marginal Way S, Seattle. 206-767-3012. telcomhistory.org

- Museum of Flight. Non-profit aerospace museum; private and military aircraft. 9404 E. Marginal Way, Seattle. museumofflight.org

- Museum of History and Industry. State history, culture. Smithsonian affiliate. 860 Terry Ave N, Seattle. 206-324-1126 mohai.org

- Museum of Museums. Contemporary art center. 900 Boylston Ave., Seattle. museumofmuseums.com

- Museum of Pop Culture (MoPOP). Rock & roll, popular music memorabilia, interactive exhibits. 325 5th Ave N, Seattle. 206-770-2700. mopop.org

- National Nordic Museum. Heritage of area Nordic immigrants. 2655 NW Market St, Seattle. 206-789-5707. nordicmuseum.org

- Neely Mansion Association. Stories of farm immigrants who resided here. 12303 Auburn-Black Diamond Road, Auburn. 253-833-9404. neelymansion.org

- Northwest African American Museum. African American heritage in the Northwest. 2300 S Massachusetts St, Seattle. 206-518-6000. naamnw.org

- Northwest Nikkei Museum. History of Pacific Northwest Nikkei community. 1414 S Weller St, Seattle. 206-568-7114. jcccw.org/museum

- Northwest Seaport. Historical maritime vessels and events. Historic Ships Wharf at Lake Union Park, 860 Terry Ave N, Seattle. 206-447-9800. nwseaport.org

- Olympic Sculpture Park. 9 acres of monumental artworks. 2901 Western Ave, Seattle. 206-654-3100. seattleartmuseum.org

- Pacific Bonsai Museum. Living art in an outdoor setting, native trees 2515 S 336th St, Federal Way. 253-353-7345. pacificbonsaimuseum.org

- Pacific Northwest Railroad Archive. Maintains historic railroad document collections, makes those available online. 425 SW 153rd St, Burien. 206-349-6242. PNRArchive.org

- Pacific Science Center. Science education, exhibits, programs for all ages. 200 2nd Ave N, Seattle. 206-443-2001. pacificsciencecenter.org

- Photographic Center Northwest. Contemporary photography gallery. 900 12th Ave, Seattle. 206-720-7222. pcnw.org

- Pioneer Association of the State of Washington. Museum for historical memorabilia, records, genealogy. 1642 43rd Ave E, Seattle. 206-325-0888. wapioneers.com

- Puget Sound Maritime Historical Society, Maritime Research Center. 5933 6th Ave S, Seattle. 206-812-5464. pugetmaritime.org

- Renton History Museum. Located in a historic Art Deco firehouse. Renton, past and present. 235 Mill Ave S, Renton. 425-255-2330. rentonwa.gov

- Seattle Art Museum. Collections and exhibits from around the world. 1300 First Ave, Seattle. 206-654-3100. seattleartmuseum.org

- Seattle Asian Art Museum. Extensive Asian art collection. 1400 East Prospect St, Seattle. 206-654-3210. seattleartmuseum.org

- Seattle Central College M Rosetta Hunter Art Gallery. 1701 Broadway, Seattle. 206-934-3800. artgallery.seattlecentral.edu

- Seattle Children's Museum. Hands-on exhibits, programs for kids. 305 Harrison St, Seattle. 206-441-1768. seattlechildrensmuseum.org

- Seattle Mariners Hall of Fame. History of Seattle Mariners baseball. T-Mobile Park. 185 S Royal Brougham Way, Seattle. 206-650-5795. mlb.com/mariners/history

- Seattle Pinball Museum. Vintage pinball machines. 508 Maynard Ave S, Seattle. 206-623-0759. seattlepinballmuseum.com

- Seattle University Galleries. Hedreen Gallery, Vachon Gallery. Lee Center for the Arts, 901 12th Ave, 206-296-5360. seattleu.edu

- Steamship Virginia. Operating example of Puget Sound Mosquito Fleet steamer. South Lake Union, Seattle. 206-624-9119. virginiav.org/ship

- Suquamish Museum. Suquamish history back to the last ice age. Baskets, carvings, artifacts. 6861 NW South St, Suquamish. 360-394-7105. suquamish.nsn.us/suquamish-museum

- The Unity Museum. Exhibits depicting a variety of social issues. 4341½ University Way NE #210, Seattle. 206-390-9982 unitymuseum.org

- Vashon Heritage Museum. Vashon-Maury Island Heritage Association. 10105 Bank Road SW, Vashon Island. 206-463-7808. vashonheritagemuseum.org

- Washington State Jewish Historical Society. Preserves the stories and events that shaped Jewish life in Washington State. 3801 E Mercer Way, Mercer Island. 206-774-2277. wsjhs.org

- White River Valley Museum. Puget Sound history, Native American, Japanese culture, research resources. 918 H St SE, Auburn. 253-288-7433. wrvmuseum.org

- Wing Luke Asian Museum. Culture, art, and history of Asian Pacific Americans. 719 S King St, Seattle. 206-623-5124. wingluke.org

Kitsap County

- Aurora Valentinetti Puppet Museum. Showcases craftmanship of generations of puppet artists. 257 4th St, Bremerton. 360-728-2840. valentinettipuppetmuseum.com

- Bainbridge Arts & Crafts Gallery. Non-profit gallery of contemporary works by Northwest arts. 151 Winslow Way East Bainbridge Island. 206.842.3132. bacart.org

- Bainbridge Island Historical Museum. History of the island. 215 Ericksen Ave NE, Bainbridge Island. 206-842-2773. bainbridgehistory.org

- Bainbridge Island Museum of Art. Contemporary art and craft of the Puget Sound region. 550 Winslow Way E, Bainbridge Island. 206-842-4451. biartmuseum.org

- Bremerton Naval Museum. Pacific Northwest naval heritage. 408 Pacific Ave, Bremerton. 360-479-7447. pugetsoundnavymuseum.org

- Bug Museum. Free. Bug and reptile museum. 1118 Charleston Beach Road West, Bremerton. 360-373-7691. bugmuseum.com

- Naval Undersea Museum. Combines naval history, undersea technology, marine science. 1 Garnett Way, Keyport. 360-396-4148. navalunderseamuseum.org

- Poulsbo Historical Society & Museums. Four museums exhibit history, heritage, and culture of the area. 200 NE Moe St, Poulsbo. 360-517-5037. poulsbohistory.com

- Puget Sound Navy Museum. National museum of the U.S. Navy. 251 First St, Bremerton. 360-479-7447. pugetsoundnavymuseum.org

- Sidney Museum and Arts Association. Operates local history and art facilities: Log Cabin Museum, Sidney Museum, Art Gallery. Free. 202 Sidney Ave, Port Orchard. 360-876-3693. sidneymuseumandarts.com

Mason County

- Mason County Historical Society Museum. Local history, records detailing families in Mason County. 5th St & Railroad Ave, Shelton. 360-426-1020. masoncountyhistoricalsociety.org

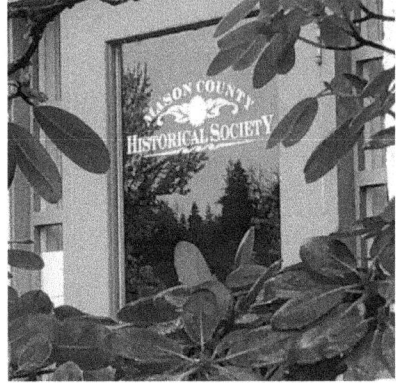

- McReavy House Museum. Restored historic mansion on the Hood Canal. 10 E 2nd St, Union. 360-898-7714. mcreavyhouseofhoodcanal.weebly.com

- Peninsular Railway and Lumbermen's Museum. Restoring the Simpson Timber Railroad to operate as an excursion railroad. 10138 W Shelton Matlock Road, Shelton. 360-589-9201. simpsonrailroad.org

- Squaxin Island Museum Library and Research Center. 150 Kwuh-Deegs-Altxw, Shelton. 360-432-3839. squaxinislandmuseum.org

Pierce County

- Anderson Island Historical Society. 9306 Otso Point Rd, Anderson Island. 253-884-2135. anderson-island.org/hs

- Browns Point Lighthouse Park. Historic lighthouse and park. 201 Tulalip St NE, Tacoma. 253-927-2536. metroparkstacoma.org

- Buffalo Soldiers Museum. Museum honoring the all-black regiment of the U. S. military. 1940 S Wilkeson St, Tacoma. 253-272-4257. buffalosoldierstacoma.org

- DuPont Historical Museum. Exhibits include former DuPont Company and impact on region, Fort Nisqually, period home, village and school displays, Buffalo Soldier display. 207 Barksdale Ave, DuPont. 253-964-2399. dupontmuseum.com

- Fife History Museum and Cultural Center. Fife history, changing exhibits. 2820 54th Ave E, Fife. 253-896-4710. fifehistorymuseum.org

- Fort Nisqually Living History Museum. Recreation of first Puget Sound European settlement with a fort, costumed interpreters. 5519 Five Mile Dr. Point Defiance Park. 253-404-3970. fortnisqually.org, metroparkstacoma.org

- Fort Steilacoom. Preserved pre-civil war fort. Events sponsored by Historic Fort Steilacoom Association. Western State Hospital. 9601 Steilacoom Blvd SW, Lakewood. 253-756-3928. historicfortsteilacoom.org

- Foothills Historical Museum. Depictions of early life in Washington state. 130 N River Ave, Buckley. 360-829-1291. cityofbuckley.com.

- Foss Waterway Seaport. Working waterfront maritime museum. Showcases Tacoma's maritime history. 705 Dock St, Tacoma. 253-272-2750. fosswaterwayseaport.org

- Fox Island Museum. Historical artifacts and exhibits of the island operated by Fox Island Historical Society. 1017 9th Ave, Fox Island. 253-549-2461. foxislandmuseum.org

- Fred Oldfield Western Heritage & Art Center. History of Western lifestyle and advancing Western art. 9th Ave SW & 4th St SW, Puyallup. 253-267-5582. fredoldfieldcenter.org

- Greater Bonney Lake Historical Society. Preserves knowledge about history of Greater Bonney Lake and State of Washington. 19306 Bonney Lake Blvd, Bonney Lake. 253-447-3268. gblhs.org

- Greek-American Historical Museum of Washington State. Online museum of visual history captures life stories of Greeks in the state. 1515 E Olin Place, Seattle. greeksinwashington.org

- Harbor History Museum. Regional history, artifacts, library, and research facility. 4121 Harborview Dr, Gig Harbor. 253-858-6722. harborhistorymuseum.org

- Henry M Jackson Visitor Center. Exhibits, films of the area. Paradise Road East, Ashford, Washington. 360-569-6571. visitrainier.com

- Heritage League of Pierce County, Tacoma. 50 area heritage organizations dedicated to preserving the history of Pierce County. 253-588-6354. heritageleaguepiercecounty.org

- Historic Tacoma. Preserves Tacoma's architectural character through education, advocacy, and preservation. historictacoma.org

- Job Carr Cabin Museum. Tacoma history. Museum of Job Carr, founder of Tacoma. Tacoma history. 2350 N 30th St, Tacoma. Old Town Park. 253-627-5405. jobcarrmuseum.org

- Karshner Museum and Center for Culture & Arts. Artifacts of Native American cultures, local and world history, science, and technology. 309 4th St NE, Puyallup. 253-841-8748. karctr.puyallup.k12.wa.us

- Key Peninsula Historical Society & Museum. Preserves history of Key Peninsula. Key Peninsula Civic Center, 17010 S Vaughn Rd, Vaughn. 253-888-3246. keypeninsulamuseum.org

- Lakewood Historical Society. Lakewood History Museum. Preserves and shares history of Lakewood. 6114 Motor Ave SW, Lakewood. 253-682-3480. lakewoodhistorical.org

- LeMay America's Car Museum. Recognized as one of the World's 10 best automotive museums. 2702 East D St, Tacoma. 877-902-8490. americascarmuseum.org

- Lewis Army Museum. Army equipment, weapons, and memorabilia. Building 4320, Main St, Joint Base Lewis-McChord. 253-967-7206. Certified U.S. Army Museum. lewisarmymuseum.com

- Longmire Museum. History of Mt. Rainier National Park. Admin Bldg. Tahoma Woods Star Route, Longmire. 360-569-6575. nps.gov

- McChord Air Force Base Museum. Aviation and restored military aircraft exhibits. McChord Air Museum. 100 Joe Jackson Blvd Ste 517, Joint Base Lewis McChord. 253-982-2485. mcchordairmuseum.org

- Meeker Mansion Museum. Restored historic mansion restored and preserved by the Puyallup Historical Society. 312 Spring St, Puyallup. 253-697-9468. meekermansion.org

- Museum of Glass. Premier contemporary art museum dedicated to glass and glass making. 1801 Dock St, Tacoma. 253-284-4719. museumofglass.org

- Pioneer Farm Museum & Ohop Indian Village. 1880s homesteading in Washington, seasonal Ohop Indian Village. 7716 Ohop Valley Rd E, Eatonville. 360-832-6300. pioneerfarmmuseum.org

- Shanaman Sports Museum. Artifacts and exhibits of Tacoma's athletics history. 2727 East D St, Tacoma. 253-272-8543. tacomasportsmuseum.com

- Slater Museum of Natural History. Collections of bird, mammal, reptile, amphibian, plant, insect, and geological specimens. University of Puget Sound, 1500 North Warner St, Tacoma. 253.879.3356. pugetsound.edu

- Steilacoom Historical Museum. Steilacoom history, historical homes. 1801 Rainier St, Steilacoom. 253-584-4133. steilacoomhistorical.org

- Steilacoom Tribal Cultural Center & Museum. Tribal history, group tours and storytelling. 1515 Lafayette St, Steilacoom. 253-584-6308. steilacoomtribe.business.site

- Sumner Ryan House Museum. Historic building houses local history museum. 1228 Main St, Sumner. 253-863-8936. sumnerhistoricalsociety.com

- Tacoma Art Museum. Major museum for art of the Pacific Northwest and western region. 1701 Pacific Ave, Tacoma. 253-272-4258. tacomaartmuseum.org

- Tacoma Historical Society Museum. Tacoma Historical Society preserves, presents, and promotes Tacoma's history. 406 Tacoma Ave S, Tacoma. 253-472-3738. tacomahistory.org

- Tacoma-Pierce County Genealogical Society. Diverse group of descendants of early settlers and others with an interest in area genealogical history. Tacoma. tpcgs.org

- Washington Museum Association. Provides online directory of Arboretums/Botanical Gardens, Art Galleries/Museums, Children's Museums, Cultural Centers, Historical Societies, History/Heritage Museums, Natural History Museums, Science Centers/Museums, Zoos, and Aquariums. washingtonmuseumassociation.org

- Washington State Genealogical Society. Directory of Museums in Washington. 1901 S 12th Ave, Union Gap. List of museums throughout Washington State. wasgs.org

- Washington State History Museum. Washington State Historical Society. 1911 Pacific Ave, Tacoma. 888-238-4373. washingtonhistory.org

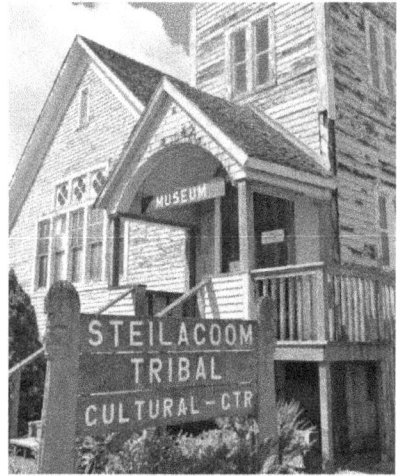

Thurston County

- Bigelow House Museum. Early history of Olympia and Washington Territory, operated by Olympia Historical Society. 918 Glass Ave NE, Olympia. 360-753-1215. olympiahistory.org

- Evergreen Gallery. Art from diverse cultures, philosophies, discipline, and media. The Evergreen State College, Olympia. 2700 Evergreen Pkwy NW, Olympia. 360-867-6413. evergreen.edu

- Hands On Children's Museum. Interactive exhibits and learning experiences. 414 Jefferson St NE, Olympia. 360-956-0818. hocm.org

- Lacey City Museum and Cultural Center. Located in a former fire station and Lacey's City Hall. 829 Lacey St SE, Lacey. 360-438-0209. aceyparks.org/lacey-museum

- Monarch Contemporary Art Center and Sculpture Park. Art center with gallery and 80-acre outdoor sculpture park. 8431 Waldrick Rd SE, Tenino. 360-264-2408. monarchsculpturepark.org

- Olympia Historical Society. Collects and preserves Olympia area historical resources, including the Bigelow House Museum. Historic locations and buildings featured on website. olympiahistory.org

- Olympic Flight Museum. Restored vintage military aircraft and helicopters. 7637-A Old Highway 99 SE, Olympia. 360-705-3925. olympicflightmuseum.com

- Tenino Depot Museum. Local history museum. 399 West Park Ave, Tenino. 360-264-4321. teninodepotmuseum.net

- Thurston County Historical Journal. Online publication of local history sponsored by various Thurston County heritage groups. laceyparks.org/lacey-museum/thurston-county-historical-journal

- Tugboat Sand Man. Restored early 20th-century tugboat museum ship. Percival Landing, Olympia. tugsandman.org

- WET Science Center. Exhibits and games for all ages focus on water – conservation, wastewater treatment, reclaimed water use and protecting Puget Sound.

RESOURCES: MUSIC ORGANIZATIONS

Below are listings of area organizations that promote music, hold concerts and festivals, and provide lessons and provide volunteer opportunities for members and fans. Visit their websites for more information.

Kitsap and Mason Counties

- Bainbridge Community Piano Association. Presents `jazz and classical music in First Sundays Concerts. firstsundaysconcerts.org

- Bainbridge Island Youth Orchestra. Training orchestra for all levels young musicians. Bainbridge Island. biyo.us

- Bainbridge Performing Arts. Offers year-round live on-stage music, theater, and dance. 403 Madison Ave N, Bainbridge Island. 206.842.4560, bainbridgeperformingarts.org

- Bainbridge Symphony Orchestra. Diverse volunteer orchestra. bainbridgeperformingarts.org/bso

- BARN. Makerspace, learning place, offers tools and knowledge to enable anyone to make, create, upcycle, and repair. 8890 Three Tree Lane NE, Bainbridge Island. 206-842-4475. bainbridgebarn.org

- Bremerton Westsound Symphony. Consists of an orchestra, chorale, and youth jazz ensemble. Bremerton. 360-373-1722. bremertonwestsoundsymphony.or

- Mason County Concert Association. All types of live music, theater, and musicals. Brings world-class entertainment to small towns. PO Box 1602, Shelton. 360-463-2746. masoncountyconcerts.org

- Great Bend Center for Music. Center for music lessons for all age children; music event, community gatherings, therapeutic music. Union. greatbendmusic.org

Pierce County

- Auburn Symphony Orchestra. Live orchestra music in various local venues. 253-887-7777. auburnsymphony.org

- Gig Harbor Peninsula Civic Orchestra. Variety of music including classical, recent classical, contemporary, show tunes. PMB #64, 5114 Point Fosdick Dr, Ste F, Gig Harbor. 253-686-0491. ghpcorchestra.com

- Kareem Kandi World Orchestra. Jazz performances, free classes and workshops by world class musicians. 253-307-4057. kkworldorchestra.org

- Narrows Music Society. Umbrella organizations for various area bands, jazz combos, chamber groups, and young artists. 5114 Point Fosdick Drive Ste F, PMB 35, Gig Harbor. narrowsmusicsociety.org

- Northwest Sinfonietta. Professional chamber music blended with power of a full symphony orchestra. 917 Pacific Ave, Ste 304, Tacoma. 253- 383-5344. nwsinfonietta.org

- Orchestral Recital Series of Tacoma. Provides music students of all levels with opportunities to perform with professional musicians on stages. Spring, fall,and benefit concerts. orstacoma.org

- Pacific Northwest Folk Harp Society. Promotes folk harp music, newsletter, events, harp circles, harp music. hreigningharps.com

- Pierce County Community College Music program. Regular performances by Concert Band and Orchestra. Check Pierce Events Calendar for upcoming performances. pierce.ctc.edu/music

- Puget Sound Youth Wind Ensemble. Concert band of region high-school-aged musicians. Tacoma. facebook.com/people/Puget-Sound-Youth-Wind-Ensemble/100068002072429

- Second City Chamber Series. Promotes live chamber music. Various venues throughout Tacoma 253-572-8863. scchamberseries.org

- South Sound Blues Association. Committed to preserving and promoting blues music. Concerts and festivals. southsoundblues.org

- South Sound Symphonic Band. Various concerts throughout south Puget Sound, amateur and semiprofessional musicians. southsoundsymphonicband.org

- Symphony Tacoma. Classical, choral pops, choral concerts. 901 Broadway, Ste 600, Tacoma. Performances at Pantages Theater. 253-272-7264. symphonytacoma.org

- Tacoma Community College. Free concerts in jazz, orchestral, and vocal ensembles. 6501 South 19th St, Tacoma. tacomacc.edu

- Tacoma Community College. Offers free concerts, art exhibits. Creative writers. Artist and lecture series. tacomacc.edu

- Tacoma Concert Band. Symphonic Band. Performs variety of music, from classical to pop, traditional to modern. Pantages Theater. 901 Broadway, Tacoma. 253-591-5894. tacomaconcertband.org

- Tacoma Pierce County Jazz Band. Big band. plays a wide variety of music and styles. Parkland. pccbb.com

- Tacoma Youth Symphony. Symphonic education and performance. 901 Broadway, Ste 500, Tacoma. 253-627-2792. tysamusic.org

- Washington Blues Society. promote, preserve, and advance blues music as an art form. Concerts, resources. wablues.org

Thurston County

- Olympia Chamber Orchestra. Plays music suited for a smaller orchestra, opera, or ballet orchestras and chamber music. Olympia. 360-350-1299. olympiachamberorchestra.org

- Olympia Highlanders Pipes and Drums. Scottish music and tradition with bagpipes and drums. South Union Grange, 10030 Tilley Rd SW, Olympia. olympiahighlanderspipesanddrums.org

- Olympia Jazz Central. Supports the local jazz musicians and vocalists who perform in Olympia. Events calendar. olympiajazzcentral.com

- Olympia Symphony Orchestra. Semi-professional orchestra. Regular, summer outdoor, and seasonal concerts. 3400 Capitol Blvd SE Ste 203, Olympia. 360-753-0074. olympiasymphony.org

- Saint Martin's University. University and community sponsored music events. See Calendar. Worthington Center. stmartin.edu

- Sound Puget Sound Community College Jazz Band. Comprised of students, Evergreen State College students and community members. 2011 Mottman Rd SW, Olympia. 360-596-5200; 4220 6th Ave SE, Lacey. 360-709-2000. spscc.edu/arts-comm/music

- Sound Puget Sound Community College Symphony Orchestra. Comprised of students and community members. 2011 Mottman Rd SW, Olympia. 360-596-5200; 4220 6th Ave SE, Lacey. 360-709-2000. spscc.edu/arts-comm/music

- South Puget Sound New Horizons. Music program for adults 50 and over. Wanta-be's included! Concerts. olynhb.us

- South Sound Classical Music Meetup. Gatherings for happy hours, live concerts. Olympia. meetup.com/south-sound-classical-music-meetup

- Student Orchestras of Greater Olympia. Four groups of young South Sound musicians, seasonal concerts. 1629 22nd Ave SE, Olympia. 360-352-1438. studentorchestras.org

- Washington Bluegrass Association. Calendar, newsletter, listing of bands in the state. Toledo. washingtonbluegrassassociation.org

Vocal

- Amabile Choir of Bainbridge. Mixed-voice ensemble of area singers, teens through retirees. Performs eclectic repertoire; 2 annual concerts. Rolling Bay. amabilechoir.org

- Bainbridge Chorale, Community Chorus. Bainbridge Island. 206-780-2467. bainbridgechorale.org

- Bridge Music Project. Uses song writing to provide youth with tools for self-expression and understanding. Classes, performances. 120 State Ave NE #1417, Olympia. bridgemusicproject.org

- Capital City Chorus of Olympia. Community-based chorus; chorale and mixed choir, standard choral repertoire. cccolympia.org

- Cascade Foothills Chorale. Non-audition, diverse group. Enumclaw. 253-261-4889. cfchorale.org

- Cora Voce. Tacoma-based community chorus. 11706 Larson Road. Anderson Island. coravoce.org

- Eastside Midday Singers. Mixed voice community choral group. First Congregational Church of Bellevue 11061 NE 2nd St, Bellevue. eastsidemiddaysingers.com

- Great Bend Chorale. Non-auditioned choral ensemble open to all adults (14+) regardless of training. Great Bend Center for Music. Union. greatbendmusic.org

- Harstine Island Community Choir. All ages, themed concerts of choral masterworks, music from various countries, and more. Harstine Island, near Shelton. harstinechoir.org

- Kitsap Community Chorale. Community chorus. St. Bede's Episcopal Church, 1578 SE Lider Rd, Port Orchard. kitsapchorale.org

- Kitsap Peninsula Opera Guild. Showcases West Sound arts and provides educational outreach to area schools. Bremerton. 360-876-4373. mightycause.com/organization

- Masterworks Choral Ensemble. Community Chorus. Free concert tickets to selected schools. 360-491-3305 Olympia. mce.org

- Normanna Male Chorus. Male Norwegian chorus Scandinavian culture music. Tacoma. 253-272-7286. pcnsa.org/local-groups/tacoma

- Northwest Repertory Singers. Mixed Voice Community Ensemble. 2522 N Proctor St, Tacoma. 253-265-3042. nwrs.org

- Olympia Chorus. Female Barbershop chorus. All styles of a cappella music. Olympia. 360-436-6313. olympiasweetadelines.org

- Olympia Musical Theater. Musical performances and education for voices of all ages. Olympia. olympiamusicaltheatre.org

- Olympia Peace Choir. Eclectic -- themes of peace, justice, optimism, and earth stewardship. All ages. Olympia. theolympiapeacechoir.org

- Olympia Youth Chorus. Youth chorus of all backgrounds. 120 State Ave NE #102, Olympia. 360-701-4518. olympiayouthchorus.org

- Pierce County Community College Music program. Regular performances by Concert Choir and Chamber Choir. Check Pierce Events Calendar for upcoming performances. pierce.ctc.edu/music

- PLU Choral Union. Community choir. Pacific Lutheran University. 12180 Park Ave S, Tacoma. 253-7411. plu.edu/choir

- Puget Sound Revels. Celebrates community through multi-cultural song, dance, and story. 621 Tacoma Ave S, Tacoma. 253-756-1804. pugetsoundrevels.org

- Puget Sounders Men's Chorus. Men's a cappella barbershop chorus. 360-754-9397. facebook.com/PugetSounders

- Sonoro Choral Society. Wide variety, from Bach and Brahms to cutting edge music. Tacoma. sonorochoralsociety.org

- Sound Puget Sound Community College Percival Choir. Community-based choral ensemble open to everyone in the college and community. 2011 Mottman Rd SW, Olympia. 360-596-5200; 4220 6th Ave SE, Lacey. 360-709-2000. spscc.edu/arts-comm/music

- South Sound Classical Choir. 253-531-0102. facebook.com/southsoundclassicalchoir

- Spectrum Choral Academy. Community choir program for children, teens, and college age singers. 7700 Skansie Ave, Gig Harbor. 360-271-8086. exceptionalchoralevents.com

- Tacoma Barbershop Harmony Chorus. Men's Barbershop chorus. Tacoma. 253-237-7464. facebook.com/totemaires

- Tacoma Community College. Free concerts in jazz, orchestral and vocal ensembles. 6501 South 19th St, Tacoma. tacomacc.edu

- Tacoma Opera. Professional opera company offering traditional and non-traditional operatic productions. 1720 S 7th St, Ste 105, Tacoma. 253-627-7789. tacomaopera.org

- Tacoma Refugee Choir. Rich combination of over 700 participants representing 65 countries. refugeechoir.org

- Tapestry Singers. Adult community choir based in Puyallup Tacoma. 253-820-4505. facebook.com/TapestrySingers

- Washington Bluegrass Association. Calendar, newsletter, listing of bands in the state. Toledo. washingtonbluegrassassociation.org

Music Festivals, Events

Below are examples of popular music festivals in the South Sound. Visit the festival website for current information.

- Bluegrass From the Forest. South Mason Youth Soccer Park. Shelton. July. bluegrassfromtheforest.com

- BREW FIVE THREE: Tacoma's Beer & Music Festival. Broadway & 9th St, Tacoma. August. tacomaartslive.org

- Classical Tuesdays in Old Town Tacoma. September - March. classicaltuesdays.blogspot.com

- Dock St, Blues Festival. Waterway Stage. August. Tacoma.

- Highline Classic Jazz Festival. Landmark on the Sound. March. Des Moines.

- Olympia Music in the Park. downtownolympia.org. Port Plaza and Sylvester Park, Olympia. July, August. downtownolympia.org

- Olympia Old Time Festival. Festival shares the learning, teaching of old-time fiddle music. February. Olympia. olyoldtime.weebly.com

- Port Gamble Maritime Music Festival. Sea Shanties, pirate-themed. August. portgamblemaritimemusic.com

- Port Townsend Acoustic Blues Festival. July. Ft. Worden State Park. centrum.org/program/acoustic-blues

- PLU Jazz Under the Stars. Russell Music Center. Tacoma. July. plu.edu

- Sumner Music Off Main. Music series. July Heritage Park, Sumner.

- Tacoma Guitar and Drum Festival. Tacoma Dome. Tacoma. tacomadome.org/events

- Tacoma Jazz and Blues Festival. Tacoma. July.

- Yelm Jazz in the Park. August. 115 Mossman Ave SW. Yelm. facebook.com/YelmJazzFestival

RESOURCES: SENIOR SERVICES

The following are examples of organizations that provide many different services for older adults, and opportunities for volunteering in Kitsap, Mason, Pierce, and Thurston Counties. Visit their websites for more information. See also listings of organizations in *RESOURCES: COMMUNITY SERVICE ORGANIZATIONS* on page 172.

Senior Assistance Organizations

Statewide

- AARP. Offers three volunteering programs that provide services to members through its state offices. Tax-Aide volunteers provide free tax-filing help to those who need it most. Driver Safety volunteers help others get on the road to safety as an AARP Driver Safety instructor or coordinator. Volunteers in AARP Experience Corps tutor children in reading. aarp.org

- AARP Create the Good. Helps seniors search for local volunteer opportunities. Search by keywords and zip code. createthegood. aarp.org

- AARP Tax-Aide Program. Volunteers assist seniors preparing tax returns in Washington State. aarp.org/washington

- AARP Washington state volunteers. Volunteer opportunities in avoiding fraud, outreach, advocacy, state legislative issues, driver safety, and more. states.aarp.org/washington/make-a-difference-volunteer-with-aarp-washington

- AmeriCorps Seniors. Network of national service programs for Americans 55 years and older. They serve communities in many ways, including tutoring and mentoring students, assisting and caring for the elderly, and supporting relief teams when disasters strike. nationalservice.gov/programs/senior-corps

- County Programs on Aging. These local agencies ways to provide senior services in your communities. They rely on volunteers in areas such as caregiver support, light housekeeping and yard work, emergency and disaster shelters, foster grandparent programs, meal sites, senior centers, companion programs, and similar services.

- Meals on Wheels. (wheelsamerica.org). A nationwide network of community-based, nonprofit programs that provide seniors in their communities with support that enables them to remain living in their own homes. This support is typically a nutritious meal, a friendly visit, and a quick safety check. To sign up, visit the website, or contact the local organization that provides services. Examples are churches, senior centers, and other nonprofits.

- Seniors Mobility. Site that lists options for free transportation for senior throughout the State of Washington. Search by city. seniorsmobility.org/free-transportation

- State of Washington. Discounts and benefits programs for seniors. Services include volunteer chore services, for seniors and adults with disabilities. Volunteers provide light housework, laundry, transportation, household repairs and more. ccsww.org

- Washington State Senior Games. Olympic style multi-sport event at various sites throughout the South Sound. July, August. Open to everyone. Volunteers. 360-413-0148. washingtonstateseniorgames.com

Kitsap and Mason Counties

- Community Action Council of Lewis, Mason & Thurston Counties. Connects people to community resources; partners with governments, nonprofits, faith organizations, corporations. 360-438-1100. caclmt.org

- Island Volunteer Caregivers. Provides services to senior adults including transportation, companionship, light housekeeping, life enrichment activities and more. Bainbridge Island. 147 Finch Place SW, Ste 4, Bainbridge Island. 2-6-842-4441. ivcbainbridge.org

- Kitsap County Aging and Long-Term Care. Serves needs of older or disabled adults. Volunteers assist seniors and those in need of long-term care; serve on Kitsap County Area Agency on Aging, and as Long-Term Care Ombudsman. 614 Division St, MS-4, Port Orchard. 360-337-4650. kitsapgov.com

- Lewis-Mason-Thurston Area Agency on Aging. Provides information on senior services and services and adults with disabilities. 2008 Olympic Hwy N, Shelton. 360-664-2168. lmtaaa.org

- Lutheran Community Services Northwest. Volunteers serve as senior friends or with the RSVP program. 645 4th St, Ste 202, Bremerton. 253-272-8433.

- Meals on Wheels Kitsap. Delivers hot nutritionally-balanced meal to adults 60 years and older on weekdays. 2817 Wheaton Way, Ste 208, Bremerton. 360-377-8511. mealsonwheelskitsap.org

Pierce County

- Catholic Communities Services. Volunteers assist elderly adults with transportation to medical appointments. 1323 S Yakima Ave, Tacoma. 253-502-2741. ccsww.org/drivers-pierce-county

- Lutheran Community Services Northwest. Volunteers assist with dementia related activities and services through RSVP program and other activities. 3848 S Junett St, Tacoma. 253-272-8433. lcsnw.org/office/bremerton

- Pierce County Aging & Disability. Provides links to a wide variety of organizations offering volunteer opportunities in senior and disability services, and various county advisory boards. piercecountywa.gov/1985/Employment-Volunteering

Thurston County

- Catholic Community Services. Volunteers assist elderly and disabled adults with household tasks, transportation, shopping, minor home repairs, etc. 3545 7th Ave SW, Olympia. 844-851-9380. ccsww.org/volunteer-services-volunteer-thurston-county

- Community Action Council of Lewis, Mason & Thurston Counties. Connects people to community resources, partners with governments, nonprofits, faith organizations, corporations. 360-438-1100. caclmt.org

- Lewis-Mason-Thurston Area Agency on Aging. Provides information on senior services and services or adults with disabilities. 2404 Heritage Ct SW, Olympia. 360-664-2168. lmtaaa.org

Senior and Community Centers

Below are listings of area senior and community centers that serve seniors with a variety of services, classes, social opportunities, and activities. Visit their websites for more information.

Kitsap and Mason Counties

- Bainbridge Island Senior/Community Center. 70 Brien Ave. SE, Bainbridge Island. 206-842-1616. Arts and crafts, cultural, educational, arts, reading, fitness activities. biseniorcenter.org

- Bremerton Senior Citizens Center. Arts and crafts, games, specialty programs, health, welbeing, and wellness activities. Travel and trips. 1140 Nipsic Ave, Bremerton. 360-473-5357. bremertonwa.gov

- HUB Center for Seniors. Games, art, music, fitness activities, community resources. 111 NE Old Belfair Hwy, Belfair. 360-275-0535. hubhappenings.org

- Kitsap County Givens Community & Senior Center. 1026 Sidney Ave, Ste 110, Port Orchard. 360-337-5700. facebook.com/people/Port-Orchard-Senior-Center

- Mason County Senior Activities Center. 50 and Better Activities Center. Fitness and health, nutrition, dancing, walking, trips, personal enrichment, services. 190 W Sentry Drive, Shelton. 360-426-7374. mcsac.net.

- North Kitsap Senior Citizen's Lounge. Activities include crafts, games, outings and more. 18972 Front St NE, Poulsbo. 360-779-5702. poulsboseniors.blogspot.com

Pierce County

- Bonney Lake Senior Center. Variety of activities for fitness, hobbies, health, personal enrichment, and entertainment. 19304 Bonney Lake Blvd, Bonney Lake. 253-863-7658. ci.bonney-lake.wa.us

- Buckley Senior Activity Center. Variety of classes and activities, healthcare services, special events, trips. Senior van. 811 Main St, Buckley. 360-761-7894. cityofbuckley.com/seniorcenter

- Center at Norpoint. 4818 Nassau Ave NE, Tacoma. 253-404-3900. MetroParks. metroparkstacoma.org/place/center-at-norpoint

- City of Tacoma. Provides variety of services, active lifestyle classes. Beacon Activity Center. 415 S 13th St, 253-301-3369; Lighthouse Activity Center, 5016 A St, 253-301-3369. cityoftacoma.org

- Dupont - Adults & Seniors. City offers senior programs, events, and activities to enhance skills, keep fit, and meet others. 253-964-8121. dupontwa.gov/545/Adults-Seniors

- Eatonville Family Agency. Provides food, clothing, and resources for the community. 305 W Center St, Eatonville. 360-832-6805. eatonvillefamilyagency.org

- Fife Community Center. 55 & Older Adult Programs. Provides fitness, personal enrichment, and social activities. Senior lunches. 2111 54th Ave E, Fife. 253-896-8654. cityoffife.org

- Gig Harbor Senior Center. Provides food, fun, friendship, fitness, crafts, games, and fitness classes. 6509 38th Ave, Gig Harbor. gigharborfoundation.org

- Graham-Kapowsin Community Council. Community enrichment classes, projects, and programs. Frontier Park, 21718 Meridian Ave E, Lodge Room B, Graham. 253-921-2914. g-kcc.org

- Greater Maple Valley Community Center. Senior activities, trips, and services. 22010 SE 248th St, Maple Valley. 425-432-1272. maplevalleycc.org

- Key Peninsula Community Services. Senior Center provides senior meals, classes, activities. 17015 9th St, Ct NW, Lakebay. 253-884-4440. keypeninsulacommunityservices.org

- Lakewood Senior Activity Center. Exercise classes, personal enrichment, and social activities. Weekly walks. 9112 Lakewood Dr SW, Lakewood. 253-798-4090. cityoflakewood.us

- Mid-County Community Center. Senior services, fitness, personal enrichment classes. 10205 44th Ave E, Tacoma. 253-531-8412. mccctacoma.org

- Milton Senior Center. A variety of senior programs. 1000 Laurel, Milton. 253-922-6586. cityofmilton.net

- Mountain View Community Center. Various exercise and personal enrichment programs. 3607 122nd Ave E, Ste A, Edgewood. 253-826-4329. mtviewcommunitycenter.org

- Multicare Celebrate Seniority. Free program of education, social activities, and volunteer opportunities at senior centers, retirement homes, and community centers in King and South Pierce Counties. 1004 East Main, Ste C, Puyallup. 253-697-7385. multicare.org

- Orting Valley Senior Center. Various senior activities for seniors, meals. 120 Washington Ave N, Orting; 112 Varner Ave SE, Orting. 360-893-5827. facebook.com/OrtingValleySeniorCenter

- PenMet Parks. Community Recreation Center. 2416 14th Ave NW, Gig Harbor. Educational, fitness, and recreation programs. 5717 Wollochet Dr NW #3, Gig Harbor. 253-858-3400. penmetparks.org

- Point Defiance-Ruston Senior Center. Broad range of services, games, classes, crafts, health, personal enhancement, and trips. 4716 N Baltimore St, Tacoma. 253-756-0601. franketobeyjones.com

- Puyallup Activity Center. Variety of activities, classes, games, social times, exercise. Trips and tours. 210 W Pioneer Ave, Puyallup. 253-841-5555. cityofpuyallup.org

- Salvation Army Puyallup Valley Senior Activity Center. Provides social, recreational, and educational opportunities for seniors. 4009 9th St SW, Puyallup. 253-841-1491. seniorcenter.us/sc

- South Park and Community Center. Senior programs, trips, and sports. 4851 S Tacoma Way, Tacoma. metroparkstacoma.org

- Spana-Park Senior Center. Various activities including crafts and games. Senior meals. 325 152nd St E, Spanaway. 253-537-4854. facebook.com/spanaparkseniorcenter

- Sprinkler Recreation Center. Indoor, outdoor activities, sports, classes, all ages. 14824 C St S, Tacoma. 253-798-4000. piercecountywa.gov

- Steilacoom Community Center. Various programs and activities including exercise and games. 2301 Worthington St, Steilacoom. 253-983-2599. townofsteilacoom.org

- Sumner Senior Center. Various programs, activities including Music Day, arts and crafts, games, exercise, and senior services. 15506 - 62nd St, Ct E, Sumner. 253-863-2910. sumnerwa.gov/senior-center

- Tillicum/American Lake Gardens Community Center. Social, educational, cultural and health programs, services. 14916

Washington Ave SW, Tacoma. 253-584-1280. tillicumcommunitycenter.com

- University Place Community Connection and Senior Center. Senior health care services, educational activities, cross-generational programs. 2534 Grandview Dr W, University Place. 253-564-1992. communityconnectionplace.org

Thurston County

- Olympia Senior Center. Classes and activities in arts and crafts, exercise, personal growth, and far more. Trips and tours. 222 Columbia St NW, Olympia. 360-586-6181. southsoundseniors.org

- Senior Center of Rainier, WA. Meal program. Community activities. 108 Michigan St S, Rainier. 360-446-2258. seniorcenterofrainier.org

- Tumwater Old Town Center. Senior programs. Meal program, music, games, arts, and crafts activities. 215 North 2nd Ave S, Tumwater. 360-252-5467. ci.tumwater.wa.us

- Virgil S. Clarkston Senior Center. Classes and activities in arts and crafts, exercise, personal growth, and more. Meals. 6757 Pacific Ave SE, Lacey. 360-407-3967. southsoundseniors.org

- Yelm Senior Center. Various activities including exercise, arts and crafts, and games. 16530 103rd Ave SE, Yelm. 360-458-7733. yelmseniorcenter.comcastbiz.net

RESOURCES: THE GREAT OUTDOORS

The following is a list of area paddling, rowing, and sailing clubs near or within Mason, Kitsap, Pierce, and Thurston Counties. Visit their websites for information.

Paddling, Rowing, Sailing Clubs

Below are examples of area outdoor clubs and Meetups that focus on paddling sports adventures and classes.

- Bainbridge Island Rowing. Multi-generational rowing community. All levels. Waterfront Park, Eagle Harbor boathouse, 281 Brien Dr SE, Bainbridge Island. bainbridgerowing.org

- Gig Harbor Dragons. Dragonboat club, paddling and racing. Sponsored by PenMet parks. gigharbordragons.com

- Gig Harbor Sailing Club & School. Beginner and experienced sailors. 3226 Harborview Dr, Gig Harbor. 253-858-360-3626. gigharborsailing.com

- Hui Heihei Wa'a. Outrigger Canoe Club. Races throughout Pacific Northwest. Silverdale. hhwsilverdale.org

- Hui Wa'a O Wakinikona. Outrigger canoe club. 2157 N Northlake Way, Seattle. wakinikonaclub.com

- Key Peninsular Kayakers. All ages, levels explore local waterways in Kitsap area. Lakebay. meetup.com/key-peninsula-kayakers

- Kikaha O Ke Kai. Outrigger canoe club. 1930 E D St, Tacoma. 253-237-4425. kikaha.com

- Mountaineers. Year-round paddling program all over Puget Sound. Programs and activities in Seattle and Tacoma. mountaineers.org

- Olympia Community Sailing. Diverse sailing community, lessons for all ages. olympiacommunitysailing.org

- Olympia Dragon Boating Meetup. Dragon boating for all backgrounds and fitness levels, coaching and equipment provided. 1700 Marine DR NE. Olympiameetup.com/olympia-dragon-boating-meetup

- Seattle Canoe and Kayak Club. Paddling classes, teams. Green Lake Small Craft Center, 5900 W Green Lake Way N, Seattle. 206-684-4074. seattlecanoekayak.club

- Seattle Outrigger Canoe Club. 18 N Northlake Way, Seattle. 206-289-0090. Six-person outrigger canoes. Weekly practices. Waterway 18, N Northlake Way, Seattle. 206-289-0090. seattleoutrigger.com

- Seattle Sea Kayak Club. Small social kayak club. Short or long trips and expeditions. Mercer Island. seattlekayak.org

- Sound Rowers. Water rowing and paddling club. Conducts open water races for world class and weekend athletes in any sea-worthy human powered watercraft. soundrowers.org

- South Sound Sailing Society. Sailing education, racing, and cruising programs. Olympia Yacht Club, 201 Simmons St NW. ssssclub.com

- Washington Kayak Club. Trips, events, education, skill development. Redond. wakayakclub.clubexpress.com

RESOURCES: THEATER, PERFORMANCE

South Sound Performing Arts Companies and Venues

Below are listings of performing arts companies and venues in or near Kitsap, Mason, Pierce, and Thurston Counties where you can choose to enjoy performances, participate in, or work behind the scenes.

Visit their websites for current information, show descriptions and schedules, auditions, and volunteering opportunities.

Kitsap and Mason Counties

- inD Theatre. Produces independent theatrical events that inspire social change. Bainbridge Island. 206-486-0290. indtheatre.org

- Kitsap Forest Theater. The Mountaineers Players brings Puget Sound audiences outdoor spring and summer theater. 3000 Seabeck Hwy, Bremerton. 206-542-7815. foresttheater.com

- Lesser-Known Players. Performs new, rare, unusual, and/or out-of-mainstream theatrical works. 321 High School Rd NE, Ste D3, #26, Bainbridge Island. lesserknownplayers.org

- Port Gamble Theater. Live theater. 4839 NE View Dr., Port Gamble. 360-977-7135. portgamble.com

- Peninsula Dance Theatre. Young artists committed to high-quality live dance performances. 515 Chester Ave, Bremerton. 360-377-6214. peninsuladancetheatre.org

- Shelton Junior Programs. Volunteers who sponsor live theater for students. PO Box 2501, Shelton. sheltonjuniorprograms.com

- Shelton Performing Arts Center. Shelton High School, 3737 N Shelton Springs Rd. 360-426-1687 sheltonschools.org/community

- Western Washington Center for the Arts. Promotes theater arts in Port Orchard and surrounding communities. . 521 Bay St, Port Orchard. 360-769-7469. wwca.us

Pierce County

- Centerstage Theatre Arts Conservatory. New plays and musicals. Dumas Bay Centre, 3200 SW Dash Point Rd, Federal Way. 253-661-1444. centerstagetheatre.com

- Dukesbay Productions. Independent Theatre in Tacoma. Local Playwrights. Merlino Art Center, 508 S. Sixth Ave #10, Tacoma. 253-350-7680. dukesbay.org

- Hilltop Elder Performing Ensemble. Singers, movers, storytellers, and actors who develop works for live performances. Tacoma Urban Performing Arts Center, 1105 Martin Luther King Jr Way, Tacoma. 253-327-1873. tacomaupac.org/events

- Puget Sound Revels. Theater productions of multi-cultural song, dance, story for all. 621 Tacoma Ave S, Ste 402, Tacoma. 253-756-1804. pugetsoundrevels.org

- Lakewood Institute of Theater. Theater classes and instruction for all ages. 10330 59th Ave SW, Unit A, Lakewood. 253-588-0042. lakewoodinstituteoftheatre.org

- Lakewood Playhouse. 5729 Lakewood Towne Center Blvd, Lakewood. 253-588-0042. Lakewoodplayhouse.org

- Northwest Sinfonietta. Classical music for diverse audiences. 917 Pacific Ave, Ste 304. Tacoma. 253-383-5344. nwsinfonietta.org

- Pacific Lutheran University. Performances by Dept of Theater and Dance. Karen Hille Phillips Center for the Performing Arts, 12180 Park Ave S, Tacoma. 253-535-7772. plu.edu/theatre-dance

- Puget Sound Revels. Multi-culture song, dance, story. 621 Tacoma Ave S, Ste 402, Tacoma. 253-756-1804. pugetsoundrevels.org

- Symphony Tacoma. Classical concerts and education programs. 901 Broadway, Ste 600, Tacoma. 253-272-7264. symphonytacoma.org

- Tacoma Arts Live. Home to Tacoma's Resident Arts Organizations that form the core of the performing arts in the South Puget Sound region: Northwest Sinfonietta, Puget Sound Revels, Tacoma City Ballet, Tacoma Concert Band, Tacoma Opera, Symphony Tacoma, and Tacoma Youth Symphony Association. 253-346-1721.

- Tacoma City Ballet. Performances and Instruction. 508 6th Ave, Tacoma. 253-272-4219. tacomacityballet.com

- Tacoma Concert Band. Symphonic band. P.O. Box 64922, Tacoma. 253-353-237. tacomaconcertband.org

- Tacoma Little Theatre. All types of live theater performances. 210 North I St, 253-272-2281. mtacomalittletheatre.com

- Tacoma Musical Playhouse. Performs musical theater; offers education programs. 116 6th Ave, Tacoma. 253-565-6867. tmp.org

- Tacoma Opera. Professional opera company offering traditional and non-traditional operatic productions. 1720 S 7th St, Ste 105, Tacoma, 253-627-7789. tacomaopera.org

- Tacoma Performing Arts Center (T.U.P.A.C). Provides culturally relevant dance training, community events and classes in performing arts to Black and BIPOC youth in Hilltop Community. 1105 Martin Luther King Junior Way, Tacoma. 253-327-1873. tacomaupac.org

- Tacoma Urban Performing Arts Center. Performances by Black and BIPOC youth who receive performing arts training in Tacoma's Hilltop Community. 1105 Martin Luther King Junior Way, Tacoma. tacomaupac.org

- Tacoma Youth Symphony. 901 Broadway, Ste 500, Tacoma. 253-627-2792. tysamusic.org

- The Changing Scene Theatre Northwest. Cutting-edge fringe theatre; original, unconventional productions, and innovative adaptations of the classics. Performances at Dukesbay Theater, 508 S Sixth Ave., Tacoma. facebook.com/changingscenenw

- University of Puget Sound. Various theater productions. Norton Clapp Theatre, Jones Hall. 1500 N Warner St, Tacoma. 253-879-3555. pugetsound.edu

Thurston County

- Harlequin Productions. Live theater. 202 4th Ave E, Olympia. 360-786-0151. harlequinproductions.org

- Kenneth J. Minnaert Center. Puget Sound Community College, 2011 Mottman Rd. SW, Olympia. 360-753-8586. washingtoncenter.org

- Oly Arts. Multi-platform publication covering live theater, arts, and culture in the South Sound via print, online, podcasts, and mobile apps. olyarts.org

- Olympia Family Theater. Multipurpose performing arts for all ages. 612 4th Ave E, Olympia. 360-570-1638. olyft.org

- Olympia Little Theater. Olympia's oldest live theater. 1925 Miller Ave NE, Olympia. 360-786-9484. olympialittletheater.org

- Olympia Musical Theater. Musical performances and education for voices of all ages. Olympia. olympiamusicaltheatre.org

- Standing Room Only (SRO). Community theater group. Triad Theater, 102 E Yelm Ave, Yelm. 856-677-8243. srotheater.org

- Theater Artists Olympia. Performs creative theatrical pieces under-represented in the community. theaterartistsoly.wordpress.com

- Washington Center for the Performing Arts. Performing arts facility. Multi-genre and styles. 512 Washington St, SE, Olympia. washingtoncenter.org

Dance

- Peninsula Dance Theatre. Young arts committed to high-quality live dance performances. 515 Chester Ave, Bremerton. 360-377-6214. peninsuladancetheatre.org

- Tacoma City Ballet. Classical ballet performances and instruction. 508 6th Ave, Tacoma. 253-272-4219. tacomacityballet.com

RESOURCES: VOLUNTEERING

The following lists sources of volunteer opportunities that welcome senior volunteers. Also included are volunteer websites that connect volunteers to multiple opportunities within their communities and organizations. Visit their websites for more information.

Also listed are organizations that match volunteers to multiple community needs.

Find Opportunities in Your Area
Washington Statewide Programs

- AARP Real Possibilities. Helps seniors search for local volunteer opportunities. Search by keywords and zip code. createthegood.aarp.org

- AmeriCorps Program - Serve Washington. Links to a variety of ecological and other community service projects by county. servewashington.wa.gov/programs/americorps

- Just Serve. Search by community for all types of volunteer opportunities in your area. justserve.org

- Point of Light Engage. Hundreds of volunteer opportunities throughout the world. Search database for local organizations seeking volunteers. engage.pointsoflight.org/

- Serve Washington's Get Connected system. Website search for or post volunteer activities in the state by county. servewashington.galaxydigital.com/need

- United Ways of the Pacific Northwest. Regional Association of local United Ways in Washing, Oregon, and Idaho. Information on community programs; links to local United Ways. uwpnw.org

- VolunteerMatch. Volunteer website that helps volunteers search locally for nonprofits, government agencies and causes that need them. volunteermatch.org

- Washington State Retired Senior Volunteer Program (RSVP). Volunteer network, projects by nonprofits, local government agencies in 15 counties. servewashington.wa.gov/programs

- Washington State How-to Guides. Volunteer or Give to a Charity. Information on volunteering with state agencies, outside, during disasters, at food banks; lists organizations that match volunteers with opportunities. wa.gov/how-to-guides/volunteer-or-give-charity

Kitsap and Mason Counties

- Bainbridge Community Foundation. Links to organizations that make a difference through hands-on-service. 299 Madison Ave N, Ste B, Bainbridge Island. 206-842-0433. bainbridgecf.org/giving

- Kitsap County Volunteer Services. Links to volunteer opportunities with various area non-profits, advisory boards, emergency management, government agencies, hobby clubs, environmental organizations, youth advocates and more. 614 Division St, MS-4, Port Orchard. 360-337-7080 itsapgov.com

- RSVP of Lewis, Mason, and Thurston Counties. Lutheran Community Services Northwest. 645 4th St, Ste 202. Bremerton. 253-272-8433. csnw.org/office/Bremerton

- Shelton Mason County Chamber of Commerce. Volunteer for chamber and community events. 215 W Railroad Ave, Shelton. 360-426-2021. masonchamber.com/volunteer

- United Way of Kitsap County. Connects volunteers to opportunities with community partners to meet community needs. 645 4th St, Ste 101, Bremerton. 360-377-8505. unitedwaykitsap.org

- United Way of Mason County. Volunteer organization providing wide variety of human services; works with other non-profits. 790 E Johns Prairie Rd, Shelton. 360-426-4999. unitedwaymason.org

Pierce County

- Pierce County Human Services Volunteers. Links to opportunities county's advisory boards and human services organizations. piercecountywa.gov/714/Volunteer-Opportunities

- RSVP of Pierce and Kitsap Counties. Connects volunteers to a variety of community organizations. Volunteer sites in Pierce Co. are in greater Tacoma, Puyallup, Graham, Edgewood, and Gig Harbor. In Kitsap County, volunteer sites are in Bremerton, Silverdale, Port Orchard, and North Kitsap County. Sponsored by Lutheran Community Services Northwest. Tacoma. lcsnw.org/office/south-puget-sound

- United Way of Pierce County. Connects volunteers to opportunities with community partners to meet community needs. 1501 Pacific Ave, Ste 400, Tacoma.253-272-4263. uwpc.org

Thurston County

- United Way of Thurston County. Connects volunteers to local organizations to meet community needs. 3525 7th Ave SW, Ste 201, Olympia. 360-943-2773. unitedway-thurston.org/volunteer

Sharing Wisdom

Options for retirees looking to apply their life experiences are nonprofits that tap into the experience of seniors to carry out their missions. These programs recognize the valuable contributions of older adults who make a difference in our communities. Some examples are:

- AARP Experience Corps. Senior volunteers work with children one-on-one and in groups to help kids in grades K-3 develop literacy skills and build self-confidence. aarp.org/experience-corps

- AmeriCorps Seniors. A network of national service programs for Americans 55 years and older. They serve communities by tutoring and mentoring students, assisting and caring for the elderly, and supporting relief teams when disasters strike. nationalservice.gov/programs/senior-corps

- Boy Scouts and Girl Scouts. Volunteers are leaders, and mentor and help youth learn a variety of skills, many outdoor related. scouting.org

- City and County Governments. Many have established retiree volunteer programs for their communities. Nearly all welcome the life experience and wisdom retirees bring on various advisory committees and boards. *See CHAPTER 13: GOVERNMENT SERVICE* on page 89.

- Encore.org engages older adults in programs that encourage connection and collaboration across generations to address society's greatest problems. Encore.org provides fellowships that match seasoned professionals with social sector organizations.

- National Park Service. Through the NPS VIP program, retirees volunteer in national parks in exchange for a free RV camping site. See details and opportunities on their website. volunteer.gov

- SCORE (Service Corps of Retired Executives). Retired businesspeople provide free business mentoring services to entrepreneurs throughout the county. Volunteers offer specific knowledge based on professional skills or industry, lead seminars and workshops, and expand outreach through alliances in local communities. (score.org)

Find Opportunities in Your Community

Examples of other organizations with local operations that value the experience and skills of seniors include:

- Bainbridge Island Resource Directory. Provides lists of, and links to organizations that welcome senior volunteers. resourcedirectorybi.org/category/activities/volunteering

- Boy Scouts and Girl Scouts. Volunteers are leaders and help mentor and help youth learn a variety of skills, many outdoor related. (scouting.org)

- City and County Governments. Many have established retiree volunteer programs for their communities. Nearly all welcome the life experience and wisdom retirees bring on various advisory committees and boards. For a list of websites, see *CHAPTER 13: GOVERNMENT SERVICE* on page 89.

- Junior Achievement. A national nonprofit dedicated to educating students in grades K-12 about entrepreneurship, work readiness and financial literacy through experiential, hands-on programs. (juniorachievement.org)

- Serve Washington - Retired Senior Volunteer Program (RSVP). Volunteer network for people 55 and over in nonprofits and government agencies. servewashington.wa.gov.

ABOUT THE AUTHOR

Janet Farr (Jan) is a self-proclaimed authentic Boomer on the loose. Typical of Baby Boomers beyond that "certain age," Jan is re-inventing a 40+ year career experience as a business and technical writer. She also shares that boomer-typical desire to pursue meaning in her next phase in ways that make a positive difference in the lives of others.

Jan is the author of *Boomers on the Loose*® published in 2021 and *Boomers on the Loose*® in Portland, the second edition published in 2020. Enhancing what she learned about the abundance retiree interests, aspirations, and options everywhere, she created *Boomers on the Loose*® *South Sound* to help retirees in South Puget Sound discover meaningful ways to enjoy retirement.

Jan is a transplant from the Kansas City area, and before that, central Michigan. In 2009 she finally took steps to realize her dream to experience the unique Pacific Northwest outdoor lifestyle, and took off for Portland, Oregon. She currently resides in Olympia, Washington.

She loves exploring northwest forests, wetlands, mountains, gardens, the coast, wine country, cities, towns, and villages, large and small. And she especially enjoys experiencing the homegrown arts, music, and culture scene – thriving side-by-side with the high-profile – the caring-for-people attitude, the amazing summers and yes, even the rain making the elegant ruggedness possible.

She's cursed with an eagerness to research and organize vast amounts of information into useful chunks that delight, surprise, and help her Boomer retiree audience find meaning in their own lives.

She hopes that *Boomers on the Loose*® *South Sound* accomplishes that.

INDEX